windy city queer

windy city queer

LGBTQ Dispatches from the Third Coast

Edited by

Kathie Bergquist

The University of Wisconsin Press

The University of Wisconsin Press
1930 Monroe Street, 3rd Floor
Madison, Wisconsin 53711-2059
uwpress.wisc.edu

3 Henrietta Street
London WCE 8LU, England
eurospanbookstore.com

Printed in the United States of America

Library of Congress Cataloging-in-Publication Data

Windy City queer: LGBTQ dispatches from the Third Coast / edited by Kathie Bergquist.
p. cm.
ISBN 978-0-299-28404-6 (pbk.: alk. paper)
ISBN 978-0-299-28403-9 (e-book)
1. Gays' writings, American—Illinois—Chicago. 2. Lesbians' writings, American—Illinois—Chicago. 3. Bisexuals' writings, American—Illinois—Chicago. 4. Transgender people's writings, American—Illinois—Chicago. 5. Gays—Illinois—Chicago—Literary collections. 6. Lesbians—Illinois—Chicago—Literary collections. 7. Bisexuals—Illinois—Chicago—Literary collections. 8. Transgender people—Illinois—Chicago—Literary collections. 9. Chicago (Ill.)—Literary collections. I. Bergquist, Kathie.

PS508.G39W56 2011
810.8′092066—dc22
2011011632

Contents

Acknowledgments

The editor would like to thank the following for their help and support during the assembling of this anthology: Raphael Kadushin and the acquisitions, editorial, and rights staff at the University of Wisconsin Press for all their hand-holding and encouragement through the entire process; Nikki Rinkus, Paige Kelly, and Liz Mordarski for their patience, positive attitudes, discriminating taste, and helpful input; all the terrific writers who submitted work, only a small fraction of which is represented here; and the writers who generously agreed to have their work appear in this collection.

Introduction

> A façade of skyscrapers facing a lake and behind the façade, every type of dubiousness.
>
> E.M. Forster

Back in the days when men cruised each other openly in Towertown; back when Jane Addams and her lover, Mary Rozet Smith, were tucking in for the night at Hull House on the near west side, and when Henry Blake Fuller skipped stones into Lake Michigan from the Evanston Beach while the radicals and anarchists were congregating at the Dill Pickle Club in Old Town; back when lovers Margaret Anderson and Jane Heap were publishing all the new modern writers in *The Little Review* from the Fine Arts building on Michigan Avenue, and a researcher named Jeanette Foster was studying *Sex Variant Women in Literature* at the University of Chicago; back when mannish women and sissy boys juked it up at Tiny & Ruby's Gay Spot on south Wentworth, and when a young playwright from Washington Park named Lorraine Hansberry took classes at Roosevelt University and a boy named Edmund White landed, temporarily, on the Evanston shores; back when a writer named Valerie Taylor penned dimestore novels with titles like *Stranger on Lesbos* and *A World Without Men* from her home on Surf Street in New Town; back through all those thens and thens, through seemingly isolated occurrences and across a spectrum of more than sixty years, a culture was taking root, and it was a very queer culture indeed: a Chicago-based queer literary culture.

What distinguishes LGBTQ writing from Chicago from its well-documented counterparts in New York or San Francisco? It's poking fun at stereotypes to say we Midwesterners are a guileless and plainspoken people, that we are unworldly in some way that is precious and valuable, and *so* adorable. In fact, we're pragmatic. We're diligent. We believe in the merits of hard work. In a way, we're like the middle child to New York's beloved eldest and San Francisco's *infant terrible.* ("What the heck is that crazy San Francisco getting into now?") We say "heck."

Chicago's broader literary legacy—the legacy that includes Sherwood Anderson, Richard Wright, Ernest Hemingway, Nella Larsen, Saul Bellow, Theodore Dreiser, Carl Sandberg, Upton Sinclair, Nelson Algren, Gwendolyn Brooks, and, more recently, Sandra Cisneros and Sara Paretsky (among so many others, of course)—is characterized by grit and tenacity. Chicagoans are shrewd and scrappy, steely-eyed dreamers who share a collective agrarian memory, a sensorial recollection of hayseed and thrift. We are the children of farmers, of laborers, of industrialists, of immigrants, of diaspora. And, I say it again, we are dreamers. With the frigid, shut-in winters, lazy summer nights, and expansive sheet of Lake Michigan that meets the sky at the horizon, we are geographically prone to reverie, to yearning. In each of us is the farmboy dreaming of adventure, the immigrant dreaming the American Dream, the laborer yearning for a human connection. The Cubs fan.

The writings that comprise this collection—poetry, memoir, fiction, essay, performance texts—cover terrain as wide and diverse as the city itself. We visit an illusionist nightclub in Little Village, and a blues bar in Grand Crossing; we ride the El, walk down Glenwood Avenue in Edgewater, and hit I-90 on the way to Wisconsin. We visit the northern suburbs in the 1950s, enter a downtown gay disco in the 1970s, and stroll through gentrifying Uptown in the very present now. The characters and narrative voices who act as our tour guides are tender and fierce and outrageous and hilarious. They work and dance and cry and mourn and make love and lose love; they rage, ponder, muse, ache, and yearn.

The seven parts of *Windy City Queer* are organized by themes interpreted both literally and metaphorically. In part 1, "Emergence," culture and identity take shape. From Sharon Bridgforth's incantatory celebration of generations, "*con flama*," and Edmund White's thirteen-year-old aesthete in 1950s Evanston, through the decadence of the gay '70s, and up to an all-ages queer dance party in pre-gentrified Logan Square, these stories explore the ways we come into our culture, our identity, and ourselves.

The stories and poems in part 2, "In Transit," are thematically linked by the idea of motion, and the space we inhabit between our points of origin and final destinations. Robert McDonald's "Elevated Postcard" and Carina Gia Farrero's "the wife and the bride" both take place on Chicago's iconic El train. "Darla Speeding" by Deb R. Lewis is a rollicking thrill ride across suburban and state lines with the unforgettable Darla Rausenstaadt, an S&M diva with a need for speed and an Adam's apple. In Karen Lee Osborne's "Survivor," a lesbian travels home after the suicide of her gay sister. The section ends with cin salach's "Cheese, Gifts, Fireworks! (A Wisconsin Sonnet)," a love poem featuring Chicago's favorite local getaway.

Cultures cross and expectations are subverted in part 3, "Intersections." Couples and singles, gays and straights flock to an illusionist club in Little Village to pay tribute to Gabrielito, a Juan Gabriel impersonator, in Achy Obejas's "Juanga Forever." In Aldo Alvarez's hilarious "The Anarchist Potluck," nothing goes according to plan when the eager-to-please narrator is invited to a gathering of overly dogmatic young anarchists.

From ad copy to academia, from Brian Bouldrey's outrageous account of delivering business cards to the doorways of suburban strip malls for his 12-step sponsor, to Yasmin Nair's urban ramblings in a gentrifying Uptown, the stories in part 4, "The Grind," tackle the daily grist of life in the Windy City. Part 5, "Family Matters," sheds light on the conflicts and compromises inherent in queer parenting, including Emma Vosicky's wrenching tale of confrontation between a transgendered parent and her adult son.

The euphoria of new love, the forging of romantic attachments, the itch of lust, and the profound ache of regret are all chronicled in part 6, "Hooking Up." C.C. Carter's memoir, "The True Story of S/Him and Femme," charts the circuitous geography of the road to love. In "The Liar" by Sheree L. Greer, a duplicitous protagonist gets a taste of her own medicine when she falls for a sexy blues musician. The collection concludes with part 7, "Winter," examining it both as a season of life and a season of the heart.

Many of the contributors to *Windy City Queer* are writers of national renown and distinction. Among them are several award winners, authors with such lengthy lists of publications and accolades that our contributors' notes only skim the surface. To their combined credit are several Lambda Literary Awards, two National Book Critics Circle Awards, and an Officier de l'Ordre des Arts et des Lettres of the French government. Joining these are several emerging voices, the vanguard of Chicago's queer literary tradition. What unites these writers is more than the statistical detail of location; indeed, while the majority of writers in this collection do call Chicago home, for others it is the vestige of a past life, a temporary encampment. Rather, the union is in that commitment to continue the traditions of language and craft, of truth telling and record keeping. It is in the claiming of a queer space on the literary continuum, a queer cartography of the places we inhabit.

And these are, ultimately, the goals of this book. To chart a map of Chicago's queer landscape in the second half of one century and the first decade of another; to claim our queer space in the city's literary legacy; to testify that we are here, we are queer, this is how we live, and this is how we love.

1

Emergence

con flama

A Performance Text

Sharon Bridgforth

An Excerpt

my earliest memory is of my grandmother's laughter when i was three and
we lived in
chicago/and i stole her beer and drank it down
before my mother got across the room to take it away
georgia sweet georgia on my mind/was on the radio.
my mother was very upset   but i didn't care
'cause i liked the taste of beer
and grandmother's laughter.

grandmother smelt like sweaty stockings and day old beer. every night
i climbed into a sweet sleep encased in that smell/and grandmother's thick
damp skin/big belly snores and covers.
i loved no one more than my grandmother.

who are our Ancestors, grandmother?
i used to ask her
'cause i was hoping i had more grandmothers somewhere.
she'd say

kassa shaka mutu.

my mother told me grandmother
was 15 when she picked the chicago streets over her own child
who she sent back south to the home house/so

i knew grandmother loved no one more than me 'cause we were in chicago
and she was there
to tuck me in at night.
i loved my grandmother
even though she made my mother cry.

who are our Ancestors, grandmother?
i'd ask on rainy days or nights i wasn't sleepy

kuta mako mo

she'd say
and i'd make believe for hours that they were visiting us.

we got evicted 'cause grandmother drank up three months' rent money and my mother
didn't know/and that's how we ended up in los angeles 'cause right when we got on the
street grandmother's sister came by on her way to los angeles
and me and my mother got in the car/went with her.
grandmother stayed on the street waving

bye babies
i love you.

my mother is still angry about that   but i didn't care
'cause i knew grandmother would join us when the next great-aunty car came by.

four years later my mother sent me south to stay at the home house until she finished
night school   i didn't care
'cause grandmother was back at the home house too and as soon as i saw her
i loved her more again. more than ever.

who are our Ancestors, grandmother?
i asked happy to hear her voice

kaba zula we

she said

grandmother
you said our Ancestors were
kassa shaka mutu and kuta mako mo you never said there was a kaba zula we
this can't be right grandmother
who are our Ancestors!

she said

shit gal
i don't know.

that was a very unsettling moment.
why
didn't she know i wondered.
why don't i know
i wonder
i wonder
why/i am crying/i am crying now/now i cry . . .

my daughter is a beauty queen.
so was my mother
'cept nobody told her. she was a singer and a dancer too
but at the home house down south
they said

ain't no Coloured gal
gone ever make it in this world
singing and dancing

but what about
ma rainey and bessie smith and ethel waters and florence mills and josephine baker and lena horne and dinah washington and marian anderson and ella

fitzgerald and mahalia jackson and big maybelle and big mama thornton and sarah vaughan and billie holiday and lavern baker and gladys bentley and ms. snuggie down the street

she said

well you ain't them

they said.

fear took a seat inside her/gradually
replacing the light in her eyes

you ain't good enough

they said and they hit her and they hit her to make sure she heard

you ain't good enough

they said remembering all they had left of aunt vera was her braid
which lil tootie found bloody on the tracks last year

you ain't good enough!

they said
knowing how dangerous it was for a Coloured girl
to dream

i
ain't
good
enough

she said
not really understanding
why . . .

i love no one more than my mother
except my daughter who i sent to live down south with her father

and his home house people when she was little/and i was learning how to enjoy laughter without beer.

i know that my mother she loves no one more than me even though she never said it/i
know my mother she loves no one more than me 'cause she put me on the bus
and there is no better place to dream
than on the bus
in los angeles.

my daughter she don't ride the bus/she gets rides
but we all
my mother and even the down south at the home house folk tell her
how beautiful she is and how she can sing and dance and do
anything
she wants to do.
and when she asks who her Ancestors are
i tell her
Missouri Kirk and Calvin Mitchel Black and Joseph Hadley Black and Georgia Ana Hicks and Georgia Lee Black and/i go on and on naming them all and i tell her i don't know the names of the Africans but your daddy's daddy can name all the names on that side of your tree/including the Indians and the Africans.

my daughter you see
gets to keep all her dreams
because we have made it so
and through her
my mother gets to dream again too.

bye babies
i love you . . .

Record Time

Edmund White

Loneliness can be a full state or an empty one, by which I mean that when I was thirteen in 1953 I usually felt forlorn but occasionally—especially in the presence of a work of art—triumphant. Most of the time, at school, on the bus, on the street, I thought I was embarrassingly conspicuous if I was alone. I was convinced everyone was burningly aware of my isolation, almost as though I were trapped in one of those sweating grinning embarrassment dreams. In the high school corridors, gliding from one class to another, grazing the walls, I didn't retreat into a comfortably grim resignation, waking up only when I was seated once again in the biology lab or in honor civics. No, I suffered and smiled and mentally debated whether I should try to walk along with that girl I knew from choir practice or join those guys from gym class, who weren't all *that* popular, after all. My loneliness was ready to sizzle and explode as it leapt from one electrode to another: high-voltage emptiness.

There was the amniotic sloth of a long bath or the agitated mindlessness of reading the back of the cereal box over and over or the sadsack squalor of sitting on the floor in the sunroom, listening to all the clocks ticking in an empty apartment.

But mainly, every day, there was the same sort of highly anxious inactivity I'd felt the previous summer looking for a part-time job, waiting in the reception room in a starched collar, hoping to catch the eye of my potential boss, wondering why my appointment had already been pushed back forty minutes, observing the hands of the wall clock millimetering toward five, closing time. That's the way I felt alone at school, as though I were ready at a moment's notice to go into action, smile, charm, display my wares—but until then forced to wait and hypothesize the worst.

The other kind of loneliness, the full, self-sufficient kind, never came on me with lightning suddenness but had to be slowly wooed. I'd bring records and scores home with me from the public library, and behind my door, which I'd outfitted with a flimsy hook and latch, I'd listen to the old vinyl 78s with the gleaming outer-space black grooves and round burgundy labels printed in gold as though they were Ruritanian medals for bravery. I'd listen to Vincent D'Indy's *Symphony on a French Mountain Air* (I can't bear him anymore, now that I know he was an active, hate-driven anti-Semite) or all forty-eight records of *Tristan and Isolde* (the work of another anti-Semite, one whom I admire, alas). The *Tristan* records were in four matching leather-bound volumes that looked like snapshot albums. Most classical records were numbered so that a good pile could be stacked on the spindle, then flipped, though real connoisseurs were against stacking.

I'd worked three months at that summer job to earn the money necessary to buy a three-speed record player, which would accommodate the 78s borrowed from the library as well as the new 33⅓s and 45s I was buying at a dispiritingly slow rate. My very first record had been a 45 of Chet Baker playing "Imagination" on trumpet and singing in his high voice stunned by heroin into expressionless neutrality.

The speed had to be changed and the needle flipped when I went from 78s to the other speeds. If the records were battered, the scores were often pristine—I held in my hands a first American edition of Puccini's *Tosca* with its *art nouveau* cover design of the passionate Italian heroine all wasp waist, long gauzy gown, imploring hands, and hornet's nest hair. I saw from the dates rubber-stamped on the orange card inserted into its own glued-in pocket that these scores had scarcely circulated in the last half-century. These cards made me realize how neglected and private and chancy was musical history. Just as I could check out the first English translations of Anatole France and Pierre Loti with their white leather bindings tooled in gold and braided flowers on the spine, in the same way I was in direct physical contact with these early musical scores of *Cavalleria Rusticana*, of Verdi's *Requiem*, of Massenet's *Thaïs*, of Wagner's *Lohengrin*, of Strauss's *Der Zigeunerbaron*. I was equally intimate with these scratched recordings of Lauritz Melchior (whom I'd heard sing a solo concert in Dallas when I was nine), of Jussi Björling (whom I'd seen, corsetted and tiny, flailing his arms on the stage of the Chicago Lyric Opera as he sang Rodolfo in *Bohème*), even of "Madame" Schumann-Heinck, whom my mother had seen in some Texas cow palace during one of her innumerable farewell tours just after World War I.

I'd come home from school by way of the library, my biceps aching from my burden of records, scores, and books, and I'd barricade myself in my room. As the Chicago night began to fall earlier and earlier each December evening and the snow on my sill would melt and refreeze, I took comfort in my room with the sizzling radiator, the chocolate brown walls, tan burlap curtains, gleaming maple chest of drawers, comfortable arm chair, and the old brass lamp from my earliest childhood, originally designed before my time as a gas lamp but now rewired with its glass chimney still intact and its luminosity still capable of being dialed down into yellow dimness. I loved the coarse red wool blanket with its big Hudson Bay dull satin label sewn into the upper left-hand corner like a commemorative stamp showing a moose and a canoe. I loved the pale celadon green pots I'd bought in Chinatown, their raised designs nearly effaced under heavy glazes, their wide cork tops sealed shut with red wax that had to be chipped away to reveal the candied ginger slices within, floating, slimy, in a thick, dark sugar syrup. Now the ginger had long since been eaten and the bowls washed clean, but they were still faintly redolent of their spicy, mysterious original contents. I loved my seven bronze Chinese horses, which were stored in a brown velvet box cut into exact silhouettes into which the little statues could be wedged. Each horse was different, head lowered in a gentle arc to graze or thrown back to gallop, each weighty and cold in the hand. I loved my music boxes given to me one by one, Christmas after Christmas: the turning brass cylinder under glass plucking brass tines that played the Gounod waltz from Faust; the unpainted wood Swiss chalet with the mirrors for windows that played "Edelweiss"; the miniature grand piano; the revolving water mill. But I was less impressed by the look of each box than by the richness of its sound. The Gounod I liked the best since the sound wasn't tinny but resonant, and the box, if I held it, throbbed in my hand with expensive precision.

I loved the smell of the boxes of tea I collected and scarcely ever drank—I'd inhale the dry, smoky perfume of the lapsang souchong leaves, the Christmassy clove and orange odor of the Constant Comment, the acrid smell of Japanese gunpowder green tea, not really like a tea at all but a kind of grass, or so I imagined. I loved the way the hard metal lids fit snugly into these square boxes and had to be pried open with the handle of a spoon. I loved sitting on the floor, my back propped against the bed as I turned the broad, smooth pages of the opera scores in which the original words were translated, very approximately, into the same number of English syllables so that one could sing along. I'd keep changing the stacks of 78s, some of them so badly gouged that I'd have to nudge the needle out of a deep crevasse, others so worn down that my needle, itself not ideally sharp, would just slide over the bald surface in a split-second condensation of long minutes' worth of music.

But more often than not the records were still in good shape, perhaps because they were so seldom checked out. Sometimes for extra protection they were even inserted into translucent envelopes that were then closed and tucked into heavy, yellowing paper sleeves. The early 1950s record jacket designs were rarely printed with more than two colors and were pert or jaunty—black musical notes zigzagging like bees around a mauve cut-out of Wagner's head, surmounted with his baggy beret, or all of Respighi's Fountains of Rome picked out in yellow and pink dashes and dots as though they were birdcages soldered in Morse code—or else the covers were just dumbly romantic (a huge red rose superimposed over a brown violin for Brahms's violin concerto).

I was alone with classical music, just as a reader was alone in the library or a museum-goer in those days was alone with paintings. Everyone else in America was listening to Perry Como and Dean Martin or looking at Arthur Godfrey's breakfast program on the flickering black-and-white television screen. American popular culture was cozy, queasily banal, pitched at everyone in the family—there was no Elvis yet, nothing tough or twangy or raunchy, just all these bland white people, the men in jackets, dark knit ties, and white dress shirts, the women in fluffy skirts and long-sleeved sweaters, acting out cute little skits week after week on a hit parade show as they thought up new variations on story lines that might fit the unchanging lyrics of a song that lingered for months in the top ten. People twenty or twenty-five or thirty-five all looked and acted alike in their dress-up clothes as they cracked their cute jokes and simpered and skipped between giant cut-outs of sunflowers or waved from the flimsy back platform of a papier-mâché train.

One day I discovered the collection of circulating art books at the library and came home with a volume of ukiyo-e prints introduced by a spirited, seductive text. I liked it that these prints recorded the look of famous Kabuki actors or courtesans in the "Floating World" of 18th and 19th century Edo, that no one in Japan had taken these wood-cuts seriously until French painters had discovered them. I liked the refinement of tall ladies standing in a boat, opium pipe in hand, sailing past the strutwork supporting a bridge. I liked the intimacy of a beauty coquettishly blackening her teeth while her cloudy gray cat tiptoed over her makeup table. I liked the ecstasy of a monk in his hermitage, the paper wall thrown open, contemplating snow-capped Mt. Fuji reflected in a black lacquer-rimmed round mirror. The crevasses descending down from the snow cap looked like the lines radiating out from a toothless mouth. I especially liked the young lovers running on high wooden shoes through the visibly slanting morning rain, a faint smile on their lips, their slender bodies nearly interchangeable, the umbrella grasped in their joined hands . . .

It seems to me now that I had few judgments about music or paintings or poems and if works of art were difficult that didn't put me off. I worked my way through almost all the titles listed inside the paper dust jackets of the Modern Library. I'd figured out that these books were classics, and if my attention wandered while reading *Nostromo* I simply started again and concentrated harder. It was not up to me to declare Conrad a bore or to wonder how a professional writer could allow himself to use so many words such as "indescribable," "ineffable" and "unspeakable." Similarly I felt it necessary to know something about Vlaminck *and* Van Eyck, about Rembrandt *and* Cézanne, as though I were preparing for God's Great Quiz Show in the Sky rather than piecing together a sensibility.

When other people, older people, took a strong stand for or against a Sung vase or T.S. Eliot's "The Waste Land" or a Jackson Pollock "drip" painting ("Pure charlatanism!"), I was so impressed by their opinions that I immediately adopted them as my own and sometimes repeated them for years to come without always realizing they were internally inconsistent and needed to be reconciled. I was so ecstatic as I sprawled on the rough red Canadian blanket, dialed my brass lamp down to its dimmest wattage, listened to Flagstad's "Liebestod" in which a human body was sublimated into pure spirit, as I smelled the smoky tea leaves or brightened the light and looked at my Japanese lovers in the rain, each wearing a matching black cloth hat that formed a wimple under the inconsequential chin—so ecstatic that I didn't think to judge these experiences any more than a starving man turns up his nose at food. I didn't judge things, but I was delighted when other people did. I was so shocked that I laughed, scandalized, when other people said, "This Sung vase with its pale raised peonies and delicate *craquelure* is worth more than all of Michelangelo's sculptures," or "Eliot is a fussy old maid with his royalist politics and furled umbrella but he has brought all of world culture together into a fragmented collage—fragmented because all collages necessarily are fragmented, but wonderfully suggestive and *systematic*, finally."

I was thrilled by so many sleek, purring opinions, I, a self-invented Midwestern public-library intellectual who ate books and records and art reproductions the way other people ate meat and potatoes. My kind of art meal was always eaten alone, just as I improvised on the piano alone, and I had only rare contacts with other art consumers. My mother's friends who had all the quirky, nuanced opinions seemed to have drifted out from New York or Boston. Their take on my favorite authors and composers ("Wagner certainly has his *longeurs* and if he is the greatest composer we can only add, Alas, just as Gide sighed, *Hélas*, when he named Hugo the greatest poet") seemed to me almost sacrilegious, as though they were discussing sales figures for the relics and relic-derived products of a saint whom I actually believed in.

To judge a work of art depends on a certain fastidiousness, just as to taste a wine properly requires not being actually thirsty. But I was hungry and thirsty as well as a true believer in art's miracle-working properties. For me artists and writers and composers did not exist in time any more than general truths can be dated (later, of course, I learned that each epoch produces its own truths, but we didn't know that back then). When I was reminded of the *age* of a work of art (by the fresh look of the *Tosca* score, or by a story about Pollock's recent death in *Time* and time), I was disturbed, as when a headline-grabbing geologist claimed he could now confidently date the Flood and had even found the exact landing site of Noah's Ark. This intersection of the mythic and the temporal struck me as indecent. I myself was ageless, unformed, an ungendered eye and I, too, resisted definition.

I had never played with toys as a child. I'd improvised on the piano, I'd invented complicated scenarios for my puppets or for my imaginary friends and me, I'd wandered through nature, receptive as a nose and eyes on a stem, thunderstruck by the smell of the lilac bush next to the Congregational Church, awed by the glassy tranquility of Lake Michigan as I waded into it on an August evening and stood there, white and stark as a single soprano note, and watched the raised waves radiate out from my slow steps.

Now, at age thirteen, guiltily, I dropped the latch on my bedroom door and played with toys. Not real toys, not store-bought toys, but my own invented toys. I organized triumphal marches on the red Canadian blanket between ranks of tea-box military tanks, noble processions of the seven bronze Chinese horses, of a pink jade bodhisattva and a soapstone Buddha, of giant floats of music boxes all playing at once while the hordes shouted their approval (a sound-effect I provided with my whispered roars as I hovered over the whole scene, invisible and manipulative as God). Finally I donned the red blanket as a cloak and put on a recording of the Coronation Scene from *Boris* and made my royal entrance, imagining the rows of bearded, brocaded boyars. I heard the clangor of all Kiev's bells.

I thought to myself, This is what little kids go through, this total immersion into fantasy, this self-sufficient solitude, the good kind, the triumphant kind. I was ashamed but not so much that as the school day would draw to a close I wouldn't become excited by the thought that soon I'd be able to start playing again—not exactly with toys, but with my fetishes, whose ludic aspect had dawned on me only recently.

My favorite games were all about power, benign power, the same games I played outside in the snow by constructing ice palaces, a Forbidden City for my solitary empress, an Old Winter Palace for my ailing Tsarevitch. From the opera records I borrowed I'd learned all about Boris's coronation and the pharaoh's triumphal march in *Aida* as well as about the people in *Turandot* wishing the Son of Heaven ten thousand years of life. I was so highstrung that Mimi's death—and especially Violetta's—could make me tremble all over and sob hysterically (I wasn't your basic baseball-playing, freckled little kid); what I preferred, what I found soothing, were royal processions, and if I'd been Queen of England I would have managed to "process" on a daily basis, my raised gloved hand describing small circles in the air.

One day I read in the paper that Greta Garbo's *Camille* would be showing at a remote movie theater. My mother agreed to drive me way out there if I'd come home on the train by myself (she verified the times). In fact my mother indulged me in nearly all my whims. It was she who'd let me decorate my room as I'd wanted, who bought me my Chinese horses and my yearly music boxes and who'd driven me all the way down to the South Side that one time when I'd wanted to attend a Japanese Buddhist Church. When I pleaded to go to a military school camp (I'd just read biographies of Napoleon and Peter the Great and was suddenly attracted to power even in its less benign forms), she enrolled me against her better judgment; halfway through the summer I was begging her to let me come home, which she even more reluctantly allowed me to do.

It was a spring night when I went to that distant community to see *Camille*, a town which I couldn't name now and which I never saw again. It appeared to have been built all at once in the same manner in the 1920s or even earlier in what was even then a nostalgic style with converted gas lamps, cobblestone streets, and half-timbered store fronts. The spring was not advanced enough to have produced any flowers beyond big, gaudy sprays of forsythia.

It was raining and the cobblestones were as slick and even as dragon's scales. There was no one on the street. At last we found the movie, which was being shown in a narrow church, perhaps as a fund-raiser. If so, the programming was a disaster, since the only other member of the audience was an old man seated two rows away on a folding wood chair.

But once *Camille* began I was absorbed. Not by the humble, scratchy black-and-white look of the thing (it was a bad print, but my borrowed 78s had taught me to overlook that); I was used to Technicolor, even three-dimensional movies, and I'd never seen a vintage film before. Garbo's acting style would no doubt make kids laugh now, but I was used to melodrama from the operas I'd seen. Anyway, this was an exaggerated style but unlike anything I'd ever witnessed before. She could change in a second from a sadness as piercing, as physical, as light directed into the eyes of someone suffering from a massive migraine to a joy that shook her as agitatedly as though her big, lovely face were as bright and faceted as her pendent earrings. In one scene she was sophisticated and skeptical, one eyebrow raised, and in the next tender as my mother when I was ill with a high fever. Her voice would go from a fife's excitement to the bagpipe drone of her grief, a grief that really was just like a migraine that requires drawn curtains and deepest solitude.

I didn't quite understand why she had to give up her lover. What had she done wrong? Wasn't she even, all things considered, too good for him? Nevertheless, I liked the idea of sacrifice in the abstract and hoped to make one soon. Her lover had a straight nose and oily black hair, but I disliked his long sideburns and thought his acting was as unconvincing as his morality was caddish. That didn't matter—after all, Jussi Björling had had all the allure of a waddling duck, but he had sung with the clarion tones of a trumpet calling reveille.

I knew how the story turned out from *La Traviata*, the very first opera I'd ever seen, but this knowledge made my tears flow all the hotter as the end approached. When the lights came up the old man was snoring peacefully. No usher was in sight, although I could hear the operator in his projection booth rewinding the film. I pushed open the main church door. The rain had stopped but the bare, budding trees were still dripping and the sound of my lonely footsteps rang out.

I found the little suburban station easily enough. A sailor was also waiting for the train, playing a mouth-harp, quietly, to himself, as though he were rehearsing a speech, trying to get it by heart, or evoking a sentimental tune for his ears alone. I felt washed clean and faded almost to the point of transparency. I was very old and wise, not in need of a great love since I'd already had one, afraid that something might jostle my mood, which I wanted to carry without spilling all the way home. The night was conspiring graciously to help me—the deserted, dripping village with the gas lamps and cobblestones, the sailor with the mouth-harp, even the sight of forsythia blazing in the dark on the hillside next to the station.

The train came, just two cars long. The only other passenger was an old black woman, asleep and smiling, split shoes too small to contain her feet. The sailor kept playing and I looked at the few dim lights that suggested the depths of these old suburbs with their huge wood houses in which everyone was asleep.

Back in my room I drank a glass of cold Welch's grape juice in the dark and pretended it was wine. I opened my window and toasted the wet spring night, which didn't feel like the beginning of anything but the very last plucked note at the end of a long, soft, slow coda.

’78

Gregg Shapiro

This was back when Boystown
was still called New Town.
When fierce drag queens held
court in the window at the Golden
Nugget at the corner of Belmont

and Broadway, starting knife fights,
and when there were no knives,
they’d bust coffee cups on the tables
and wield the broken ceramic shards
like blades. Before Donna Summer

went Jesus-crazy and only the gays,
dancing until near collapse at Crystal’s
Blinkers and the Broadway Limited,
knew about her, too generous to keep
her a secret. The Village People

were still macho men and hadn’t checked
into the Y.M.C.A. yet. We were college
students with hungers new and familiar.
For food, before the clubs, Joel catered
to our needs from his post at the host

stand at The Brewery, making sure
that we had enough nourishment from
the abundant (and fern hung) salad bar

After the disco we dined at the Medinah
(now a Gap!) in the wee smallest hours

of the morning. When we kissed each
other like friends and went our separate
ways, we never asked about what happened
after sunrise. When we kissed like lovers
in the rambling apartment on Sheffield,

doors slammed and windows rattled, but
we nestled in each other's arms, eager
to learn whatever we could teach other,
anxious for homework that was meant
to be done naked, between the sheets.

Marriage and Commitment

Owen Keehnen

The kid had heard about the place. Last week he'd come to Old Town and parked across Wells Street and watched and waited and let fear and worry dissuade him. He hated being afraid. That wasn't going to happen this week.

The doorman was too drunk to ask for a fake ID. Actually the kid wasn't sure if he was the doorman, or just some drunk sitting by the door. The kid went around the heavy black curtain. A narrow hallway opened onto a kaleidoscope floor of pulsing tiles. Smoke hung in the air. The kid entered as an underground prowler—slowly, cautiously, but with an undeniable hunger. Neon bars and scattered stars covered the black brick walls. Stars populated the dance floor was well. Some stars were shirtless and some were dancing on platforms. One star was in a sequins jockstrap. These stars were named Ted, Rick, and Bruce—Mitch, Mike, Butch, Bart, and Stefan (not Steven). It was glamour with puka shells and big man bells, platform shoes and more. This was disco and this was NOW!

When he ordered a beer, Eddie the bartender smiled and asked if he was new. The kid said "*No*" a bit too loudly, forcing a laugh as though the suggestion was absurd. Eddie smiled. "Well, this is a gay bar—so just be yourself. In a gay bar no one wants you to be anything other than what you are." Looking back the kid realized that was probably the comment he *should* have found amusing.

The kid looked around. It was a rare instance of having his expectations not only met, but exceeded. Moderation was for the mediocre. This fabulous world was all about more, more, more. There were designer clothes and designer colognes, the blatant use of drugs, public drunkenness, partial nudity, and an overall sleazy feel. It felt more like home than home had ever been, and he hadn't even discovered the back room yet. For the first time the kid could remember, he felt he was exactly where he was meant to be.

Doc was the hottest gay disco DJ in Chicago. That first night he pistol-shot him from the glass DJ booth and dedicated "Heaven Must Have Sent You" to "that kid in the checked pants." It took a second to register. When it did the kid did one of those "who me" finger-to-chest gestures. Guys turned and eyed him like a tender flank of veal. Thankfully his blush was hidden by the rotating color wheel.

Doc was a stone fox with a handlebar moustache and fanning sideburns that reached all the way to his mouth. His hair crunched when touched, but Doc's hair was never touched intentionally. He was a clone's clone with shirts open low and jeans so tight that the kid could clearly make out thirty-five cents in his front pocket. It looked like a nice chunk of change. Doc smoked Tiparillos and his Trans Am had reclining bucket seats. Clearly he'd been around the block (and up the alley) a few times. He swept the kid off his feet, onto his back, and out of those hideous checked pants that first night.

That's how it began.

Theirs was a rolling bulb romance of dancing and fucking and drugs. Doc rang his bell, made him feel mighty real, and took him down . . . to funkytown. Before heading to the bar they'd go to Doc's. Sex came first, but instead of getting dressed they'd lie on Doc's waterbed and listen to 12″ disco singles he got for free just for being a DJ. The kid looked at himself in the gold-veined headboard. His life had become a throbbing all-male fairy tale, an adventure in semen and song.

Doc's swinging pad was a seventh floor pie-shaped slice of heaven in Marina Towers. It was almost entirely chrome and white. Cream colored shag carpet covered the walls. Doc had a half-moon minibar and a zebra-print rug. In his fridge were a lemon, a lime, and a partial jar of olives. The kid imagined Burt Bacharach and Angie Dickinson's place to be somewhat similar.

Looking through the ghost of himself and out Doc's high-rise windows the kid smiled. For once the world was down and he was on top. Now they'd see. From here the life he'd known was far below and a world away. It was then that he knew he was in love with Doc. For a gay Catholic boy from the West Side, love and salvation were synonymous. Love was a delirious escape that transformed him at a time when he so needed to be something else, or someone else, or at least something more.

The kid envisioned white tux nuptials at Studio 54. The VIP guests would arrive in limos and include the usual vials and velvet ropes crowd—Bianca, Liza, Diana, Halston, Andy, Grace Jones, maybe Britt Ekland. Fog would roll over a huge dance floor with a bridge of mirrored tile arching above it. At the intro of a "not yet designated song" they'd approach from either side. In the black light strobe they'd be flickering specters. A pin light color wheel would dance across them. All heads in the crowd would be upturned as they reached through the beads of light to join hands. At that point there'd be an explosion of glitter.

They'd serve champagne labeled with their names and the date. He and Doc surrounded by a heart—today, tomorrow, forever. They'd give away lighters and tiny spoons and have special beverage napkins. They'd wear foil boutonnieres of silver and red with two ribbons; the silver with their names, the red with the date. Naturally, there'd be paparazzi.

With the promise of jet set glamour, walls of glass, and hot man-on-man sex, the future was filled with possibilities. Seeing through such moon and starry eyes the kid turned to Doc and gushed, "I love you." His declaration came too early, too easily, and ultimately too expectantly. Doc didn't love him back. Doc said nothing at the time; he only smiled, slipped on his Jordache jeans, and said he had some errands to run before heading to the bar.

He broke up with the kid that night on the dance floor. He put on the extended version of "Enough is Enough (No More Tears)" to be sure to have ample time. Doc offered the kid a whiff of poppers. Poppers were the best. Well, not the best—but definitely not something to pass up. Liza would never turn down poppers. Doc handed him the bottle for a second snort. Somewhere amidst the purple spots and the throbbing Doc said it isn't you, it's me. He said he thought he was a great kid and that it had been fun, but that they should just be friends. He said someday he'd find the right one. The kid was young so none of this was cliché to him.

This all happened so quickly the kid didn't know what to feel—mostly he just couldn't believe how weird it was to break up on poppers. Sure it was sad and unexpected, but still kind of sexy.

At the end of it all Doc said, "No hard feelings," and told the kid to have Eddie comp his drinks for the rest of the night. Doc was back in the booth by the time the kid's peripheral vision had returned.

The first person the kid told was Eddie when he ordered a beer. Eddie nodded like it was no surprise. The second person he told was Jake, a guy at an adjoining barstool who nodded because he was jelly neck drunk.

Eddie said guys like Doc—DJs with facial hair who wear sunglasses in restaurants, who order netted underwear from International Male, and who subscribe to *After Dark*—aren't looking for a mate. Eddie said it was just a law of the 1979 man jungle. He said Chicago was full of men and indeed it was.

The kid met Reggie tossing a Frisbee in Roger's Park. A parked Camaro was blaring Pink Floyd. He noticed Reggie's Disco Sucks T-shirt and smiled. Time hadn't *quite* healed his wounded heart. Hunched over to catch his breath, Reggie's spine was visible through the thin fabric of the shirt. He resembled a pimply whippet—but in a cute way.

The kid's gaydar read full speed ahead. He approached and asked for a smoke. "A smoke . . . or a *smoke*?" With a loopy grin Reggie flipped his long hair back and pulled a joint from his Levi's pocket. The kid loved guys who were generous with drugs. It was very Christian and very decadent at the same time. Grace and sin were a winning combination.

When the kid suggested going back to his place, Reggie said, "Definitely!" They messed around that afternoon serenaded by Journey and Mötley Crüe. Sex didn't last long, but they got high before and after.

That summer they hung out. Smoked. Listened to tunes. Smoked. Watched TV. Smoked. Listened to music while watching TV with the sound down. Ate pizza. It was a full life. The kid felt he'd arrived without even having to leave the couch. He never realized happiness was an inhalant. He and Reggie made each other smile, or rather the pot they smoked made them smile, and since they were together it was easy to think it was the other and not the pot.

They were most in love at a Cheap Trick concert at Navy Pier. They'd had a couple of Reggie's magic brownies beforehand. "One'll do ya, two'll undo ya," he'd warned. They'd had two.

Reggie's eyes were red slits when he scratched his head, pointed towards the stage, and said, "I can't see for shit." Without thinking the kid lifted Reggie onto his shoulders. It was a moment of gay empowerment greased by a lot of weed. Reggie was shoulder-riding another guy—devil's horns high, dopey smile wide, fist pumping the sky to "Dream Police"—and no one cared. With a metal band up there, there was nothing else. There was no gay or straight or he or she or them—just one glorious cluster of black T-shirt clad cells joining to form a rock and roll beast.

The kid's eyes may have been red and glassy, but they were starry nonetheless. He heard the wedding march on electric guitar. He imagined a backyard kegger wedding at Reggie's place in Edgewater, with special vendor cups that would say "He and Reggie" and then something like "Can't Fight This Feeling Anymore" or maybe "Don't Stop Believin'." They'd drag the couch out back and arrange some chairs. They'd have a deli spread on a folding table. There'd be pale salads in plastic and burnt and blackened meats on foil. There'd be horseshoes and Frisbee, a confederate flag and Lynyrd Skynyrd. There'd be big-ass speakers on the back porch so you know there'd be air guitar.

There'd be trashy drama. Reggie didn't get along with his folks. He called them "intense," but it was a word Reggie used a lot. The kid wasn't sure what it meant in the context of Reggie's parents, but he was really high so whatever it meant didn't matter for long. Anyway, his parents wouldn't be invited so they'd raise a ruckus and call the cops. It would be a day to remember, though probably no one would. It would be the sort of wedding where half the guests *arrived* in a blackout.

He and Reggie would've had major problems. They already did, but bringing it up would be bogus, so it was all sucked in and held until the kid's mouth could only slacken into a dopey grin. The kid saw that the easy life was definitely easy, but it wasn't enough. He could feel his dreams start to suffocate. He could never come right out and tell Reggie this wasn't what he wanted. Instead he decided to leave a note. It was much easier to be direct if he didn't have to be in the room at the time.

He taped the note to the turntable:

> I want you to want me.
> I need you to need me.
> I'd love you to love me.
> I'm begging you to beg me.

When Reggie found it he said, "Great song!" He never asked why the kid had left the note, and the kid was too embarrassed to explain. Even he had too much pride to explain a plea. A week after he left the note, he left Reggie.

Every day with Reggie was wasted, yet that summer wasn't a total waste. He'd learned some valuable things. He could now roll an amazing joint and de-seed in his sleep. He had a working knowledge of heavy metal, lots of tie-dyed T-shirts, and could make killer Rice Krispies Treats out of almost any brand of cereal. He also learned that going to a basketball game on acid is never the wise choice.

After leaving Reggie the kid entered a blurry stretch of sluttiness, moving up and down Halsted and Broadway with his eyes closed and his thighs open. Since he now called himself an artist, he figured it was all life research. He couldn't *possibly* write without living first. He loved being an artist. It excused everything, *plus* he looked really good in black.

For the next few years boyfriends came and went and came and went. He probably would've married a couple more, but he was no longer quite so idealistic. He'd still fall in love, but love was something he grew wary of sharing. It was a secret, an embarrassment, a weakness to hide. He didn't want to get hurt and hurt had taken on new forms.

The plague had come to waste and mark and cast a gaunt gaze upon the world. It changed everything and nothing seemed harmless anymore. Life became medieval and distorted, shadowed and unspoken. So the kid hid in a faster and faster blur of drugs and drink and dick and a distance that soon frightened him more than death.

Staggering down the Christopher Street steps he collided with a volunteer organization table. The table tipped, leaflets scattered, and a clipboard skittered down the sidewalk. He felt like an idiot and sobered up enough to scrawl his name as a volunteer when the quilt came to Navy Pier.

It wasn't the pier of the Ferris wheel and the IMAX, Shakespeare and tourists . . . this was the dilapidated shell, the great hollowed husk of Navy Pier circa 1988. He was a floating quilt monitor. His task was to answer questions, protect its borders, and be there for people. They gave him a box of tissues to distribute even though he'd never been good around emotions or people who displayed them.

He walked the edges of beautifully stitched tributes and looked over the panels by those who learned to sew for the sake of love and sanity. Everyone was so young—31, 36, 42, 23, 32, 19, 26, 25, 22, 32, 47, 40. Then he came upon Doc's three-by-six-foot panel. It was covered in black felt with a sequined disco ball off center. Beside it was a picture with his birth and death dates. Thirty-eight. Doc was so handsome. Below was the cursive title "Never Can Say Goodbye." They couldn't use Gloria Gaynor's other disco hit, "I Will Survive"—because Doc didn't. He'd lived, but he hadn't survived. The panel of Eddie the bartender was on his left.

He imagined what the disco would be like now. Empty. A place as black as night with only the ghost of all those stars fading in and out and in and out before finally fading to black. Now all the stars named Ted, Rick, and Bruce—Mitch, Mike, Butch, Bart, and Stefan (not Steven)—were here. Even Halston was in the room. Doc would be pleased about that.

On the other side of the room he saw the quilt for Reggie. He'd been right—two'll undo ya. His panel was white with his name in block letters—blue purple black, blue purple black. Below was written "Beloved Son." Along the border were pictures—a laughing baby, a toddler at the beach, arms around the neck of a carousel horse, thin and acned and taking a *girl* to homecoming, and finally thin and old and clearly sick—blowing out candles atop the numbers two and seven and looking as though the numbers should be seven and two or eight and two or nine and two and that even the idea of candles and celebration was tragic.

He'd never met Reggie's parents but doubted they were as bogus as Reggie believed. They'd come through in the end. They were on either side of him in that last two and seven birthday photo, wearing smiles that belied a premature grieving, hoping their mouths might hide the grief in their eyes.

He and Reggie were most in love somewhere near here. The ghost of it flooded him. Reggie on his shoulders, fist pumping the sky, not looking up, not needing to, knowing there was space there, believing eternity was there—both in the moment, into the music, and high out of their minds.

I want you to want me,
I need you to need me,
I'd love you to love me,
I'm begging you to beg me.

Time had only added to the urgency of the lyrics. Now there was no need to explain that plea.

For much of the day he thought about Doc and Reggie and so many friends and fucks and men who came and went—husbands and tricks. There was Stu, whose love of gay porn was only surpassed by a love of sucking cock but who adamantly denied being gay. Stu hated labels.

There was Will, who picked him up at The Crafty Beaver with the line, "Is that caulk in your shopper's basket for filling cracks?" How could he not fuck him after a line like that? When he showed his friend a picture of Will and called him his new beau, his pal had laughed and said, "Oh my God, you're dating the Crafty Beaver guy? He came up to me and said he was looking for a large pounding tool. He hits on everyone there."

There was Bobby, who played meditation tapes all night, and Steve, who never slept, and Kellan from Ireland, with the habit of saying "Oh, for fuck's sake" and making it sound like the opposite of profanity.

And Marvin, whose penis was curved so severely that even on the bottom Marvin was almost a top. Sex with him was the closest the kid had come to using the high school geometry that Sister Catherine had told him he would use someday.

How many more were here and how many had been forgotten? Dozens? Names forgotten, dicks remembered. It was all a game. Sure he was keeping score, but he wasn't counting. In those days the kid was falling in love at the drop of a hat or the drop of his pants.

Life was so different. He'd been so alive, but it had all gotten smothered beneath shrouds of worry and guilt and anger and resentment and the thickest, heaviest shroud of all—that of fear. A plague will back you in a corner if you let it, and take your life regardless of whether or not it kills you. It was no way to live. He still hated being afraid, but sometimes fear is eclipsed by something greater. Sometimes to be someone more you need to face the bully in your brain.

He looked across the room at the flat linen sea of the lost, and for the first time in years he knew he was exactly where he was supposed to be.

He spent the rest of the day guarding against footfalls, saying "No" to soft drinks in the area, and blocking any falling rot from the roof. No scourge from the heavens was going to touch them, not on his shift. They were beyond his protection, but maybe he could still help preserve their memory.

He handed a tissue to a middle-aged woman on his right and another to a young man leaning on a cane. He handed out an entire fucking box, and then got another. He reached through years of hesitance to put a hand on a stranger's shoulder.

Leaving that hallowed shell of a building, that transformed cathedral, he looked to the sky. The stars above Lake Michigan shone bright against the darkness, so bright that when he closed his eyes he could still see them fading in and out and in and out until he didn't need to see them to know they were there. After so long he'd finally come home.

We are family,
Get up everybody
And sing.

Nights at Dugan's Bistro

Dancing with Angels, Dancing with Ghosts

Gerard Wozek

I cried the day they demolished Eddie Dugan's Bistro in Chicago. Wailed unapologetically as the bulldozers ripped up the colored lights under the Mondrian-inspired disco floor. Stood with tears in my eyes as the wrecking ball tore through the dance hall walls that seemed to expand out one hundred feet or so every night Cheryl Lynn wailed on "Starlove" or the Weather Girls predicted a rainstorm of sexy men or when Chic definitively proclaimed it to be "Good Times."

Dubbed "Chicago's Super Bar," the glittering disco palace, once situated in the North Loop at the corner of Dearborn and Hubbard Streets, rivaled the decadent glory days of the Ice Palace and Studio 54 in New York City. Throngs of people came to this flagship nightclub in order to inhabit a world where they could lose their conservative façade and be utterly consumed by the rush and torrent of flashing lights and contagious dance beats. Torn down in 1982, this landmark city institution that attracted an eclectic, mostly queer identified crowd, has never been truly replicated.

I wept on demolition day because my old orchestral-inflected diva anthems were still coiled around those sacred wooden rafters, the shrill high notes from "Two Tons of Fun" and Donna Summer were tenuously clinging to the strobe lights in the ceiling, wrapped around whatever bar glasses and empty liquor bottles still remained on those imploded shelves. In the crush of brick and plaster, I paused to listen for Ami Stewart's percussive "Knock on Wood," Grace Jones begging the dance tribe to "Pull Up to the Bumper," and Karen Young taunting all the dancers to indulge in a long overdue "Hot Shot." The day they tore Dugan's Bistro down, I could almost hear Evelyn "Champagne" King's gravelly voice singing the lyric "It's a lowdown dirty, dirty, shame," still hovering in the air, the way it used to over hundreds of stomping, shirtless males at midnight.

Wandering into Chicago during the late seventies at the pitch of disco fever, I had my share of memorable dances. Sneaking out of my bedroom window and driving into the limits of the jewel-encrusted downtown, I came to the city to inhabit a world where I could brazenly embrace an unbridled, empowered stance as a queer youth. A carefully forged identification card and a shy wink at the bouncer allowed me access into the Bistro's black and silver main dance room. Whirling colored spotlights and a massive, oversized mirrorball prevailed over a continuous walloping beat that seemed to permeate every cell of my body—it was this percussive pounding coupled with a euphoria-inducing tribal hum that insisted that I unconditionally accept the individualist I was becoming.

For years, Lou Divito sat in his disc jockey booth above the dance floor with a stack of vinyl and a poster of Diana Ross on the back wall and guided his willing supplicants through a drumbeat-inflamed journey. Divito became locally famous for being one of the first Chicago spin masters to have his hot mixes played on the radio, Chicago's own WDAI Dance Radio. Whenever I was at the club and heard a record that I loved, I would ask him for the name of the song. He would write the title of the spinning vinyl disc on a sheet of paper that could be redeemed for a discount at a neighborhood Sounds Good record store, which was how I built a vast collection of twelve-inchers. This way, at home, with my headphones securely planted over my ears and my eyes tightly shut, I could reconstruct my vision of slender, male dancers shrink-wrapped into their Lycra hot pants, balancing on the vinyl cushions of Bistro barstools.

In my mind I became Vicki Sue Robinson, Sylvester, Gloria Gaynor, and Teena Marie all rolled into one. I sipped cocktails with fellow divas while wearing the Viking-inspired headdress Cher wore on the cover of her "Take Me Home" album. I was the dolled-up backstreet girl on the inset of Donna Summer's "Bad Girls" LP. Or the suave. zoot-suited Kid Creole stepping out for an all night conga. Later, as the party stumbled on in a psychedelic trance, I became the stereotyped and much maligned disco bunny who survived the homophobic dance music backlash, the destruction of thousands of vinyl records in Comiskey Park in the summer of 1979, but who still, somehow, never got over the addictive hop.

When I fell in love for the first time, wicked disco was my soundtrack and my teenage libido was securely braided into every extended remix. Giorgio Moroder's trademark synthesizers were darting through the speakers. Santa Esmeralda was imploring, "Please Don't Let Me Be Misunderstood"; Carol Douglas was entreating me into a "Midnight Love Affair." Candi Staton's anthem called out for "Young Hearts to Run Free." Dan Hartman begged heaven to "Relight My Fire." And I believed anything was possible, including finding a kindred soul on the teeming dance floor. I exchanged my first penetrating glance with a stranger, experienced my first male-to-male kiss, and discovered my first searing heartbreak, as so many other neophytes did, right inside Eddie Dugan's nonstop disco playground.

All of gay Chicago came to feel the communal electricity of the illustrious dance hall, press their bodies against one another in the smothering heat, lip-sync to the lyrics of an infectious disco chorus, and get stupefied in the ubiquitous scent of amyl nitrite. Each night that I showed up at the monster palace on Dearborn proved to be a melding of half-clothed bodies, unleashed reckless spirits, and orgiastic, elated drunkenness. We were buoyed up on the pulse of Latin congas and hissing tambourines, discombobulated by swooping laser beams and the trademark blinking neon red lips that blew French kisses over the heads of dervish dancers. A seductive, brown-haired "bearded lady" would often whirl across the floor, arms flailing through descending confetti and silver glitter snowflakes before collapsing into the arms of a receptive muscled stranger. Cymbals clanged, heavily perfumed drag queens from the nearby Baton Show Lounge would giggle and flirt, a disco goddess belted out an irresistible tribute to romantic love, and the whole world gently sambaed and slid sideways.

In a kind of pagan, tribal love knot, men came to Dugan's Bistro to satiate their submerged desires. We recognized each other's raw pulse on the dance floor or in the shadows of the back cruise room, and we were irrevocably ignited. We came to the Bistro in order to become transfigured by a live performance of Melba Moore, consumed by Loletta Holloway's epic "Love Sensation," or find passion consummated in the Trammps's "Disco Inferno." Our supple bodies swayed and spun and turned to flame and in the crescendo of one of Sylvester's declarative anthems: "Everybody is a star!" We insisted, there was nothing that could possibly extinguish the intensity of this crazed mob as we shimmied and stomped into the beat, the beat, the beat, the beat, the beat, the beat, the beat, the beat.

This was Queer Chicago circa the late seventies and early eighties at its finest. The hedonistic toga parties at the Bistro were infamous with both men and women taking great liberties to check out and sample what was wrapped beneath the swaddles of ripped bed sheets. Theme parties were frequent, with "Sleazy Nights" being a crowd favorite. And it was common to watch men "falling out" of their torn jeans, or see women slipping their tongues into bartenders' mouths or tearing up their indigo fishnet stockings and hairline thongs during a passionate gyration.

After the closure of Dugan's Bistro, a dancehall that had celebrated the gay community at a time when we desperately needed sanctuary and affirmation, it felt like the whole city mourned. I think for a whole year or so, I didn't go out dancing, preferring rather to stay home with my makeshift turntables and my amateur attempts at emulating Lou Divito's intricate mixes. A few sobering years later, the Paradise Bar and Bistro Too opened up in north side Chicago neighborhoods and they both tried heroically to recapture the romantic dazzle and glamorous sheen of the original Bistro. But nothing could match the legendary icon that once magnetized and entranced every dance devotee in queer Chicago.

Even now, I still want to do the Bus Stop with the remembered ghosts of my well-spent youth. Though I never became acquainted with the impresario who was Eddie Dugan, I still wish I could thank him somehow for providing a safe haven in Chicago, a city that at the time, for me, seemed all too conservative, and even at times hostile. This risqué discothèque had somehow midwifed my arrival into social circles and wholly assisted my maturation as a gay man. The festive, welcoming atmosphere helped me to trust my own developing sexuality and come to terms with my emerging identity. It would be impossible to fully calculate the transformative resonance a place like the Bistro had on the Chicago queer landscape at this time.

Though I am much older now, I still listen to my favorite dance music, and I keep on moving my body, only occasionally losing myself in clanging synthesizers, overdubbed vocals, and bellowing drums. I still crave that naive era when the only thing that mattered was the extended dance cut Mister DJ happened to be spinning at the moment. I still ache for the "Solid Gold"-inspired dancers who once ruled Dugan's dance floor, the omnipresent syncopated electric bass line that flooded the entire complex, and the artificial snowflakes and tiny sponge balls that fell from the rafters, covering us in shimmer and gloss and hope.

Give me back my silver sparkle skinny tie, the one I wore on New Year's Eve the night I kissed a half-naked go-go boy. Give me back my abandoned record collection, the lost West End and Casablanca labels, those obscure limited edition pink vinyl discs, those endless bumpin' bubble remixes, the ones that drove us onto the floor for hours at Sunday afternoon tea dances with Eddie Dugan himself presiding over the slowly sloshing crowd. Give me back my sunglasses with the crimson lenses and glow in the dark side rims. Give me back my striped polyester shirts—the ones with the extra long collars and a sheen that reflected back those giddy flashing lights. Give me back my John Travolta brass belt buckle. My original "Staying Alive" T-shirt. My Bee Gees pendant and chain.

Give me back my Bistro life. The long Saturday night lines to get in the front entrance, the fevered crush and mash of sweaty chests on the dance floor, the exotic umbrella drinks from handsome bartenders, and the slow, sad retreat back into dusty streetlamp-lit Chicago boulevards. Give me back those long drives afterwards with a backseat overfilled with newfound friends, my head still throbbing from all the tambourine beating, chanting, spontaneous screaming, and hip thrusting. Give me back my makeshift map to locate my favorite all-night hamburger stand on Clark Street, the one serving up the most exquisite helping of cheese fries, or that familiar summertime cruise out to the cavernous hedges of the Lincoln Park Lagoon at three a.m.

Give me back the urge to merge with taboo disco fire. My breathless leap into the unknown, into first hand experience, into absolute trust. Give me back the boy I used to be. The boy who "looped-the-loop" with angelic beings hovering over a kaleidoscopic floor. The boy who thought he would remain so young, so infatuated with dance fever, so hopelessly enthralled with being a winged free spirit in Chicago, entranced by the glamorous party life, so pretty in the cocaine soot atmosphere of the Bistro's back bar, so captivated by the underground terrain of an all-night paradise the whole world thought would last forever.

rhythm is a dancer

kay ulanday barrett

Growing up, I do remember "THE ROYAL"
(pronounced like the first names
"Roy" & "Al," for usual big gay pyrotechnics)
thursday nights as younger
queers teemed in logan square
armed with body lust that could
squeeze out teenage awkwardity
in just one dance.

Being in 1998
& under 21
for $5
we could outwit our
muscles, discover them, boys
with eyeshadow glitz to match their
grafs on avenue walls, the
pants or shirt you were forbidden
to wear at home
(due to whatever that check box said
on your birth certificate).
Our mamas probably would have
slit their wallets
if they only knew where
their work hours went.

We kissed hard.
We held hands.

Speaking our mother tongues
cheek to cheek, with our *bestfriends*
who were really our girlfriends,
even though being 16
meant a new best friend
oh every 6 months.

Managed "it's time for the peculator,"
in the veins way before hipster
upswing tattered property taxes,
disemboweled hearts
of brown queers everywhere.
Way before white and straight folks
took our moves, bought
our clothes or put holes
in their own to call "vintage."

Some like Joanna aka Johnny,
depending if you were her father
or his lover,
banished shadows with cig butts by 3 a.m.
and gave this glare like he knew
exactly how to hold you
if you needed it enough.

Or Celía who could out pop AND lock
any b-boy and move her hips
stunning to freestyle
swerving more than kicked snare drums.
The following morning,
girls would itch the lines of
their palms for those
angles

or the kids that assembled rum
and sugary juices
to forget whatever
they were or weren't coming
home to

or the bois
who laid down their guns
at the door for a long
slow dance

or her,
that one girl who had The Cure
and Depeche Mode buttons all over her jean jacket,
too cool in the corner
who shook her legs a bit
particularly in appreciation of
salt-n-pepa, and maybe it was
a trick of the strobe lights
—but she even smirked a little.

Or us—
rounding out summer stars
& sky with soprano notes.

How glorious could we have been
lodged in lockers by school day,
scared of the lies that mirrors
and windows told?

We came home breathless
from dancing our queer bodies
back to valid,

each time we'd make
a ruckus
as queer
as brown
—not to reinforce
stereotypes, but to take back the
space that is ours,

the space in our ribcages
and in Chicago's sidewalks
that would coax us,
to love.

We come from ancestors who drum and dance,
who made sweat rivulets alongside the tears
because movement had to start first on the body,
before the noose,
before the well-intended missionaries,
before the semi-automatic rifles,
before the rich studied our rhythms,
before the empty and angry,
before the straight and the narrow
beat us.

We found beats.

Now when I ask you,
Giiiirrllll? What was the last jam you danced to?
I mean reeaaallly danced to?
Sometimes I want to hear your song,
sometimes I'll listen to your beat and say, *eh, it's aiiight.*

But mostly
I want us to celebrate, honor, love
our movements.

2

In Transit

Elevated Postcard

Robert McDonald

I love the sweet loping boys, their corduroy jackets
with threadbare elbows, a scorched-open hole
on the leg of their jeans. Transparency,
I tell you, can be a kind of gift; this might
be one definition of a ghost: someone who desires
the things of the world but cannot
be seen and desired in turn. I haunt
this city or I become the one haunted
by the rush and return, the repetition of trains,
each car bearing a lanky and oblivious stranger—
dark-eyed, pensive, he might dream of the lover
waiting at home, or just wonder
if there's any ice cream left
in the fridge—a mist
rises off the graveyard between Wilson Avenue
and Montrose, you can see it from the El—
and if the dead in their still
and snowbound village
glare with longing
at this clattersome train,
it's because in every season
the breath of eros
sparks the best
and most dangerous
weather.

the wife and the bride

Carina Gia Farrero

i met her on a train
she said she belonged
somewhere to someone
that she too had been cooked up in a ladle
and could do nothing without her maker

she told me that her husband was also her bride
and that she wouldn't let him visit all the time
though he tried
almost every lunch
to bring her meat or milk
and beg for her to stay

the wife that took me cooked me
she said
my dress is too red
my mouth too red
my mind too tight

who am i
i keep record

she seemed to think it was fate
we met like this
on a train
we are divine and homesick
she said

the self is a tricky monster
and love is a gorgeous monster

but not to worry
somebody somewhere will pack your lunch

i watch her
it rains
we sit on trains
and sleep
we eat our belongings

it's night
she's still
i'm forcing the whole of the lightbulb into my mouth

Cold Cab

Byron Flitsch

It was one of those first dates you'd totally tell your grandkids about. Sort of.

His name was Jason and his hand was all the way up my thigh at this Chicago west-loop sushi joint where we're finishing dinner. You know the place: lowly lit, airy, abstract beats spun by a DJ, and tables so small and so close putting your hand on someone's inner thigh looks like no more than leaning in.

"I think we should take this back to my place," he says in a raspy whisper, looking me straight in the eye. Meanwhile his hands are inching towards my groin and it felt . . . right. I mean, he was a professional photographer with a nice BMW and some chocolate brown eyes that make you think of the sweetness of dairy cows. Okay, so that might be a Wisconsin thing to think of.

Yes, it was our first date. Yes, I barely knew him. Yes, I was horny and at least wanted some heavy make-out action. You know, some good second-base stuff. Truth: I hadn't gotten anything in months . . . ahem, six months to be exact.

"Let's get the check," I whisper back with that tingle that shoots through your body when you know you're about to get something good. We grab the waitress. I watch as he slaps his AMEX on the bill without looking at the amount. God, it's sexy when people don't look at amounts before they pay! I swig the rest of my Shiraz while putting on my coat, preparing for the January cold.

Have you ever messed around in a cab?" Jason asks while he lifts his muscular arm to hail one. The snow decorates his dark pea coat. From a distance, he looks like Jake Gyllenhaal.

"Heh . . . no . . . phew . . . no . . . I can't say I have . . ." I try not to come off desperate, but Jason was the first guy in months to make me pant. He winks, and within a few seconds a yellow cab rolls up and crunches the freshly fallen snow with its wheels.

"After you," Jason says, holding open the door.

In the cab, he places his hand on the left knee of my jeans while slowly dancing his fingers to my thigh. The cab slows to take a sharp turn. Then his hand is at the point where your thigh meets your hips. The cab speeds down a one-way street. Then he's about to cup my balls. I can feel his breathing slow down as mine speeds up. It feels like it's the first time again. The smoking cab driver continues to whip around corners and speeds down streets as if he were being timed on his arrival. The fogging of the glass makes it seem like it's only Jason and me in this whole snowy world. For an instant, we make eye contact. I can smell him, mint mixed with the smell of red Shiraz coming from his breath. His trimmed facial hair and smile and his laugh and then in the backseat of a yellow cab I get a hot kiss that was going to change everything . . . or at least lead to something.

He presses his perfectly wetted lips to mine and we moan a long moan.

Instantly, the cab slams on its brakes, veering to the curb while cutting across a lane of traffic. Jason rolls to the wet floor of the cab. I ram my elbow on that plastic partition that separates driver from passenger.

"What the . . . !" Jason screams toward the front of the cab. It's the first time I get a look at our cab driver—a white guy with a thick beard and a mole on his right cheek. He's wearing a ski cap and has a cigarette dangling from his lips.

"Get out!" the man barks in an accent I can't decipher. Russian?

"I'm sor . . . sorry . . . ," I stutter.

"Get out of the cab!" he snaps again. French?

"Why are we getting kicked out?" Jason nervously asks.

"Men don't kiss in my cab," the driver barks back to us over the radio playing. Oh, then I pick up his accent: he speaks asshole!

"I'm . . . I'm sorry? You . . . pulled over because . . ."

"Get out!" he interrupts. "No fags!"

The "F" word. Now, I'm not talking "fuck" here. That's a whole different story. "Fag." Fag is a whole lot worse than the other "F" word. It's like calling Prada Old Navy. It's like calling Madonna just a pop singer. It's like telling someone he's not worth the breath he takes, especially when it's being used to judge someone.

The "F" word means I'm fourteen; Chad Ello, a fellow Boy Scout, corners me with two other guys at Boy Scout camp near Eagle's Lake.

"You're a fag. We all know it," he says, pushing me into the wet sand.

"I'm sorry . . . but we're not getting out . . . We didn't do anything wrong," I politely respond. Plus it's cold out. We're in the middle of an industrial area where getting another cab will be impossible.

"Get the fuck out of my cab, faggots," the driver barks again. His lit cigarette bounces like a firefly in his mouth.

The "F" word means Ryan Sellers, my dorm roommate my freshman year of college in Wisconsin.

"Dude, if you watch me get dressed, I'll kick your ass. Everyone on the floor knows you're gay. No one likes you," Ryan says after a week of knowing me. "And if I catch you checking me out, I'll hurt you."

"Byron, let's just get out. He's obviously an ass . . . We'll get a different cab and . . . ," Jason says.

"NO!" I yelp at Jason. He throws his head back and leans in to the seat. He's already frustrated with the situation and it seems like I'm only getting started. Sidebar: I'm not a confrontational guy. But whether I was buzzed on wine or if it was that I wanted to get laid, I was feeling the testosterone.

"We're not getting out," I say to the cab driver, pressing my ass firmly into the seat as if he could feel the pressure.

"I will getchu out, you faggots."

The "F" word means gay people not allowed to get married.

"Then . . . do something about it . . . ," I say, not really knowing where this is going.

The cab driver doesn't respond.

In that moment I realize how cold the leather cab seats are and how the heat has suddenly been turned down, but the radio turned up. A cheesy, soft pop song plays in the background. My stomach drops. I look at Jason. He has his fists clenched in his lap and tucked near his thighs. He's staring out through a part of the window where he has wiped some fog away. His face spells anger, but the way his lip quivers . . . he looks like he is going to cry.

"Get out. Don't worry about tab. Get out!" the cab driver yells, breaking the silence over the radio.

"Don't worry about the tab . . . ," I whisper back. DON'T WORRY ABOUT THE TAB? That's the last thing I'm thinking about right now.

My mind is racing. My stomach is flipping. Cars are whipping outside the cab while cold wind punches the exterior of the car. All I concentrate on is breathing and Jason's silence.

"Let's just go," Jason pleads as he raises his hand to open the car door. "Please . . ." The entire night, the dinner, the wine, the kiss . . . it's all dead now.

I look at Jason's face and in that instant, I see me ten years ago as a Boy Scout being picked on for the way I walked, the way I talked, and for what people thought I was.

"No . . . ," I plead while grabbing his thigh to keep him from getting out the car.

"Get out!" the driver screams.

"I'm not doing this. I refuse to do this," Jason says to me. He doesn't look me in the eye.

"I have to be to work early . . . I . . . ," he continues, and with that he jumps out of the cab and darts into traffic.

He left me. He left me alone.

"Leave with your friend," the driver says, laughing.

"He's not a friend!" I snap back. "And no!" I adjust my legs in the cab and stare forward.

"Fine! I call cops!" he yells while picking up his cell phone, and I can see him start to dial.

I play with my fingers in my palm. I feel my face turning warm. My throat gets scratchy. I want to cry . . . I want to cry because this is the first time I'm actually standing up for myself as a gay man.

I try to listen to the conversation the cab driver is having on the phone. It's hard to hear over the radio. "Won't pay tab!" I hear him lie. "I want him out!" I hear him say next. "Quick!" I hear him say before he hangs up. "They're on way," he laughs. "You should get out."

I don't know whether he's telling the truth or the call is to scare me. It works.

But, as stupid as it sounds, I don't really feel alone. I feel like all the past Byrons are in the backseat of the car with me. The young Byron who quit Scouts because he was teased so much is sitting in the middle seat wearing a little Cub Scout hat. The Byron who refused to try to make friends his freshman year of college because he was terrified of his dorm mate, he is sitting on the other side of the car with an eighteen-years-naive look drawn on his face. Crammed in that backseat with us is all our bulky baggage—no marriage, being harassed, being judged, being ignored, gaining rights and then losing them. This backseat isn't empty—not at all.

We sit in silence with just the radio playing and the sound of the wind trying to make it through the cracks of the cab. Each car that zips by flashing its headlights through the fogged windows startles me . . . Are those the cops? My heart races. I've never stood up to anyone. I've always given in. I've always been the first to apologize.

Ten minutes go by. I can hear the cabbie grunting in frustration. The car is still running. I get a text message from Jason that reads: *You home OK?*

I don't respond.

Fifteen minutes go by. Still no cops. My head starts racing. Shouldn't they be here by now? Another text from Jason: *Dude, are you still in the cab?* I give no response.

Finally, I get frustrated. "Where are the police?"

No response.

"Where are the police?"

He's still silent while lighting another cigarette.

"Where are the police!" I snap.

"Just get out, please . . . ," the driver says calmly.

"They aren't coming, are they?" I laugh in realization.

"Please, just get out," he says, almost desperately.

Then I see him shift, turn his head and eyes to meet mine. It is the first time I see his eyes. In the dark, I can't tell the color . . . I can only tell the emotion. He is frustrated. He is defeated. He is . . . scared.

I stare into his eyes for as long as I can; then I realize I'm going to get out of the cab . . . not because I have to, but because I won. He never called the cops. He just wanted me gone. He was scared. For the first time, someone was scared of me.

"Fine, I'm getting out," I say. I could see the tension in his face loosen.

"Don't worry about tab . . . it's not . . ."

"Screw you!" I snap as I grab a twenty from my wallet. The fare was about six bucks. "I'm not taking a free ride from you!"

I toss the only twenty I have between the plastic partitions between the driver and me. There is so much I should have said, but as he starts to break the twenty all I can say is "Keep the change . . ." as I step into the cold winter night.

Darla Speeding

Deb R. Lewis

You ever have a friend who sounds like *National Enquirer*'s front page—but when you're not trying to put words on it, it's really fucking simple? You're you, they're them, and there's nothing more to talk about?

Get this, I'm riding shotgun with Darla Rausenstaadt from Aurora back into Chicago, for the Chicago Council of Clubs meeting—which is the oversight board for the leather community's social calendar because you don't want two dungeon parties on the same night if you can help it; the leather community's small enough that it would affect turnout. I'm in my leather vest and blue jeans; she's in a blouse, skirt, knee-high riding boots, and vest, topped off with a Muir cap—all black leather save the red blouse—like an Aryan motorcycle chieftess, complete with deep blue eyes.

We're on the East-West Tollway. Typical of Darla, we're late, so forget eighty miles per hour; we're booking ninety or ninety-five. It'd be faster but the Geo Metro's redlining. Just as we zip past the giant N building—you know, N for Naperville—flashing lights erupt out of nowhere.

The passenger side mirror is optional on Geo Metros, so I gotta turn to look through the rear window. "It's a State Trooper. Can they *bust* you for speeding on a tollway? Since you pay to use it?"

Darla opens her pouty, lipsticked lips to cackle while releasing the steering wheel with both manicured, long-fingered hands to flip her digits around in panic. Or mock panic. Hard to tell with Darla. She's grinning through the sunglasses perched on her hawkish nose as she downshifts.

The grin turns to a real shit-eater as she says, "Aw man, you know this is going to suck."

Now for you to understand I have to tell you something—but it doesn't matter. And yet, for some reason, it always fucking changes everything: Darla was born Daryl. At this point she was on enough estrogen to make her soft with a hint of curvy. She's got legs to kill and die for. If you catch on that she's not a born girl, it's only because you noticed that her hands and feet are kind of long and confirmed your suspicions by checking for an Adam's apple. For someone like Darla, a simple traffic stop is never quite as simple as it might be for everyone else.

You also have to know Darla's not one to play it safe. When she gets into trouble, it's never halfway. It's one of the things I love about her—her incredible guts and sense of humor. Running with Darla is running away with the circus without being jaded after the lights go down.

My pal Butch tried to introduce me to Darla at my first-ever dungeon party, three years before. Darla's in a dark green leather smock cinched with a cord to give her tall, slender frame more of a waist. The dark green sets off her strawberry blonde hair; her eyelids, done in reddish gold, pull it all together. Darla was going down on some chick, Holly, who was naked, strapped face-out on a St. Andrew's cross—a giant wooden X. You couldn't see, but later it turned out there was this special set consisting of butt plug and dildo, made of polyurethane with special electrical probes embedded, wired to electricity. Holly had the dildo up inside her and Darla had the butt plug in, so that whenever Darla's tongue touched Lisa's clit, the electrical current completed right at the point of contact.

It had never occurred to me that electricity and wet orifices might resemble a good idea.

Butch tips her dark buzz cut toward them and says, "Well, they're busy. Let's see what else is going on."

We killed time eyeing different scenarios from a polite distance: mostly standard whipping scenes, clothespins on nipples, and so on. But then there's stuff I hadn't dreamt of yet: a woman with dozens of needles woven into her back as a temporary piercing. Or someone tied down on a table being made to cum over and over again until shrieking—she actually passed out. *Way* beyond my scope at the time.

After an hour, Darla was still taking her long, charged sip of Holly. Never did meet her that night. Supposedly, when Holly finally came, the dildo shot out of her pussy like a cannonball, hit Darla in the forehead, completing the circuit, and electrocuted her, green smock and all. Darla's crazy, panicked digits flipped and quivered in the air when she finally told it: "And would anyone help me? No! Too much fun laughing at me convulsing on the floor." Typical Darla.

Or there's the time Darla wore white, fringed leather, going down on this school girlish vamp she'd just met in the jane at the leather bar. The SLUTS—that was the first all-women's leather club in Chicago—their big mission at the time, aside from eating and throwing dungeon parties, was to encourage dykes to use barriers for safer sex. That was out the window with Darla, apparently—the pleated skirt was on her period, which stained those blinding leathers. "I think they're ruined," Darla moaned. I knew from the outlay for my vest, they'd easily cost $800. After the SLUTS resident nurse slapped her on the ass and told her it was her own damned fault, Darla just powdered her nose and laughed.

Then there's the whole Bocephus incident. A couple of years after I met Darla, one car of the Chicago SLUTS caravan made a stop on the way home from Freeze and Sleeze—a big SM hoorah in Indianapolis. Darla, Butch, and I were on this piece of shit road with a gravel pull-off that housed Leroy's Tackle, Bait, and Gun Boutique and a stand-alone Harley dealership. Well, me and Butch thought it'd be fun to eyeball the motorcycles, and Darla was up for anything with "Gun" and "Boutique" in the same breath. Needing to pee, we decide on the Gun Boutique first. While we're acting like customers, this tractor-capped, bent-belted, flannel-bellied good ol' boy took a shine to Darla. And who can blame him? She's in her black and red outfit with cowboy boots and a black cowboy hat this time—she's a long drink of kinky and her make-up is flawless in a "Dreamweaver" sort of way.

The Hoosier got on the right track to impress her when he handed her a shotgun and said, "How d'ya like the feel o'that, little lady?"

But he'd failed to tell her that the gun was loaded.

So when Darla leveled it at a taxidermied dog, the gun went off, blowing the poor thing—henceforth known as Bocephus—to sawdust bits.

Meanwhile, the upstanding gents at the Harley dealership called the cops. Who demanded driver's licenses from everyone on the premises and separated us for individual interviews, so we couldn't hear each other's stories, though at one point I did hear Darla say, "Who on earth hands a lady a loaded shotgun?"

After weighing all the information—Darla's driver's license, which has a photo of an in-betweenie with a ponytail, still says "Daryl," and has an "M" next to sex; the fact that she didn't know the gun was loaded; that it was indeed an accident, even the shop owner said so; and that the only injury was to Bocephus, a dog made of fur and sawdust—the Indiana State

Troopers, from the kindness of their hearts, escorted us to the state line and told Darla to never sully the great state of Indiana with her presence again. Actually, considering that we were two dykes and a tranny—all leathered out, no less—and the licensed carte blanche mentality you might reasonably expect of a state trooper in an isolated place, and what kind of *Deliverance* it *could* have been, I'd say we all got off easy.

So when Darla turns to me, downshifting the Geo Metro, and says, "Aw man, you know this is going to suck," I'm not much of a bullshitter. I say, "Yeah, big ass donkey dicks."

We rot on the shoulder while the trooper runs the plates. I'm wondering if he'll use the excuse of speeding to arrest us for our queer leather aesthetic when the mirrored sunglasses arrive with a frown. "License. Registration. Proof of insurance."

"Certainly, officer," Darla says, "They're in my purse."

He stares at me—maybe checking that I, the nose-ringed bulldyke, have my seatbelt buckled—while her long fingers tip through her wallet. Her slender wrist escapes the red sleeve as she extends the papers through the open window. Darla watches him march back to his squad.

He stops half way.

"Here we go," she says. He returns frowning *more*—if that's possible. "This *your* license?" Glancing from the in-betweenie Daryl photo to her and back.

If he arrests us, will Darla and I land in the same cell? Will they cuff Darla to a bench? Or worse, stick her in the men's cellblock, trying to fend off a bunch of phobic bad-asses? I resent Ossifer Squarenuts. Of all the fuckers flying past, why'd he stop us? I'm bristling, even as Darla's face looks softer and more tired than I've ever seen it. The blue in her eyes is so fuzzy, I forget that I'm sitting next to the Queen of the Smartasses, and think to myself, *He better not manhandle her . . .*

"Yes, officer," Darla says, "I have a letter from my psychiatrist right here . . ."

We're both too shaken to speak, let alone crack jokes, as he heads back to the squad, mumbling. He runs the license and there must not be any warrants out on her—and really, I think you've heard enough to know it could've gone either way.

He swaggers back to us with those impenetrable sunglasses and barks, "This is not a car. It is a pop can on wheels. Slow it down before you kill your friend here."

"I'm sorry, officer—" Darla starts.

His lips sit like bricks, one on top of the other, as he holds up a leather-gloved hand, using the other to hand back her papers. "As for the rest, I don't really want to know."

Neither of us could believe our ears. "You mean, I can go, officer?"

"Go. And don't ever make me bust you again."

So Darla's disarmed troopers in two different states. Think about it—it all makes sense: if you're a state trooper and you make what most folks would consider a bizarro bust, how do you explain it without ending up in the tabloids? Shit, it better be worth the trouble.

I guess there's an advantage to being less than simple—to being that vulnerable, unexplainable self. Darla's miles ahead in this—I'm just striving to get there.

Survivor

Karen Lee Osborne

Leaving Chicago, she drives the wide
highway west, past glass
office buildings and shopping malls

until she sees mostly farms.
Her grip on the steering wheel
loosens. The drive doesn't seem

as long, the sun less blinding.
It gets easier, they say.
The last of a small family, she

does not know the purpose
of ease. Until her sister took
her own life, she felt

that hers was one of blessed
ordinariness. Her father left
soon after her birth, and she

barely missed him. Forty years
later, she tried to find him,
to tell him of her sister's death,

and learned he had died years before.
Her mother done in by heart and
lung trouble soon after, friends

tell her she is finally free.
No more moods
demanding attention,

sticky ropes of guilt
pulling her into an endless
pool. No more waiting

for her own time, her own
needs. *I wish your sister
had never told me.*

So she never said it. *But I'm
gay too.* Now, as she leaves
the highway and enters

the old two-lane road
to the cemetery, new houses
sprout where silos once stood.

She has never liked it here,
has never cared for this endless sky,
these cornfields she's seen her whole life.

They seem to mock the dead
with their slow triumph of growth.
On her sister's tombstone, the words

"daughter, sister, partner"
in a false semblance of cohesion.
A partner she did not know

how to say "no" to, how
to leave. A sister who never
knew of her despair, masked

by easy laughter. She knows
her sister would have preferred
no tombstone, no flowers,

but their mother prevailed.
Had the body shipped
1,000 miles "home," against

the partner's wishes. Her sister,
afraid to leave, finally free.
A tinge of yellow in the calla lilies,

pink roses and purple asters
for the other graves, names
from the old country, those

she is the last to mourn.
Just silk. From Kmart? As if
her sister is whispering behind her,

ridiculing her mother's morbid
attachment to doing exactly
this. Handcuffed to the past,

to her dead. And she is smirking,
then laughing, as she forces
wire stems into the stubborn

Illinois soil. *Tacky.* She laughs
so hard it hurts, until
laughter releases her to stillness,

though she does not know
the purpose of release. She is
not her mother. She will not

return for months, perhaps years,
preferring the city, freedom to love
whom she may, even crowds

and noise to all this space,
its canvas of absence. She stands
and turns. No one will notice

how she lets the graves go.
A big-chested black dog
with stubby legs romps

along the narrow, winding
paths, then lies down and rolls
in the grass. There is nowhere else

he would rather be. Later,
he follows her toward the car,
waits for her hand as it descends

to stroke his head. He pauses
for a moment, looks up,
sees a squirrel, and runs.

Cheese, Gifts, Fireworks!

(A Wisconsin Sonnet)

cin salach

Surely my love arranged this pinkly setting sun as a surprise
for the ride, gentle topic of conversation as we head 90 west,
smartly driving the night before, so when we open our eyes
to the sun rising, we are already there with 8 hours of rest.

We sing country until we are in it, escape down a highway
blessed with cheese and fireflies, when a deer enters bright
in our headlights, shining, then dismissing the old cliché,
crosses both lanes graceful and goes quick into the night.

O! I feel it before I see it, then out of the darkness it appears,
I haul duffle, cooler, laptop, one hand tied behind my back.
Solar powered! Moon charged! I fly up the big-hilled stairs,
and with an entire state behind me, slip into the green I lack.

The cabin embraces two wholly, we do nothing but sleep, wake.
Tomorrow brings cheese and rain, wine for champagne's sake.

3

Intersections

The Incorrect Tattoo

David Kodeski

Later, I would ask myself, "Where did that guy come from? Did he come off the bus?" I had been walking home from the El station on one of those precious few still cool but warmly sunny days somewhere there in the month of March. The light had just changed and I was standing on the curb, and I could hear the bus I did not take pulling up to the stop behind me. I think.

At this point there's some "nothing" happening here. So, to try to remember that span of nothingness is difficult. Time passed and I had some thoughts. One thought concerned noticing the angle of sunlight on the building across the intersection. Which made me think about sundials. Latitude. These tangentially connected thoughts occurred within the blink of an eye and may not have even occurred at that exact same moment, but rather, may have been the *memory* of having these thoughts in some sequence, one upon the other, sometime in the past. It's a common enough thought sequence in my brain: sunlight's angle—sun dial—latitude. Oftentimes this thought sequence will drift toward "garden plant," "flower box," "budget"—as in: can I afford to buy new flower boxes or will it be cheaper to build my own?

Another thought I might have had at that moment concerned the flashing WALK / DON'T WALK sign. Again, this was an extremely unfinished and very loose thought or memory concerning Diana Slickman describing someone who wasn't properly using the crosswalk being struck down in traffic. I see crosswalk, I think "Diana Slickman." I think "jaywalker." I'm having this thought—or this memory of these thoughts—about the crosswalk, and Diana Slickman, and flower boxes, and latitude, and the shaft of sunlight all within the same eye-blink. There's traffic passing. The bus brakes hissing behind me. Vague impressions of other commuters standing nearby. I'm in that state of being that is not being at all. Aware, but not *aware*. Nearly unconscious. And even as this unaware awareness is occurring I'm deciding whether I'll stop in at the grocery store just up the street.

This state of being eventually transforms itself into a state of remembered being. It all comes out in the wash of days passing one after another with nothing to mark them beyond something unexpected occurring. Getting caught in the rain. Dropping a bottle of vodka. Falling off your bike. Noticing a tattoo on the wrist of a young man riding the bus. A tattoo that reads "Revelations 11:7," and sitting there thinking, "Do I tell this idiot—who has gone to the trouble of finding a sentiment from the Bible that is suitably insolent and Goth-y enough to get tattooed onto his wrist—that he's gotten it wrong? That it is Revelation, singular. Not Revelations, plural. The Single Book of Revelation not the Book of Twenty-Hundred Revelations. The one Revelation as revealed to the Apostle John by Jesus's personal and private angel and not a series of 'mysterious' quatrains written by Nostradamus or Jeanne Dixon. That if he's serious about advertising his allegiance to Satan and his minions, that he's got to get that 'S' lasered off." This you remember. This makes the day special. Try to remember what you had for dinner last night and it can be a brain-choking chore. Yet you recall with ease the crazy person screaming high-pitched heebie-jeebies in the alley, whose own special brand of crazy is so completely crazy that regaling party guests with the wild-eyed, foaming-at-the-mouth details becomes story-telling badge-of-honor fodder for years after the fact.

I'm looking at the shaft of sunlight and waiting for the traffic light to change, and I feel someone coming up behind me, actually walking directly into me from behind. This startles me and occupies my thoughts for a second and distracts me from the shaft of sunlight but not nearly as much as something I can feel moving back and forth between my calves. It feels like it might even be a puppy. But it is not a puppy. It is a white stick. A white cane to be more specific. A white cane with a red tip, waving back and forth between my legs as I feel the wielder of this cane falling onto me. Gently, slowly, almost with the familiarity of a lover or a stranger who wants to be my lover. Clumsily. Stumbling.

I turn and look and I see it is a man about my age and height. I look directly into his eyes and notice that he is blind. All thoughts of the shaft of sunlight, the grocery store, Diana Slickman, crosswalks, the Book of Revelation, flower boxes, and everything, including old arithmetic problems, vaporizes. A flash of Bobby Foley, the blind man who lived down the street when I was a child, bobbles up from somewhere deep and disappears again just as quickly. There is more nothingness of thought as the blind man apologizes profusely, and we simultaneously reassure one another that no harm's been done. He tells me that the light should be changing any minute. Would I let him know when it does.

Of course I would. Who wouldn't?

I offer to help him across the street. Who wouldn't?

This was my second "good deed" of the week.

A few days earlier, there I was, walking down the sidewalk in Evanston, Chicago's bland little neighbor to the north, my mind filled with simultaneous thinking on a very windy day. I may have been thinking about the wind and kites and tearing up sheets to knot to their tails, but was probably also wondering what time it was and calculating whether I had enough time during what remained of my lunch hour to see if any of last season's shirts were on sale, now that it was March, and the new spring stuff was on display in all the shop windows. And was I entitled to buy myself a birthday present? I may have also been thinking that winter might never release its grip. However, the wind was really quite warm, and I may have been thinking "lion" and "lamb," which invariably fills my brain with Androcles and Mary had a little. As I approached the corner I noticed, as I waited for the WALK/DON'T WALK sign to change (Diana Slickman, jaywalker), I noticed, out of the corner of my eye, a windblown little old lady clinging to a light pole.

Now, when I think "little old lady," I picture in my mind's eye little old ladies of yesteryear. High-button shoes. Lace collars clasped closed with a cameo. Beaded reticule. Ear trumpet.

You know, Tweety Bird's mom.

The kind of little old lady who has not been seen—certainly not un-escorted—on the streets of Evanston in a generation or two. This little old lady still had some vestiges of the little old lady of yesteryear—dowager's hump, cane, scarf tied under her chin. However, her sweat suit was right out of late last century. Very *Golden Girls*. Very early-bird all-you-can-eat country buffet.

"Sir? Sir?" she called out. "Sir? I hate to ask this. I really feel ridiculous. But could you help me across the street?" and suddenly I found myself living a Boy Scout cartoon cliché. Actually helping a little old lady cross the street. And as we made our way across she apologized profusely and was telling me she never thought she'd end up feeling so helpless, " . . . but the wind!" And all the while I'm thinking, "Hey, look at us! We ought to be a cartoon in the *New Yorker*—or *Boy's Life*—with a caption beneath us!" I told her I'd never dreamed I'd find myself actually helping someone across the street either, so we were almost even. She said, "Well, you're very sweet."

I have spent my whole life trying to be a good boy. For as long as I can remember, it was drilled into my head that it is good to do good. To do good things for people, no matter who they might be; to be there for them, if they need you—before they even ask; and that it's not tit-for-tat. At all. That not every good deed has a merit badge attached to it. That, in fact, if you're keeping score, you are not helping someone out for their sake, but rather for your own.

Still, I'm certainly no better than anyone else. I'm no saint. For instance, I lie to the Greenpeace kids. When they try to stop me in the street and ask me if I'd like to do something bigger than myself for the planet, I bald-face lie to them. I tell them, "Oh, I've been a member since you were a glimmer in your mama's eye."

It may be easier to simply ignore them, but it's not quite as satisfying.

I urge other people—I urge you—to lie to the Greenpeace kids.

I was not always a good child, but I was not really a bad child either. Mischievous but not malicious. My grandmother, whether she believed it or not, always said, "You good boy." This was never a question. It was a statement. A demand. A requisite. Whenever I saw her, saying hello or saying goodbye and sometimes in between, she would hug me with her sturdy Polish arms and say, "Ooooooo. You good boy!" and seconds later she'd bend over, bury her nose deeply in my hair, take a hearty sniff, and exclaim, "Phew!! Stink!!" It would be quite a few years before I realized that she wasn't talking about my personal hygiene but rather the smell of stale tobacco smoke from my mother's cigarettes.

I like to think I've tried to be a good boy. One who does not stink. Literally or figuratively.

The blind man is listening for the change in the traffic. I offer to help him across the street. He says he doesn't need the help. He says he knows this corner well and would only need to know if someone is running the light. He tells me, "People do at this corner," and then adds, "People can be jerks."

The light changed, and as we crossed the street I tried to guide him as best I could because, though he expressed a great deal of confidence regarding this particular intersection and his ability to navigate through it, he didn't seem to have much skill in using his white cane. In the crosswalk, he veered ever so slightly south instead of progressing due west, to the other side of the street. I tried to guide him, using my voice, "This way. This way," only to tap into his arrogance as he snapped at me that he was just fine and had crossed this way before many, many times. And by luck, or by following my voice, he made it back into the crosswalk. However, as he did, I saw a not-very-good citizen behind the wheel of a beat-up Toyota, talking on her cell phone as her car rolled inch by inch into the crosswalk. The blind man strode with purpose toward the opposite corner. The car inched forward. Pedestrians who saw the car in the crosswalk gave wide berth—glared at the driver—walked around her car. Not the blind man. He beelined. I called out to warn him, only to watch him bang into the fender of the offending vehicle, and that is when it became clear that he was quite adept at using his white cane.

"You're in the crosswalk!" WHAM! "You trying to kill somebody??" WHAM! "What the hell's the matter with you???" WHAM!

He stomped around the front of the car, still shouting invective, and stepped onto the sidewalk. The driver of the car continued her telephone conversation as though not a thing had happened.

I was a bit dumbfounded by the whole thing. But I felt that I had sort of done my good deed, and headed home, my mind filling with fresh thoughts about the cause and effect qualities of doing well by others. Wondering, as the sun slanted further toward the horizon, whether these two events, these good deeds, would stay with me to the end of my days, rattling around in my brain, or whether they would go the way of so much that had come before it, the specifics sloughing away, becoming muddled and pressed together, joining the millions of little details that create the white hum of thought of day by day by day.

Juanga Forever

Achy Obejas

Little Village—La Villita, as it's also known—is on Chicago's Southwest Side, a cluster of bungalows with trimmed lawns and the occasional yearlong crèche or Virgin of Guadalupe standing just off the stoop. It's south of the BNSF railroad tracks, north of the Chicago River, and just east of the westernmost city limits. Traversing the heart of the neighborhood is the two-laned Twenty-Sixth Street, with parking on both sides and a jumbled soundtrack of boleros, rancheras, and Latin pop at its busiest hours, especially after Mass on Sundays, when gaggles of toddlers in miniature suits and frilly pastel dresses lead their families around by the hand from ice-cream shop to music store to elaborate window displays of a timeless sort of Western wear: cowboy hats, wide belts, snakeskin boots with buckles, and leather and silver bolos.

Juan Gabriel, probably Mexico's most popular singer of all time, croons through the speakers set outside the shops, usually winning the battle of volume: "*Cuando tú estás conmigo es cuando yo digo / que valió la pena todo, todo lo que yo he sufrido.*" (When you're with me, that's when I can say / that everything, everything I've suffered was worthwhile.)

There are taco stands here, and stores with layaway programs and showrooms of plastic-encased sofas and living room chairs, banks, legal offices specializing in immigration matters, giant supermarkets, and bridal shops whose real forte are the quince dresses necessary for Latino-style coming-out parties. There's still gang activity out here, the occasional sniper fire that fells a bystander, but this strip of Twenty-Sixth Street is said to generate more business revenue than any other in Chicago except Michigan Avenue.

The first time I went, back in the early 1980s, I missed most of the hustle and din. The street at night was a quiet fog, the piquant smell of carnitas wafting from a couple of late-night eateries. Suddenly, a mustard-colored sedan raced east and came to a squealing stop in front of a squat, white-brick building. A flash of glitter turned into a troop of sprinters that disappeared behind an unmarked steel door.

That door is important, not just because its unremarkable state has remained a constant (though it now has lettering that says proof of age is required to enter), but because it's a kind of portal. Just behind it is La Cueva, the country's oldest Latino drag bar—a mightily successful enterprise in Little Village that is, to date, conspicuously missing from the neighborhood Web page published by the City of Chicago.

Back then I was at La Cueva, fake ID in hand and shivering with fear, because, though open since 1972, its legend had already reached me in Indiana, where I grew up, certain that no place existed that could accommodate my sexuality and ethnicity. I'd been to other drag bars before: in Miami Beach and Indianapolis, where the queens reveled in classic torch songs, and at La Mere Vipere in downtown Chicago—not exactly a traditional drag place, but an eventual home base for Jim Skafish, a gender-defying punk performer who'd squeeze into a woman's bathing suit without the slightest regard for passing and serve up terrible stories of humiliation and karmic revenge on a bed of hard, angry music.

My first time at La Cueva I went alone and crossed the threshold—the door is bullet proof and the thug of a bouncer asked the cowboys ahead of me, in Spanish, if they'd left their guns in the car—standing practically on tiptoe to see beyond, waiting for my trip to wonderland to unfold.

"*No sé si es un sueño aún o es una realidad / pero cuando estoy contigo es cuando digo / que este amor que siento es porque tú lo has merecido*"—the song is Juan Gabriel's, and it's always in the background of my memories of that initial visit, although not in his voice: maybe Ana Gabriel instead, or Rocío Dúrcal, or any of the Mexican divas who routinely perform his material. (I don't know if it's a dream or reality / but when I'm with you is when I can say / that this love I feel is because you deserve it.)

On my maiden visit to La Cueva I was stunned to find myself the only biological female in the place—a large, open space with a stage that doubles as a dance floor. The men were cool and stiff, unpartnered and closed-mouthed. If the music had suddenly stopped playing, it's likely La Cueva would have been still as a church.

As a real girl, I was sniffed out almost immediately, and the men were unabashed in their staring. I made my way around the bar, creeping close to the waitress station—still the same today—where queens whirled in to fill their orders (beer in cans to this day, to avoid the possibility that someone will get feisty and want to cut somebody) and glide back out to the crowded tables. And oh, what queens! Their behinds padded beyond anything J. Lo could have ever imagined, they dripped fantasy pearls, gold, saints' medallions, earrings in the shapes of flowers and the Mexican state of Sinaloa, sequined hormone-free cleavage down to their freshly shaved navels, and hair teased and shaped into skyscraping beehives that were architectural marvels.

The show took it up a full notch. The queen that really wowed me was Caracol, who did a fierce Celia Cruz—a crazy choice given Celia's own penchant for purple wigs, space-age platforms, and that signature cry of "AZUCAR!!!!!!"

But no performer surprised me as much as Gabrielito, one of the very first acts of the night and not a queen at all, but a Juan Gabriel imitator. The real Juan Gabriel is a phenomenon: a songwriting machine, a star who breaks all conventions; he's a former delinquent, a convicted felon who briefly served time, a vegetarian, and a Buddhist who defies any possibility of reprisal by honoring Mexico's musical traditions. He respects boundaries enough not to cross the one that might really undo him. A father of four who has never married the woman who gave birth to all of them, a flamboyant showman who very deliberately plays to his effeminate manners, he was once asked, by Chicago's TeleGuía magazine, if he was gay. His answer made international headlines: "*Lo que se ve no se pregunta.*" (There's no need to ask about what's obvious.)

Gabrielito—his real name is Salvador Chávez—doesn't resemble the dark-haired, boyish original at all. "I think my only similarity might be that we pee the same way," he says. "And that's just a maybe." He's blond, big chested, and boxy, with prominent John McCain–style jowls. But his illusion is masterly. Because Juan Gabriel only occasionally breaks into extended movement onstage, imitating him requires not grandiosity but subtlety. And even that first night, as the vein in Chávez's neck vibrated to simulate Juan Gabriel's booming voice, and his left hand flitted from the audience to the heavens promised in La Cueva's twinkling ceiling, he was remarkably convincing: "*Con decirte, amor, que otra vez he amanecido llorando de felicidad / A tu lado yo siento que estoy viviendo / Nada es como ayer,*" he mimicked, his generous lips comfortably savoring every word. "*Abrázame muy fuerte que el tiempo es malo y muy cruel amigo.*" (I have to tell you, love, that yet again I woke up crying with happiness / At your side

I feel like I'm alive / Nothing is like yesterday / Hold me tightly because time is evil and a very cruel friend.)

"Abrázame Muy Fuerte" is one of Juan Gabriel's greatest hits and, years later, it's still in Chávez's repertoire. He's forty-six now, at La Cueva for almost twenty-three years, and now such a celebrity in his own right that his Gabrielito is a full-time gig, with appearances at weddings, baptisms, quinces parties, and other occasions. He's also La Cueva's headliner now, the one who finishes the revue and draws lines of swooning admirers—mostly women, of whatever sexual persuasion, who stuff bills in his hands and pockets.

"Wherever he's done in the Mexican community, 'Juanga' is big money," Chávez says, rubbing his fingers together. "Whether it's in a gay place or not, it doesn't matter. Not that doing 'Juanga' is exactly doing a man, since he's the biggest queen himself."

Chávez began doing Juan Gabriel, in part, because he was such a fan of the singer that when asked, on a drunken lark, to lip-synch to him one evening shortly after he arrived in Chicago, he was able to get onstage and fly right through an entire vinyl record's worth of songs.

"I did 'El Noa Noa,' 'Querida,' and people were giving me tips, standing up and applauding, wanting more," he remembers. "And I thought, so long as they're giving me money, I'm staying up here."

Pretty soon, he was at La Cueva and a friend asked Miss Ketty—La Cueva's grande dame, the Empress of All Queens, and the director of the show—if Chávez could "*echarse un palomazo*"—Mexican parlance for taking a guest shot. He did, and though the reception wasn't as raucous, he's been at La Cueva ever since.

This means, of course, that Chávez has seen the evolution of La Cueva from dangerous den to its current incarnation: a surprisingly wholesome place of entertainment.

"It used to be mostly boys, gay boys, very few queens, even fewer women, and no lesbians—though you hardly ever saw masculine couples, couples that were both men," he says. "Some were real tough guys," he recalls with a laugh. "For a while you'd see them in cowboy hats, boots. Then one day they'd show up wearing miniskirts, makeup. Years later, you'd see couples who'd do that, come in both looking like outlaws, then later come back as 'girlfriends.'"

"Oh, it's changed; it's changed a lot," Chávez says. "It's been here so long, parents bring their kids now. People come up to me all the time and say, 'Oh, my dad talks about you all the time,' and they give me gifts: chains and clothes, photos. It's become a tradition on Twenty-Sixth Street, practically family entertainment."

Inside, the once dark cubbyhole is now friendly and well lit. The floors are no longer a wet, sticky mess but meticulously clean. There are posters on the wall of famous La Cueva queens (and Gabrielito), and the bouncer is a woman who respectfully asks for identification.

Salsa's a rare thing here now, where DJ Dynamico churns reggaeton, banda, cumbia, disco, Mexican polkas, country, and Latin pop. The queens—now much more subdued—continue to serve, and the dance floor is packed with neighborhood residents of all ages. Tonight there are opposite-sex couples in their twenties, their loose limbs elaborately tattooed; married couples who dance in perfect step; an elderly grandma out with a frisky younger man who doesn't always seem to be all there; carefully coiffed Mexican men in couples, wearing jeans and pressed shirts, who struggle with who's leading; and a tribe of dancing girls. Next to them, two queens press against each other with laserlike eye contact.

Roberto Beltrán, forty-two years old, looks like the guy who's having the most fun here. He dances with his wife, tips the queens during the shows with outrageous gestures, waves from his seat, and grins the whole time. "I come here for the music," he says. "I like that everybody has fun here. I don't have any close gay friends—a few people from work, that's all—but, you know, I really don't give a damn about anybody's sexuality."

His wife, Elizabeth Jones, laughs. "We're from the neighborhood; we always come here," she adds.

Another local, Cristina Armenta, thirty-five, has been coming to La Cueva for four years. She's a lesbian, but the friend she brought tonight—a quiet, stoic fellow—is straight. "I invited him to see the show," she says. "I like it here. I like the vibe; I like that nobody criticizes anybody, and you can be free."

And the show—everyone's ostensible reason for being at La Cueva, it seems—is a different ball of wax now. The tippers, once shy and suppliant, are now aggressive and rowdy. They pull on the performers' arms, demand kisses. These respond by trying to undress the fans, lifting their shirts, unbuttoning them, wrestling them off the stage without missing a beat.

The queens have changed, too. Subscribers to medical progress, they bare large, fleshy breasts with a dash of glitter on the nipples; their curves are smooth, their satiny butts heart-shaped. The art of hiding penis and testicles seems anachronistic in a show where there may be very few male genitals. There's nothing metaphoric left; the show is now playfully vulgar.

Which means that the art of illusion has been left almost exclusively to Chávez's Gabrielito. In some ways, time has served him well—while singers like Emmanuel and Luis Miguel lose their popularity, Juan Gabriel never goes out of fashion. Yesterday's hits have become classics; Juan Gabriel—whatever his predilections, whatever his controversies—is a potent symbol of Mexican cultural pride through his songwriting and, especially, his interpretation of the classic ranchera, a traditional cowboy lament. Moreover, Gabrielito is disinclined to wear the sombreros or cowboy hats—he prefers the elegant Juan Gabriel, in a suit with just a splash of color or embroidery. This is Juan Gabriel as gentleman, not as parody or irony; this is a rendition done in reverence, in love.

Out in the crowd, Migue Cordero, fifty-three, watches while Gabrielito performs. He cradles a can of beer and taps his thumb against the top. He's been coming to La Cueva for years. "It's more a suggestion of Juanga, really," he says, "and, in part, because he's not trying to convince us that he looks just like him or that he's him. You know, some Juan Gabriel imitators start to think they're him—they lose their minds—I think that's why it works so well."

"*Abrázame que el tiempo es oro si tú estás conmigo,*" Chávez sings as a woman shyly tugs on his sleeve for a kiss. (Hold me, because time is golden if you're with me.) He allows her his cheek, but his lips never touch her; he's intent on the song. "*Abrázame fuerte, muy fuerte, y más fuerte que nunca. Siempre abrázame.*" (Hold me tight, very tight, tighter than ever. Hold me forever.)

Zoo Mountain

Allison Gruber

Standing in the ape house at Lincoln Park Zoo, jammed into the crowd of moms and dads and kids, I watched two chimpanzees groom one another. The larger chimp preened the smaller. The crowd cooed.

"Cutest thing ever," a woman said.

I rolled my eyes, for at no other exhibit in the zoo is one more likely to hear "cute" and "I feel sorry for 'em" than one is in the ape house. Sorry, zebras, snakes, marmosets, and camels. Sorry, lions and bats. You're all going to have to learn how to eat, frown, or masturbate like humans do before they waste a moment of their day pitying your captivity. We humans are a narcissistic species; we look for ourselves in everything.

As I turned to escape the crowd, a little boy ran smack into my knees, and apologized, "Sorry, sir."

Embarrassed, his mother quickly corrected, "*Ma'am,*" and ushered her son toward the glass so he could get a better look at monkeys doing what monkeys do.

"Isn't that the movie about the lady with the monkeys?" my mother asked. It was 1993. I was sixteen. Faked sick that day to stay home from school, smoke copious amounts of marijuana, and channel surf. Mid-afternoon, I stumbled upon the movie *Gorillas in the Mist* and for the first time in my young life, a narrative resonated with me: *woman wants job, woman demands job, woman gets job, woman does not live in quiet desperation, woman does not marry, woman saves a species, woman is decapitated by unknown assailant, cue triumphant music.*

"Gorillas," I corrected her. "It's about gorillas."

I asked my mother to rent the movie.

"I need it for school," I lied.

Mother was skeptical. "They watched that in school? Am I thinking of the right movie?"

"Yes," I insisted, "*Gorillas in the Mist.* They watched it in Biology."

"Isn't Biology the class that you and *that Josephine* skipped?"

I bristled at her use of "that Josephine," but having anticipated this response bowed my head remorsefully and replied, "Yes."

One afternoon, Josephine and I skipped fourth period Biology to drive to the forest preserve, sit in her car, smoke cloves, and make out. All my mother knew was that *that Josephine* was a bad influence. Had she known the full scope of my attachment to *that Josephine*, I would have been back in Catholic school.

Public high school was a privilege, not a right.

My mother made my father rent *Gorillas in the Mist* on his way home from work, and before the due date on the rental, I rigged up our household's two VCRs and made a pirate copy I repeatedly watched.

When the movie wasn't enough, I took to skipping evenings out at Denny's, where my friends and I would smoke and drink endless refills of dollar coffee, leaving the waitress a catastrophe of creamer cups, spilled Sweet & Low packets, and whatever change and pocket lint we could muster as tip, choosing instead to spend my nights at the library scrolling through reel after reel of microfiche and checking out books that hadn't been touched since the Nixon Administration.

I became a real smoker, first Marlboro Reds, because that's what Sigourney-Weaver-as-Dian-Fossey smoked, then Merit Lights when I learned those were what the actual Dian Fossey smoked. I listened to Billie Holiday, because that's what Sigourney-Weaver-as-Dian-Fossey listened to, but gave up Holiday for Edith Piaf when I read she was what the actual Dian Fossey listened to. Lucky for me, it was the early 1990s, and I didn't have to alter my fashion sense to fit Fossey's—save for the Doc Martens, I already dressed like her: tattered blue jeans and oversized flannel shirts.

Josephine felt threatened. "Do you love me?"

"Yes."

"But do you love me more than Dian Fossey?"

I'd laugh dismissively; I never knew the actual answer, and would end up saying something like *Give me a break, I don't even know Dian Fossey* or *That's not a fair question: Dian Fossey is dead.*

My parents were baffled by my obsession. "That movie? Again?"

My grandmother, who, when tipsy, liked to bitterly recount that her family once owned all the land between Lincoln, Lawrence, and Western, now spent her third dirty dry martini openly fretting that I would skip college and hightail it to the Virungas. "You think they want white women there, Allison? Let me tell you, they do not."

For my seventeenth birthday, gifts included one of Jane Goodall's chimpanzee missives, a sweatshirt with a gorilla's face emblazoned across the front, and a lemur hand puppet.

On the Clark Bus, I watched my reflection in the window, pale, translucent: *Could stand to lose a few pounds. Look every minute of your thirty-three years.* I tried to see the "sir" the little boy saw when he ran into my legs, and I couldn't. I tried to see the "ma'am" his mother saw, and I couldn't see that either.

The bus rolled past the old German Catholic cemetery where my grandmother is buried. Grandmother could no longer fear my escape to Africa, and as the bus moved alongside the walled graveyard, I silently assured her I was not in Africa. *I am here, somewhere between Lincoln, Lawrence, and Western.*

"Chicago went to hell in the seventies," Grandmother used to say. "At least the suburbs are safe."

Prior to the ubiquity of cell phones and the advent of the Internet, teenagers managed to clandestinely communicate in the night. Josephine and I devised a code: *two rings and a hang up* meant "call me"; *one ring and a hang up* meant "come over."

Josephine's family lived in a one-story ranch three blocks from our high school. Josephine's bedroom faced the street. When she rang once, I would sneak out, drive the Dodge Omni my parents loaned me for getting to school to Josephine's street, park three blocks from her house, walk up her front lawn, tap lightly on her window, and wait for her to lift the pane and pop out the screen so I could climb inside. By the time we graduated from high school, I'd been climbing through that window so long I could scale the wall and slip through like an athlete.

We got away with a lot because our parents were respectively worried about our brothers. My younger brother was a burgeoning stoner-pyromaniac, while Josephine's older brother, Jimmy, was forever being suspended from school for calling teachers "cocksuckers" and punching students in the halls.

Jimmy was a nineteen-year-old senior who stormed about Josephine's house perpetually shirtless, arms and chest muscular in a way I'd only ever seen before in action movies. When he wasn't lying in the driveway, swearing and tinkering with the Mustang he would never fix, Jimmy was in the basement lifting weights or locked in his bedroom blasting Nitzer Ebb: *muscle and hate / muscle and hate / muscle, muscle, muscle . . .*

On the outside of Jimmy's bedroom door hung a confederate flag underscored by a black bumper sticker that read: *AIDS Kills Fags Dead.*

The week before the presidential election, I woke to find my car and all the cars on my block papered with brochures warning residents to vote against Obama or not vote at all, warning the election of a black president would incite race riots, perhaps worse. The brochures were from *Your Local Chapter of the KKK.*

I hadn't seen racist propaganda like that since Jimmy's bedroom door. And that was a long time ago. That was the suburbs. This was a gay neighborhood in Chicago.

"Your *local* chapter of the KKK"—*there was a* local *chapter?*

The brochures made me feel uneasy, not because I feared the tracts would recruit city-dykes into the Aryan Nation, but because I always believed the city was safer than the suburbs in one very specific way.

While racism and homophobia were barely detectable in the suburb where I grew up, every so often I'd catch a ghastly whiff—enough to make me want out.

Josephine and I sat in her parents' living room watching *Gorillas in the Mist.* Regarding myself as something of a Dian Fossey scholar, I critiqued the film pompously:

"Now, her tracker's name was not really Sembagare."

"There was no such zoo broker—all Hollywood."

During the one sex scene in the movie, I shifted uncomfortably, explaining, "Dian Fossey would never say *that.*"

Josephine inched closer to me on the couch. "What *would* Dian Fossey say?"

Before I could answer, Jimmy, wearing nothing but American flag biker shorts, stomped past us, bare chest sweaty from bench presses, shouting, "Faggot niggers fucking monkeys is where we got AIDS."

Josephine picked up the remote and threw it at Jimmy's head, but her aim was off and he made it unscathed to his bedroom. The remote broke open against the wall, spilling its batteries.

One summer night, in the middle of Lawrence Avenue, the Latin Kings warred openly. People were stabbed with broken bottles, pistol whipped. Shots were fired.

The alderman, vacationing in China, was blamed. Reporting the brawl, the *Chicago Tribune* expressed disbelief: "Where was the alderman?"—as though the alderman could have prevented the violence. As though gang bangers would have run screaming from the alderman: *Oh shit! The mother-fucking alderman is here!*

The crime rate climbed. People died whether innocent, or culpable, or simply misled. Journalists and politicians speculated, pointed fingers: *aldermen, police officers, teachers, parents, the mayor.* Everyone sought a particularly human comfort in wanting to hold one person, or one small set of people, responsible for such malevolence.

Certain species of primates fuck when trouble's afoot. Humans blame.

Jimmy made Josephine's home feel unsafe, so we started hanging out in the city with Brian.

Josephine used to work with Brian at the video store. He was twenty-five, skinny, had long auburn hair, and displayed sleeves of tattoos all up and down his arms; he was the coolest guy we knew.

Brian took me and Josephine to a bar on Armitage where the bartenders let us drink. The bar played the kind of music Josephine and I liked: Jane's Addiction, Fugazi, Joy Division. We were seventeen, giddy with badassery. None of our other high school friends got to hang out in the city and drink, but we did.

One night at the bar, I watched Brian's roommate don a clown wig and snort a line of coke off a woman's thigh. Later, I watched Brian grab Josephine and kiss her on the mouth. When I saw her kiss back, I drank myself sick.

Josephine followed me into the stall, holding my hair back as I retched.

From the jukebox, Ian MacKaye wailed: *I am a patient boy / I wait / I wait / I wait . . .*

"I want to go home."

Josephine stroked my head. "Al," she said. "It's the nineties. He's just some guy. You can't take everything so seriously."

Josephine drove the Dodge back to the suburbs while, drunk on the passenger's side, I smoked and revisited her earlier comment. "I *will* take everything seriously," I slurred. "Dian Fossey took everything seriously, and she's a fucking legend. *A legend—*"

"To you, maybe," Josephine said with a laugh.

It was a habit of Josephine's to laugh when I wasn't trying to be funny. The first time we kissed, we were sophomores waiting in the backseat of a car parked in front of a 7-Eleven while our friend tried to convince a panhandler to buy us Mad Dog 20/20.

"We'll get arrested," I prophesized.

Josephine laughed uproariously.

"Why are you laughing?"

Josephine placed a hand on one of my bouncing knees, and I bucked it off. "We are going to jail."

But Josephine didn't take me seriously; she kept laughing. "I want to put you in a cage so you can make me laugh all the time."

"That's weird," I mumbled.

I used to like being laughed at, but driving home from the bar, I raged, "Not everything is a fucking joke."

"Is that a Dian Fossey quote?"

I flicked my cigarette out the window. "Fuck you."

"Al, you're drunk."

"I'm not," I blustered. "I'm serious."

"Allison." Josephine was stern now. "Shut up."

Bested, I lit another cigarette, staring out the window at the billboards along the Kennedy advertising sneakers and Old Style and baseball, things I couldn't care less about. *Dian Fossey got to look at jungle and mountain ranges.* I thought about that scene in *Gorillas in the Mist* when Sigourney-Weaver-as-Dian-Fossey painted red nail polish witches on trees to scare away the poachers; I thought about the scene where she yelled, "Get off my mountain!"

I wanted Brian off my mountain. I wanted Jimmy off my mountain, maybe Josephine too.

Two weeks before high school graduation, Josephine gave me a spider figurine. The spade-shaped body was crystal, the spindly legs sterling silver. I understood the significance. Josephine was absurdly afraid of spiders, and the first time we slept together, I "saved her" from a daddy long legs, catching it with my bare hands and tossing it out the window despite her directive to "Kill it! Kill it!"

"I gave this to you," Josephine explained, "because you aren't scared of anything."

I held the object in my hands and scoffed. I was afraid of everything.

That night as I left through Josephine's window, the porch light came on. This never happened before; figuring her parents had installed some new sensors, and fearing recognition, I pulled my sweatshirt's hood over my head.

As I walked across the front lawn, I heard footsteps and before I could think to run, I was on my stomach.

It was late spring. The grass smelled sharp and tasted of chemicals. I couldn't catch my breath. I gagged. A vice tightened around my waist; an incredible weight bore down on my back.

"Jimmy," I screamed. "Jimmy, it's me!"

Jimmy rolled me over and yanked down my hood. "What the fuck are you doing? Huh?"

I couldn't answer. He stood and swiped grass and dirt from his legs. I blinked dumbly; the vision in my right eye was blurred, and as I attempted to straighten my glasses, my nose began to bleed.

In a curiously uncharacteristic gesture of mercy, Jimmy held out a hand to help me up. Once I was on my feet, he released my hand in disgust. "Get the fuck out of my face."

I walked, stunned, to the Dodge. Inside the car, I flipped down the mirror. The entire right side of my face was red and blue beneath a slight grass stain veneer. My upper lip was moustached with blood. When I tried to correct the severe tilt of my glasses, one arm broke off the frame entirely, and I began to sob.

I drove home with one hand on the wheel, the other holding my frames to my face like opera glasses. I didn't know what to worry about first—the fact that my face was black, blue, bloodied, and grass stained, or the fact that my glasses were broken, or the fact that Josephine's brother had just decked me in her front yard at two a.m. on a school night.

The following morning, I presented my mother with my broken glasses. "I was running and I tripped."

The glasses seemed of little concern to her; she touched my bruised face and inspected the discoloration. "Did someone *hit* you?"

I jerked away. "Mom, get real. Like anyone would *hit* me."

To move Mother further from discovering the truth, I pointed to my combat boots. "You're right about these shoes. They suck."

My favorite part in *Gorillas in the Mist* was when Dian Fossey intercepts Claude Van Veeten as he sits in his van. When confronted by Fossey, Van Veeten, safe in his vehicle, laughs in her face, and as he laughs, she grabs his nearest body part, a meaty hand sporting an ostentatious gold ring. *You like this ring? You want to keep the hand this ring is on? If I ever hear, or see, or smell you anywhere near my gorillas, you'll be wearing that ring on the other hand, and I'll have a new ashtray.*

Following Jimmy's attack, I thought about this scene. I could be tough like Fossey: *If I ever see, or hear, or smell you anywhere near me, you'll be stuffing your bike shorts, and I'll have a new bookmark.*

But there was no recourse. When Josephine saw me at school, she asked about my face. Like my mother, she tried to touch the bruises. And as with Mother, I moved my head away from Josephine's hand. "I'm clumsy," I said. "Practically retarded."

I was also scared. I didn't want to sneak into Josephine's house anymore. I didn't want to go to her house at all.

The night after our graduation, we fought about my aloofness.

"What is up with you, Al? Are you mad at me or something?"

I told Josephine I wasn't mad. "But," I added, "what we've been doing is wrong."

"Wrong?"

"Against my upbringing," I explained. "I'm a Catholic."

"A Catholic? Since when? You hate all that shit."

My face burned. I wanted her to hang up on me. I wanted her to tell me to fuck off, but she wouldn't. I started to cry. "I went to Catholic School, you know?"

Josephine was utterly confused. "What is your fucking problem?"

"You're my *fucking problem,*" I spat. "You make me do things I don't want to do."

Stargaze, the dyke bar on Clark Street, went out of business. I learned this incidentally. "I feel like going out," I told a friend. "I feel like going to Stargaze."

"You can't," my friend told me. "They're closed."

I experienced a moment of incredulity: *Where are the dykes supposed to go?*

"Where are we supposed to go?" I asked my friend.

"Anywhere we want," she said. "Regular bars."

"True," I agreed. "We can be lesbians anywhere now."

Out was in.

After high school, I went away to college at a liberal arts school in Wisconsin. It was the 1990s, Ellen DeGeneres hadn't yet come out, Clinton's "don't ask, don't tell" seemed progressive, the idea of "tolerance" was downright radical, and I felt safe being gay on campus—protected by liberal friends and professors.

It is easy to be brave when you feel safe.

Josephine skipped college and moved into a dodgy part of the West Loop with Gabe, a handsome Puerto Rican who made a little money spinning records in nightclubs and a whole lot of money dealing ecstasy and heroin.

My freshman year I took the train in from Wisconsin to visit her and Gabe at the apartment they shared. Josephine apologetically explained that Gabe was more than "just her roommate," but I knew that already. I wasn't hurt. I was relieved.

At her apartment, we smoked cigarettes, reminisced about high school, and talked about how much the suburbs sucked, and I waxed arrogant about my newest obsession, Anne Sexton. I could quote her: "Live or die / but don't poison everything." I had given up on Fossey and her dumb gorillas, found a new chain-smoking alcoholic to admire, and set my sights on becoming a poet.

Josephine was addicted to heroin, but I ignored this fact. Justified my disregard by misappropriating a line from a Roethke poem: *I, with no rights in this matter, / Neither father nor lover.*

I ran my hands over her and Gabe's couch, scabbed with cigarette burns, and asked, "How did you manage this?"

Josephine squinted defensively. "Never burned a hole in your couch before, Smokey?"

I dropped the subject and stared at my hands. For the rest of the evening and into the morning, I ignored the small bunches of foil scattered throughout the apartment. Pretended the hypodermic needle lying in the bathroom sink was a glimpse of something else—a silverfish, maybe a hairpin. I told myself that Josephine's weight loss and strange acne was from waitressing too much.

"You look tired," I observed as we readied for bed.

Josephine gathered up beer bottles. Every time she leaned forward her shoulder blades poked against the back of her T-shirt like clipped wings.

She swept stray ash from the coffee table into her hands. "It looks like a zoo in here," she said. "It's like that movie."

"Huh?" I knew what she meant, but wasn't in the mood for nostalgia.

Josephine looked hurt. "That gorilla movie," she reminded me, and proceeded to quote a minor line from the film, a small line delivered toward the end of the movie. In the scene, Fossey sits in her cabin with her faithful tracker, Sembagare, stringing popcorn to hang on the Christmas tree. Sembagare chastises her for shooting at tourists, and Fossey, looking old and tired, drops her popcorn garland, lights a cigarette, and smugly declares, *They're not going to turn this mountain into a goddamn zoo. They're not.*

The Anarchist Potluck

Aldo Alvarez

I

I've always had an incautious love
for rebellion and alternatives,
but I'm cautious enough
to not attend their parties uninvited
and be branded
a Sunday driver of the soul.

So when my then-boyfriend Ken—
may he rest in peace—
invited me to come along
to an anarchist potluck,
I was delighted,
and I asked what would be
an appropriate contribution
to the buffet table.
"Anything vegan," he said,
as if it were not a big deal,
and I said, "Fantastic!"
and you could almost hear the soft ruffling
of my ambition to make a good impression
with my contribution
to his friends, whom I hadn't met,
even though I don't ordinarily
put on a toque or even cook for myself,

and the few things I cook well
involve animal suffering.

Before you think of me
as a reactionary elitist,
let me declare
that I would not think twice
about going vegan
if I lived within delivery boundaries
of several extraordinary restaurants
in San Francisco.

At the time,
I didn't think of questioning
how self-imposed and policed
dietary restrictions
are in any way an absence of state or compulsion,
although I understood the casual tyranny of taste.
Ken would cheat on his own
with White Castle cheeseburgers,
which endeared him to the contrarian Surrealist
and mass-market Pop artist in me:
it just couldn't be more kitschy
and ideologically *wrong*.
To this day,
this makes sliders more delicious to my palate.
I rarely forget to dedicate this craving
in loving memory of Ken.

II

The pimento used to be
such a party vegetable.
I wonder what happened.

I have to remember to remove the "i"
when I write it in English.

III

In the culture I was raised in,
you try your luck with a dish
that takes premeditation and time
and works in large portions
with extended family in mind.
There is nothing wan or disinterested
about our large, thick, metal cauldrons
filled with a dish worth celebrating.
A small pan of something ordinary
would be seen as stingy and discourteous.

I decided not to veganize
my father's effortful recipe for cannelloni
as I imagined pasta would already
be well represented,
and so much of its appeal depended
on the variety of meats, creams, and cheeses
he used to make it extraordinary.
My mother's recipe for arroz con pollo
has always been a hit at potlucks.
So I decided to replace, among other things,
the cubes of chicken bouillon
with a pricey vegetable stock
and the chicken with sumptuous portions
of green olives, pimentos, and capers.
Go, Goya, go, Goya;
I named the recipe arroz sin pollo,
a dish defined by an absence.

I drew the line at using brown rice.
Brown rice does not play well with others.

I made a cauldron but decided it was wiser
to transport it in two large, disposable containers
since, at the time, my carpal pain took the pleasure
out of heavy lifting.
Still, I decorated the rice in the containers

with thick slices of roasted peppers
imported from Italy
by a supermarket for pirates
named Treasure Island
which apparently doesn't smuggle
from Puerto Rico or Spain.
I placed the slices like numbers
on the face of a clock.
Ken arrived very soon after I finished,
and he exclaimed that it looked and smelled exquisite.
That he knew how to use that descriptor
is one of the many reasons why I loved
having a scruffy poet as a boyfriend.

IV

When we arrived,
three very young men sat lackadaisically
on a couch by a very busy set of bookshelves
full of the feminists and beardy intellectuals
I had been hoping to meet.
Ken introduced me to the hostess,
and we were directed to the kitchen
to drop off my contribution
to the festivities.
Then she disappeared.
It was early for this pot luck
although it was well past dinner time
and I was starving.
The kitchen lacked revelers
but held a revelation:
the small kitchenette set
appeared to be in use
as somebody's desk for papers
and spillover shelving for pots and pans.

Ken suggested we leave
the rice without chicken

on top of the refrigerator
after he made some space.
I worried about reheating later on.
I relented on my fussing
and tried to locate drinks in the refrigerator.
I found leftovers,
a half-full carafe of water
and an open box of chocolate soy milk.
Ken suggested we look on the back porch.

On the back porch
we found an open 12-pack of canned beer,
and a girl in a vintage beaded cardigan
and a sundress too thin for this weather
watching a lone veggie burger
cooking on a hibachi.
Beside her was an empty box
for four of these patty alternatives
which looked like it had been folded
to place back inside a freezer
after it was opened.

I salivated
and I said hello.
The girl shot me a look,
her eyelids frowning with contempt,
and said nothing
and returned to staring at hot coals.
I don't know if she was defending
her fake burger or herself
from some other threat
she had perceived in me,
as I was clearly twice her age.

V

Ken and I joined others in the living room.
Three young guys were discussing

which libraries were best
for stealing books,
as if they were unaware
that they were stealing from me
and from themselves.

It was hard to take
a nonjudgmental position
when I could think of
more than ten occasions
when a book I needed like air
was reported missing in action.
The beer helped, though,
especially as it went to my head
from my empty stomach.
And none of the books
on the nearby bookshelf
had telltale stickers and bindings.
I joined the conversation
by telling them about the library community
that decided to make paper arts
out of queer books that had been defaced
by a local homophobe.
"That's pretty cool," one boy said,
reeking of reefer and sweat.
"They made an artistic statement."

I wanted to ask
what statement they were making
by stealing books from the library,
but they beamed at me
like cute little puppies,
and I had to bask
in whatever coolness came my way.
Validation is my weakness.
Eventually, they started talking
about novels and poems
they would write about their parents
and, unfortunately, girlfriends.

Ken smiled just a little.
I mentioned I had written and published
a book of short stories.
They asked me if they could find it
in the library.
A couple then walked into the party
with a box of soy milk.

I said they couldn't.
I lied.
I knew exactly
which three Chicago libraries
had my book at the time.
Then one of them berated me.
"Aw, man . . . Donate a copy
so we could read it!"

"I can't afford to spare any copies,"
I said, almost groaning in disappointment.
Then a girl was let into the apartment,
carrying a small bag of chips,
the kind one keeps in a lunchbox.
"So what did you guys bring to eat?" I asked.
"Nothing," one said,
and laughed.

Last I checked,
the Chicago Public Library system
was down to one copy of my book.

VI

I excused myself
and decided to make myself
a plate of whatever I found in the kitchen,
which was only exactly what I'd brought.

I tried not to let my hunger
and the beer alter my mood.
I took a moment to relax
and make sure I wouldn't be bitchy
when I returned to Ken
and asked him what's done at these potlucks
when no one's brought
disposable plates and utensils.

Ken rose from his seat
and went with me to the kitchen.
Ken looked through
a tiny set of cupboards.
"Just use a regular plate," he said.
"Shouldn't we ask the hostess?"
I asked.
There were no clean plates.
Ken found three plates in the sink
with two salad forks and a spork.
He took them and washed them
without a second thought.
Domesticity makes me grabby;
I held him from behind
and kissed his shoulders
as he worked on the spork.
I am so bourgeois!

VII

I returned to the living room with Ken
and a heaping plate and ate until sated.
This motivated the boys
to get some themselves right away;
one returned empty handed
to wait for his turn
with the tableware then currently

in my possession.
(For the rest of the night,
people took turns to make use
of these limited means.)
Once done, I washed the instrument
and conveyance
to make the boy a nice plate.
I turned to find the bag-of-chips girl
and the fake-burger girl behind me,
hovering over my offering
on the kitchenette table.
The bag-of-chips girl
pointed at the roasted peppers
and declared them unsuitable.
"That's salmon," she said,
circling over a slice with a finger, in judgment.

Let us dwell on the complications.
Something I made with great ideological care
had been declared anathema
by people who live in these conditions.
Something I made with love and respect
had been disregarded by closed minds.
And Ken was friends with vegans
who despite their airs
could not identify vegetables.

And the rice was fucking ambrosial.
And no one reciprocated my commitment
to a party distinctly designated
as a location for sharing
and the generation of surprise and good will.
I know, it was a different culture
and I had assumptions about it
based on my prejudices.
Apparently, this one was based on a
disconnect between a statement of definition
and its performance,
and I should have respected that.

As they walked away,
not responding to my gaze,
I said, "Actually, they're roasted peppers."
They appeared to stop a moment
but wouldn't quite look back
and then continued on their way.

VIII

Soon after,
one of Ken's friends
whom I knew from the poetry scene
arrived with a zipped bag of meatballs
and a box of toothpicks.
They were delicious but cold.
I kept asking him for the recipe.
He kept avoiding answering,
until, eventually,
he said he got them from a dumpster
at the back of a restaurant.

At least the toilet was clean
when I vomited and vomited.

IX

The drive home almost immediately afterward
was uneventful.
When Ken got sheepish and shy
I used to leave him be.
And I didn't want to share
the doubts I started to have
about him through the company he kept.
Back at home, he made me forget them
for a little while
with his mouth.

Yearners

Barrie Cole

So at first, I am confounded by the woman, well, girl really . . . well, woman-girl of thirty-some-odd years in the office who talks about sex with her lovers constantly, to me alone, as I try to do my job.

My job:

I duplicate meditation CDs for eight hours a day, four days a week, Monday through Thursday, and it is fine. People order the CDs by number, and I duplicate them and send them to the people who want them. This job allows me to paint on Fridays in a little studio I fashioned in the basement of my apartment in Lincoln Square and all through the weekend too, and walk my dog by the lake, and heal from all I need to heal from, which is some but probably not much more than other people who are trying to live somewhat alive lives, whereby I mean they are not defining "alive" simply by their capacity to breathe alone. There is a more-ness they are seeking, not extra-terrestrial more

but *more*

and they seek it in the small ways they do

but they seek it as *seekers*, as *yearn-ers*, as *desire-ers.*

They seek proof of more . . .

of something else, a thrumming inside the mundane . . . the else beyond the something . . . Jazz, perhaps, and if you have no idea what I am talking about, well, then, . . . I am sorry for you.

Back to the girl from work. . . .

Trudy.

This is Trudy:

"Wanna know wanna know wanna know what I did last night? I fucked like crazy. Crazy fucking. Me, yeah. Fucking strapped man. Fucking bitch was so hot for me. Yeah. Have you had crazy fucking where you are like, yeah, this is so fucking good, and it's like you just want to ram your love in? You just want to swallow the person whole like you could just ingest them? Not like rock pizza."

"Huh?"

She looks at me incredulously.

"It's a simile," she says. "You know, sort of a, like, metaphor. Like you know . . . How could you eat rock pizza? You'd break your teeth."

"Oh," I say. "Sure." But the truth is, I'm not sure at all, not even remotely sure.

"God," she says, "I love fucking. I could fuck for days. I wanna die fucking. Like, you know what? I was in the parking lot at Jewel, and these two cars were facing each other 'cause one car needed its battery jumped, and the cars were like headlight to headlight, all open to each other . . . car pussy to car pussy and it was pretty much like porn to me. I was like, oh yeah, cars' time to fuck. All those cables crossing over, so tangled together like arms and legs. I swear I almost came. Hey, speaking of fucking, have you gotten laid since your D.I.V.O.R.C.E.?"

I'm confused as to why she's choosing to spell the word "divorce."

"I haven't," I say. "I'm more about the heart these days, not that it's any of your business."

"Ah, excuse me," she says. "Anything about fucking is my business. Want me to set you up? I could set you up. I could find you someone. Hey, you should go out with that coffee guy next door, that barista dude with the tattoos! Tell me, you find him hot, right? You wanna fuck him, right? I mean, when he makes you a latte, your pussy gets wet, right? Does it? Does it? Does your pussy get wet? Come on, does it? Does it? Does it? Does your pussy get wet? Does your pussy get wet?"

"Trudy," I tell her, "I'm gay."

"No fuckin' way! What the fuck? Why didn't you fucking tell me? I fucking can't believe you didn't tell me. Ah, hello, we're a fucking minority. I mean fuck . . . I'd fuck you. You've got a nice rack. Why didn't you fucking tell me?"

"It never came up."

"I know, I know," Trudy gushes. "You should come over tonight."

"Thanks, but no thanks," I say.

"You think I'm gonna try to fuck you?"

I look at her. "Trudy . . ."

"Okay," she says. "You know, I mean most women love having like sixteen orgasms in a row but suit yourself."

I don't respond. I find that with Trudy if I say even one word she sees it as a conversation, and she'll just keep going and going. On one of the meditation CDs I've listened to from work, the teacher talked about people like Trudy. She said on the recording that people like her are actually medicine just disguised as annoying people and that one should be grateful for their presence in life. She spoke about how people like Trudy show us where the gates of our hearts are not particularly open. I look at Trudy. I try to see her as important medicine.

"Oh, oh, oh," she says. "Checking me out, checking me out."

"No," I say. "Well, I was . . . but not in the way that you think."

"Oh, sure," she says. She winks at me. She licks her lips.

It goes on like this all day long and the next and the next. The following day is Thursday, and she tries a different approach.

"Just come over," she says. "For an hour or two. We'll hang out as friends. How about around seven? Eat before though, okay, because I don't really eat."

"What do you mean you don't eat?" I ask.

"Just come over and wear something sexy," she says. "Just jokin'." She punches me in the arm, buddy-like.

I consider not coming over, saying no yet again. I know that if I don't come over she will ask me again every day until I do relent and that seems relentless to me, and I think that if I do agree, then at least it will be over. She will see somehow that there is no way we could be lovers, or friends, either, for that matter, or anything at all other than coworkers, and it will put an end to it, and I will have taken the medicine of her once and for all.

Trudy notices me mulling it all over.

"Ah ha!" she says. "You're thinking about it. I can tell. C'mon . . . just hanging out."

"Alright," I relent. "Tomorrow night then. Where do you live?"

She tells me her address in Edgewater, and for the rest of the day she is quieter than usual and I am grateful.

That night I don't think much about going to Trudy's. I walk my dog and run into my ex-husband and his new girlfriend, who is twenty-five years old and so . . . angelic, so wispy. She is . . . lovely. They are walking out of the burrito place we used to frequent. I look at my replacement. Her skin is translucent, and I wonder briefly if I am imagining her, and then I think about another meditation recording where the speaker said that we are imagining everything anyway and that this pain in my heart is transitory too.

"Hi, how are you doing?" he asks, and although he doesn't quite care, he says this in a not-unfriendly way. He pets my dog, which I got after we split and which he does not understand me having, since when we were married, and he asked about a dog, I was adamantly against it, and then he introduces me to the woman . . . Stephanie is her name and I cannot quite bring myself to shake her hand, and right as I lift my hand up to do the right thing and finally shake it, they both just float away.

And I wish I could explain to you the space that I am in these days. It is peculiar. I have not caught up with my life, and yet in that, there is all this awareness, so I am watching myself not being caught up and not really trying to catch up, but yearning to be caught up, naturally, and see all that is, clearly *see* it if that is even possible.

The next day passes quickly, and I remember what Trudy told me about eating before, so I make some rice and vegetables and drive over to Trudy's place after that. I am not dreading the visit so much as looking forward to it being over. I ring Trudy's buzzer and before I have even taken two steps inside the door, I hear Trudy yelling at me from the top of the stairs.

"You came, you came!" she exclaims. "I thought you might blow me off, but you didn't!"

It is actually pleasant to hear how welcoming she is. She meets me in the middle of the stairs and greets me with a hug full of warmth and gratitude.

"I'm so glad you're here," she says. "I'm so, so glad."

And I believe her.

"Want some chocolate soy milk?" she asks. "It's pretty much what I live on."

"Sure," I say.

She opens her refrigerator and inside, from top to bottom, are at least twenty cartons of chocolate soy milk.

"Wow," I say.

"Yeah," she says, "I'm sort of a freak."

She pours us each a glass and we toast one another. We sit on her rug and she smiles at me again.

"You're really here," she says. "You're really here."

"So, wanna make out? Just joking," she says. "Let's play sexy *Madlibs.*"

"What's that?" I ask.

"Well," she says, "you know what regular *Madlibs* are, right?"

"Sure," I say.

"Well it's the same thing but you have to make all the words you put in sexy."

I have to tell you that at first this part of the night did not go over very well. Trudy became frustrated with both my lack of enthusiasm and agility for the game. "Noun," she'd say.

"House," I'd say.

"No," she'd say. "Something sexy."

"Bed?" I'd say.

"Jesus," she'd say. "I hate to say this, but you suck at this."

She ended up doing two on her own and reading them to me and laughing hilariously at the nouns and verbs and adjectives she put in, each word raunchier than the next. Then when I didn't laugh, she made me read them to her over and over. This finally seemed to entertain her a great deal. She'd say, "You're killing me, just killing me. Oh my God, when you say 'clit'! Read the other one! Read 'em both again!"

She slapped her thigh and shook her head. Then there was an awkward pause.

"So, Trudy," I say.

"Yeah?" she says.

"How come you're not with one of your lovers tonight?"

"Girl's gotta hang with her homies sometimes," she says.

"Gotcha," I say.

"Well, actually," she admits, "I'm not really seeing anyone right at the moment. I mean there was this one girl that I thought something was going to happen with awhile back that I met at FKA, but nothing did, and well, I mean, I do want to be seeing someone, like, . . . a lot."

"I see," I say.

"You want to see my dick collection?" she asks me." I've got, like, six."

"No thanks," I say.

"You wanna play Twister? I have Twister. It's good foreplay."

"No thanks," I say.

"Okay," she says.

"So," she says, "like, how many times do you masturbate in a week while you think of me?"

"Trudy . . ."

There is another pause, this one less awkward, more expansive.

"I haven't fucked anyone in over a year," Trudy admits.

"Really?"

"Yeah. Why'd you and your husband get divorced? 'Cause you're gay, right?"

"No, it wasn't that, somewhat I think, but not totally . . . I mean, I loved him that way too. It was . . . something important was missing, something big and . . . in me, too."

"Did you find it yet?"

"No, but I'm working on it."

"You really listen to all those CDs from work, don't you?"

"Yes, I do," I tell her.

"Huh. You want some more chocolate soy milk?"

"No thanks."

"One kiss, okay?" she asks me.

I look at Trudy. She is small and pale and her short haircut is crazily uneven, as if she did it herself. Still, I notice for the first time that she is sort of adorable. I think about what it might mean to kiss her. It worries me. I think about people as medicine again. She looks nervous, vulnerable.

"How come your eyebrows are all pressed together?" she asks me. "We don't have to kiss. I mean you probably . . ."

"No, we can," I suddenly decide.

Trudy's smile at this news is exceptional.

"Come over here," she says. "Close your eyes, dumb-ass."

"Don't call me a dumb-ass."

"Shh," she says. "Shh."

We kiss.

Now, let me tell you about this kiss I had with Trudy from work:

It was so . . . tender it
brought me to tears.
My God.
The depth.
It was . . . oceanic
and

sad but . . . hungry.
It was like a novel
epic with yearning,
with humming underneath
the yearning,
and if it had been a painting
I could have looked upon it for hours, days, and years,
never growing bored.
We bathed in the light that was ours to bathe in . . . our light
inside this kiss,
and we suffered the searing burn of new terrain
and a campfire was lit,
a luminous current ran through it.
And
the magnitude
of our
mutual desire
left us
astonished
and
made us live every drop inside of us, and
every unlived drop resurrected itself and was reborn anew
and resplendent
as we were dragged to the altar
of something that has no better word in this language
than
love.

Trudy, from work.

4

The Grind

New. Great. Revolutionary.

D. Travers Scott

Before the Internet. Before the Clintons. Before Kurt and Courtney. Before protease inhibitors. Things were . . .

In 1991, advertising had not yet become cool again. This was before *Mad Men*. In 1991, we weren't even ironic. This was before Augusten Burroughs. In 1991, we were just bitter.

"Darrin Stephens can suck my big, black dick." These were the words of my mentor at my first ad job, as a writer for the American Institution that was the *Sears, Roebuck, & Co. Catalog*.

Curtis Freeman had warned me, "Advertising's nothing like how he makes it look on *Bewitched*, sitting around all day coming up with pretty pictures and witty headlines. That's just TV, and that's all people know from advertising, because: People. Do. Not. Read."

"Great," I muttered. "I'm a writer in a world where people don't read."

"Although," Curtis said, smiling, "people do buy things. Oh yes, people do shop. But relax: 'You write for one of the largest-circulation publications in the world!'"

Those were the words of not my mentor but our copy chief, Mike Mahler. He was a third-generation member of the Sears family, and seemed to think wide distribution assuaged his team's frustrated creativity, even though "create" wasn't exactly what we did. We copied. We'd get a product fact sheet from a buyer and fit the words on it into a template: headline, subhead, product name, offering price, promotion price, color, model number, sizes, description. We only changed words to meet company style or legal guidelines. Anyone can do it. But advertising is a glamour industry, albeit the lowest rung, so it requires college degrees. And pays white-collar salaries, even though it's easy work. This is why Curtis had been a copywriter for twenty years.

Curtis's desk sported a large, framed photo of himself singing onstage with Diana Ross, and a row of six paperback mysteries with titles like *My Hands, Your Throat*, all authored by a different Curtis Freeman. We shared a cubicle, birthday, and sexual orientation. I never saw Curtis get upset over anything. When I'd be sweating multiple rounds of last-minute corrections, cussing and coding as fast as I could type, he would lean back and look over at me.

"Child, relax. We've never printed a catalog with a blank page."

Sears was just shy of one hundred years old when I joined. Finally out of college, I was grateful for a job that paid well during the first Bush recession. And it was hard to get a job there. As most of the managers saw it, once you were in, you had job security for generations. They accepted only the most succulent young graduates: a Northwestern journalist here, a University of Chicago business major there. I'd ended up there on a fluke. But none of us foresaw that the entire catalog would be shut down within a year.

Before Sears, I'd bartended my way through a BA in Russian literature at a branch of City Colleges of Chicago in an Eastern European immigrant neighborhood. The bar was a dive. Career alcoholics arrived at 10:00 a.m., nursing pitchers of Oly or Meister Bräu all day, stretching SSI checks. We also catered to retired steel mill workers, wild sons of Greek and Hungarian immigrants, and a really sweet biker club. I'd built a good setup there, treating people well, buying regulars their third rounds, free shots at midnight, keeping the clock on real time not bar time, and walking stragglers to the door at closing rather than blasting on the lights and shouting, "Get out!"

In my last year, before graduating and moving to Sears, the bar became a hip place to slum. I found myself serving other students, kids younger than me drinking underage, students from the School of the Art Institute of Chicago and Columbia College. I'd never seen them in our neighborhood, but North Shore rents must've risen higher; maybe even Wicker Park was going up. They'd giggle and smirk; I played oblivious to the irony in their voices when they ordered a Pabst Blue Ribbon. I'm not sure why they picked our place. Normally there had to be some kitsch to be cool: flaming tiki drinks, a vintage photo booth, Sinatra on the juke. I'd resisted that urge. I liked the bar the way it was, plus it would've been so gay of me to do, and I wasn't out there. (Don't give me shit. I had to maintain a certain level of respect among my crowds to keep order.) Maybe I'd kept the place *too* authentic, and that attracted the paint-spattered, horn-rimmed hipsters. I thought authenticity was passé, but maybe it had come back, and my City College ass hadn't received the memo.

I'd been too busy in my last semester fulfilling required credits in things like science and trying to comprehend a class in computer graphic design. I was struggling to learn rudimentary desktop publishing software, practicing on the computer in the school library before work. That one class turned out to be more training than anyone at Sears had taken. Management had invested in a massive transition to desktop publishing, leaving art directors scratching their heads and typographers looking for work. Although I'd responded to Sears's copywriter ad in the *Tribune*, the computer experience on my résumé got me hired graveyard, turning tracing-paper sketches into electronic page layouts.

I told them I really was a writer with a literature degree; they sniffed at my alma mater. When they eventually allowed me to take their copywriting test—a Darrin Stephens fantasy: dreaming up a campaign to sell a paper clip—it turned out I could bullshit as well as their master's degree applicants. They put me through psychological batteries ("To make sure we hire only the right kind of people!") and interviews with management, then anointed me a copywriter.

So by 1991, I was working for an American institution and dating an HIV-positive drag queen. Randy lived in a converted attic apartment at the top of three flights of a rickety narrow stairwell. Inside, crimson walls sloped upward like furrowed brows. With posters, Christmas lights, drawings, woven strands of fabric, and draping succulents, Randy had created his own burrow of a world. Beyond the thick leaves of a rubber tree plant, through a window, you'd glimpse the other world outside, rooftops and balconies, police cars and snowplows.

Instead of a couch, he had an S-shaped lounge upholstered in leopard shag. End tables were wooden LP crates, painted dark emerald and decoupaged with 1970s gay porn. He'd labeled them with musical categories like "Faggit Boogie" and "Train Wrex-n-FX." Flipping through "Butch Vibrations," I noticed the records often had surprisingly Soviet covers.

"Does Nitzer Ebb intend all these red and black graphics to be revolutionary or fascist?"

"Hmmmmmm?" Randy had a pink tulle crinoline between his teeth while he laced his combat boots. He had a cabaret that night, a performance-art fashion show on the lawn of Cook County Hospital, protesting for more AIDS beds.

"In Russia, the graphic designers, playwrights, set designers, poets, and novelists were revolutionaries. They were trying to tear up imperialist life under the czar and end the oppression of the working classes. They were successful, but that's their tragedy. Since their efforts worked, they were put to work for the revolution. When the new Soviet government formed, they supported it with new aesthetics and ideals. But the new government got gradually more and more repressive and fascistic."

Randy blinked and spat out the skirt. "I think they just think it's sexy."

"Oh yeah. Sorry. I did my senior thesis on revolutionary art and literature. It's great stuff."

"So you're a communist? Writing advertising?"

"It's not the ideology; it's the dreaming. Artists thought they were using their gifts to make a new world. And they did! They were dreamers whose dreams came true but then became a nightmare."

"What's your dream?"

"Me? Oh, well. I want to write gay skaz."

"Gay scat?"

"No, skaz! It's this Russian writing, funny stories or novels that are extreme and absurdist to make a political point. I'm trying to do one. I work on it when things are slow at Sears. I have to send drafts to a public printer and grab them before anyone sees, and they come out in 11-by-17-inch sheets, so I have to take those home and retype them on a typewriter. I hope with the money from Sears I can get a computer. But it's like this queer skaz, like looking at Queer Nation and ACT UP."

"You think our dreams will become nightmares?"

"I think you have to beware of people more interested in power and celebrity than healthcare."

"Well, I guess, in the long run, our goal is sort of self-destructive. People like me—drag queens and leathermen and trannies and freaks—we kick down the door, make noise, and create room for all the safe, nice, little middle-class queens. They're not revolutionaries. When queers are normal, when you've got a number-one gay sitcom, a drag-queen talk show, turkey-baster babies on the cover of *Newsweek*, and suburban parents saying, 'Get it, girl!'—it'll put me out of business." Randy giggled. "Maybe I won't live long enough to worry about it!"

He pulled a 12-inch single out of my hands and put it on his turntable. "You know this one?" A bass riff and synth line repeated while a guttural male voice shouted, "Guns! Guns! Guns! Fire! Fire! Fire!"

Randy bobbed his head. "Do you want to make porn? It's a revolutionary art form."

Mahler appeared at our cube. "Drew—I have an opportunity for you to get *creative*!" He put on his thoughtful face, similar to a three-year-old who didn't like her pudding. "We always say things are 'great.' 'A great new lawnmower.' Our products are great, but 'great' doesn't have enough meaning. We need you to put on your creative thinking cap and come up with a bunch of new ways to say 'great.' Lawn and Garden wants us to recommend a whole bunch of new 'greats' to them in a *presentation*—like at an *agency*!"

"Other ways of saying 'great'?"

"Yes: say 'great' with different words." Mahler leaned in, all secretive-like. "This is a great opportunity for you to make an impression."

"Don't waste your time," Curtis said after he left, wheeling over to my side of the cube. "They'll be pissed at you for not delivering something new that's exactly the same old shit. Then they'll go back to the way they've always done things, and you've just confirmed their belief that there's no new out there."

"One," I said, "by thinking that there's 'no new out there,' they really are on the cusp of avant-garde literary theory, although avant-garde literary theory really dismisses the whole concept of an avant-garde, so let's just say they are being amazingly postmodern. Two, they believe there's no 'new' out there, yet 'new' is probably the word they use most frequently to describe their products."

"Mmm . . . ," Curtis mused. "*Second*-most used word."

I raised an eyebrow.

"'Great,'" he said.

We stepped out of Club Lower Links into the rain. Randy had his drag from the evening's show in a garbage bag that he gallantly held over my head as we walked to the El. He still had some eyeliner on. It ran in the rain until he looked like some kind of goth kid.

"Might be a while for a train at this hour. How do you do all these shows and still work?"

"Work? Sweetie, the cultural elite doesn't work." Randy laughed. "I'm on disability. That's just volunteer stuff I do during the day for the gay archives. I used to do display work at the Field Museum, sculpting wax prehistoric plants and putting eyeliner on dinosaurs. But when my T-cells got low enough for me to name them all, I qualified for disability. It lets me spend time making art, like this genderfuck porno I want to make, if I could only find a leading man." He shot me a pointed look.

"I'm not sitting around watching 'Jerry Springer' and eating Combos all day," he said. "I work hard. I contribute to the culture of this city, this country. I make life richer for people. Who knows what magic we're helping create? What famous writer—*hmmm?*—might get discovered acting in an art-porn and go on to write the first bestselling revolutionary queer novel? It's your duty to figure out what you have to offer and offer it up."

"But, Randy, I get up at 5:30. Shower, shave, breakfast, iron shirt. Get to the El by 6:45. Take the Howard line to Skokie, catch the 7:22 bus, then walk ten blocks to make my desk by 8:00. Most days I do have to work all day, no lunch, and when there are slow periods, it's a spare five, ten, or fifteen minutes, and I'm looking over my shoulder so no one catches me. I'm there till 5:00 if I don't have to work late, then I don't get home until 7:00 because there's no express bus running in the evening. Dinner, groceries, laundry, messages, bills, and all the other bullshit of life takes another hour or two, which means if I don't have a social life or indulge in entertainment, maybe I get two or three hours, after running around and working for fifteen hours, to sit at my typewriter and work more! And, I know I've got the most energy I'll probably have ever in my life, no kids, no mortgage, minimal obligations, and still, Jesus, it's so fucking hard."

Randy sighed. "I know, hon. I'm not trying to trump you with the AIDS card, but the irony that kills me—ha!—is that the AIDS got me on disability, so I finally have time to do what I think I was created to do: add joy and humor and beauty to the lives around me. But because of AIDS, I often don't have energy to do anything."

"We had a visiting artist my junior year, this poet. She'd been a political prisoner in Czechoslovakia for six years, and she carved her poetry with her fingernail on a bar of soap until she committed it to memory, then she'd wash with it and write new lines on it."

"I'm going to get all spiritual on you if you don't shut up. You weren't put in prison with soap. You were put in Chicago with a drag queen romantic interest. What you make of that is what's important."

"Maybe I'm supposed to be teaching literacy to Russian immigrants instead?"

Randy tapped my chest. "Listen. Feel. Even then you won't know for sure. Trying to find out is being alive."

In our cube, I wrote "great" on a sheet of scrap paper. "Super," "fantastic," "wicked," "cool," "fun," "wonderful," "fantastic," "very," "extreme."

Human thesaurus, c'est moi. Remember this was in the early '90s. Sears had only begun leaving behind tracing paper, pica sticks, and wax rollers for the revolution of coding, text boxes, and WYSIWYG. The new software was called WriteBank, and it had no built-in thesaurus. Microsoft's Office monopoly was still nascent; I couldn't simply type "great" into a Word doc and hit command-option-R over and over. Nor could I rely on thesaurus.com. Not only was our office not online, but at that time I'd never even heard of the Internet. Sears did sell a seemingly useless service called Prodigy that, for a monthly charge, delivered shopping opportunities, sports scores, and stock quotes to people's computers.

I wrote "excellent," "terrific," "good," "groovy," "righteous," "out of sight," and "incredible."

"Curtis?"

"Yes, child?"

"Are there any black words for 'great'? I know Sears would probably never use them, but I want to throw as many things as possible into the presentation, just to impress them."

"You want something ghetto?"

"No, I mean—"

"Urban contemporary?"

"Well, I guess—"

"AM radio?"

"Yes!"

Curtis pulled his chair over beside me. Stretching tall and straight, he threw his shoulders back, pursed his lips, and rolled his eyes up to heaven, resembling a precocious fifth-grader in a spelling bee.

"Well," he said. "There's 'fine.' Or 'foyne.' 'Foxy.' 'Funky,' 'fresh,' 'phat.' 'Ultra bad,' 'badass,' 'superbad.' 'Real,' '4-real,' 'fo-real.' 'Freaky.' 'Down.' 'Hip,' 'now,' 'happenin'—"

"These aren't all black, are they?"

"Child, everything is black."

He cleared his throat and resumed, enumerating on his fingers. "'Da bomb,' 'ghetto fabulous,' 'all that,' 'macaroni wit cheese,' 'off da miz-onkey,' 'off da hinges,' 'off da hook,' 'off the heavy,' 'crazy,' 'wack,' 'straight up.'"

"Are those all real?"

"No, I made some up. Others mean something else."

"What? Which ones aren't real?"

"I ain't telling yo' cracker ass," Curtis snapped. "I work within the system to bring down the Man."

The presentation was a complete flop. As I stuttered through my litany of "great" alternatives, watching the impatience of the buyers, I'd realized this was nothing they had asked for—they were humoring Mahler. He'd dreamed this whole thing up as some way to get more attention or prestige for his little corner of the Sears empire.

Curtis had taken me downstairs to the loading dock in consolation. The soda machine there was the only one with Dr. Pepper, plus you could talk without a manager hearing.

"The head buyer was completely unimpressed. And I even used the urban ones you gave me to be edgy, but he just glared at me."

"Even for 'tossed salad'?"

"He hated them all. What's up with that one?"

"Well, I told you they didn't all really mean 'great.' Actually that one's 'tossing a salad.' It means eating out someone's ass."

"Curtis!" I said, aghast, furious, delighted. "That's why the head buyer was looking so weird; he must've known what it meant."

"He ought to. I did it to him enough times back when I started here. Back then he still had some tone going on. And hadn't married yet, I might add."

"You knew he was going to be there! What if he'd said something?"

Curtis took a deep drink of his soda. He paused thoughtfully, and we watched the forklifts pull in and out of the trucks, their backup bells sounding and yellow lights spinning.

"Because, grasshopper, I'm supposed to be your mentor, remember? And that's something you should know, in case you don't become famous or marry rich or find some other ticket out of this."

"When you're thirty-three, or forty-three, or, hell, fifty-three, it's not enough to have just gotten by, to have just endured working at a place like this and tried to minimize the indignity. To survive with your pride intact, you have to have fun with it every now and then. You have to take some risks and make this place, this time, these precious hours of your life yours somehow. If you let them take it all, you'll never get back these fifty, sixty hours you give them every week.

"They'll suck 'em away, these hours that could've been spent on your dreams and goals. These hours of drudgery represent all the friends you'll never meet, all the lovers you'll never have, all the books you'll never write, all the countries you'll never see, all the joy you'll never experience, and all the beauty you'll never contribute to the world—all because you're stuck here earning a paycheck.

"To avenge everything this place steals from you, you've got to stick it to them every now and then. Have some fun at its expense. Make it your own. Hide obscenities in a ceiling fan spread, don't tell the art director when they've forgotten to airbrush the nipples out of a bra page, then go fuck your boss. Well, no, don't fuck Mahler. But do fuck someone or something so when it's all done, you can look back and say that, at least every now and then, it was on your terms."

Curtis held up his hand. "Child, you are just precious sometimes. But I'm too tired to explain everything else in the world to you today. That little soapbox wore me out." He walked to the elevator and pressed the call button.

"I'm gonna hide out in the clipping library for a while. Don't tell anyone."

The elevator opened, and he held the door for me. "So let's go up," he said, quoting one of Diana Ross's lesser-known songs. Familiarity with her entire catalog was one of the many things I was learning working beside Curtis.

I thanked him, then said, "I need to call Randy. I think we're gonna make a movie." The door closed on us.

orientation

Carol Anshaw

From *Lucky in the Corner*

Nora's assistant, Mrs. Rathko, has ordered her standard festive platter from the Jewel: crushed, colored foil topped with bologna roll-ups, triangles of an oily, brilliantly orange cheddar, canned olives, toothpicks with cellophane tassels. She has thumped onto the table two boxes of wine—Country Red and Summer White. Cans of store-brand pop sit in ice in the fake crystal bowl she drags out for these occasions. At Christmas, she dusts off empty gift-wrapped boxes to set under the artificial tree. For Thanksgiving, she folds out an accordion-pleated crepe paper turkey. Mrs. Rathko knows how to cut celebration down to size, portion-control it.

In spite of the heat wave—which is into the third day over a hundred degrees—there are maybe fifty students at this reception in the ballroom of the Student Union, about a quarter of those enrolled for the fall semester at Access. Even this year, with her nicotine-hungry nerves and apathy toward her job, Nora is still a little fluttery and hopeful about launching the new school year. Although Access has its share of goof-off courses, it also provides a little academic trampoline. Marginal students can build their confidence and grade points here, then move into the degree program. And now there's a strong English as a Second Language department, serving a population recently arrived here, impelled by unfortunate circumstances. These foreign students seldom show up at any of the school's social events. Nora extrapolates from their serious manner, imagines them working long hours in hard jobs, places thick with steam or fumes and too few windows. They have no time for any sort of frivolity or social break. Maybe for a wedding, a birth, a religious festival, but not for a school reception.

These sorts of gatherings mostly attract the other segment of the student population—those looking to the program for distraction or redirection. They are unhappy in their jobs or marriages, or are unpartnered and don't understand why. People in a rut or at a crossroads, or hoping a crossroad will turn up along the way of their rut. Most of the students who have come tonight look as though they fit one or another of these profiles. They look dulled, worn out, as though they've come here to revive themselves, are waiting for plasma or mega-vitamin shots rather than merely for culture or hot dates.

One of them, though, is not dull. According to the block letters on her paper name tag, she is PAM. She's very tan. There's a slight list to her stance, a confident, relaxed quality in her expression. She is, Nora suspects, someone conversant in the language of seduction. She has the look of someone who has run a long gauntlet of women but come out unscathed; it's the gauntlet that has come out battered and bruised. She's post-butch—narrow black pants, black sneakers, a black rayon camp shirt. Where the collar opens at her throat, a silver chain is visible, a semi-serious chain that rides the line between jewelry and statement. There's a small hickey under the chain. Actually, it's a neck that's hard to imagine without a hickey.

She has a crew cut.

Nora tries to picture this woman in a job. Deep-tissue massage therapy. Dog training, maybe.

To the ordinary eye, she wouldn't appear to be doing anything provocative at the moment, only standing in the middle of this reception, holding a plastic glass of Country Red, name tag stuck to her shirt. It's only to Nora that she is alarming, the alarm an echo from the past. It was precisely women like this who brought Nora out. Neo-vamps adept at using mischief and mayhem to draw not-so-very-straight women like Nora out of worn grooves of marriage and fidelity. There was a time when she desperately needed these women, needed their sullen smoldering, needed the chaos they provided, needed them to call and then not call, to drive her crazy and use up all her available nerve endings on their superficial and transient interest in her. Assembled, they provided a swaying rope bridge out of some jungle movie, unraveling beneath her as she went, creating so much drama and suspense around her transit that arrival on the other side, the goal of the journey, turned out to be rather anticlimactic.

Eventually she ran through these women and arrived at Jeanne. At first Jeanne was attractive simply for who she was not. Not a morning dope-smoker, or an all-night cokehead. Not someone who flipped out in the middle of making love and left. Not someone who, if Nora talked to another woman at a party, was suddenly standing there, like a Sicilian husband, holding Nora's coat.

When Nora approached her, Jeanne stood still, waiting both to hold Nora and to steady her. And all these years since, she has maintained this unswerving posture. What she offered, continues to offer, is a connection in which love is given the opportunity to flourish. She is never capricious with Nora's heart.

They each came into the relationship looking for something big and permanent. They were in their midthirties then, old enough to be dragging around tattered histories of grim dating, awkward near-misses, hopeless affairs, less-than-successful long-term connections. In Paris, Jeanne had lived with a woman for a few years, an orthopedic surgeon she met by way of a fall on slippery steps. Nora, of course, had her marriage behind her, a terrible mistake, with Nora bearing the entire weight of its failure. Both she and Jeanne came in with complicated reasons for wanting to make good this time.

One of Nora's reasons was her daughter. She wanted to link up with someone who would help her create a new home for Fern, and from the start, without hesitation, Jeanne understood that a life with Nora would also include Fern. And somehow, with her charm and good nature, she moved into a position that wasn't presumptuously parental or even step-parental, but rather provided Nora and Fern with a buffering presence between them. Nora knows Fern's adolescence would have been even rougher going if Jeanne hadn't been there to simmer things down, smooth them out. For this alone, Nora is hugely indebted to her. No one else could ever occupy Jeanne's place, which has been achieved through so much shared history.

Not that their relationship is a monolith; it still, even after all this time, sorts out into its good and bad days. There is still a lot of push and pull—a subtle handing over/taking back of power, control, confession, vulnerability—all of which, in certain moments, seems so terribly interesting. In other moments, it seems a more fatiguing way of doing things than might be necessary.

The fundamental tone of their partnership, though, set by Jeanne in the very beginning, is one of kindness. This simple measure has made Nora a more considerate person. She used to be thoughtless in small ways—late without calling, forgetful about plans made. Now when there's something important to be done for Jeanne, Nora writes it on her palm, then checks her hand at the end of the day. She has a sign taped to her desk that says: CHECK HAND.

Sometimes they arrive at larger differences but weather these with a tacit understanding that there are borders on disagreement, that no argument will explode into something truly threatening. At the center of the love Nora holds for Jeanne is a sense of safety—from terrible craziness rising between them, and from the rough side of life. Also from women like this one here at the reception, from her attraction to these women. Which has already come into play—warm liquid flooding her joints, an intransitive sense of urgency. (Something must be done, but about what?) Nora understands that this collection of old, familiar symptoms is probably what has inspired her interior pause to mark the merits of her relationship with Jeanne.

She has to be on guard against herself because even after all the years away from women like this, Nora can still hear their soft, deliberate footfalls as they pace the perimeter of her desire. She can still, given about two seconds, come up with a fairly detailed scenario—something fast and wordless in a gas station restroom along some deserted highway. Or something in a motel room backing onto railroad tracks. Sheets still wafting up sex recently transacted as well as the promise of more to come soon. The scene also includes drinking Cokes from small, icicle-cold bottles from a red 1950s cooler outside the door. Drinking Cokes and smoking Camels.

She gathers herself up, readies her handshake, and tries to get down to the business of greeting students. Her radar is still on, though, and so there is no surprise at all, not so much as an instant of wondering whose fingers have dropped lightly on her forearm.

She turns around.

"Someone . . . ," the woman, Pam, says. "I hate to bug you, but someone told me you were the person to talk to about getting a parking permit for the semester."

"Oh. Right." Nora loses her sure footing for a moment. Pam waits patiently while Nora pulls a couple of sentences together. "Come by my office before your first class. My assistant handles the passes." She immediately regrets having used the words "handles" and "passes."

Pam nods, shyly. This shyness throws Nora off balance; she was expecting swashbuckling. Shy is trickier.

"Actually," Nora says, "come by if you have any questions or problems at all. That's what we're there for." She feels good about having come up with this bureaucratic plural. As though her office is hopping with peppy, uniformed staffers, ready to give efficient, impersonal service and Nora is merely speaking as their representative.

"Oh, I'm not expecting a problem," Pam says. "I'm only taking pottery." She looks down at the floor again.

Nora feels an old power flood through her like a narcotic. She has had so much training in this part, is so adept at its extremely small moves. Simply continuing to stand here looking at this woman who can't look back, not letting her gaze fall or drift, is, in itself, a move. The trick is to keep whatever is said or done hovering over the blurry line between something and nothing. These are skills she learned during the women before Jeanne. Surprisingly, they don't feel at all creaky or withered from lack of use. Rather, they seem greased up and at the ready, as though she has been working out in some secret gym, at night.

"With all your responsibilities," Pam is saying, "I suppose you need to introduce yourself to some of the others, the other—"

"Students," Nora says. "Yes, I suppose I should."

While Pam heads off toward the refreshment table, Nora searches for a familiar face, any colleague will do. Instead she finds herself being nodded at by Mrs. Rathko, who was apparently on her way over anyway to say "Disappointing turnout. If only you'd gotten those flyers to me a little earlier." She goes on in this rueful vein for a while (what a pity they've been sabotaged by the weather, how many withdrawals she's already gotten for the semester ahead). When Nora finally manages to disengage and is free to scan the thinning crowd, Pam is gone.

She herself stays a while, until the ice melts around the cans of pop and the buffet runs out of everything but a scattering of carrot sticks, and the students have diminished to a self-sustaining group of perhaps a dozen, chatting in small clumps. Still, even though three-quarters of an hour has elapsed, she is not really surprised when she comes out the front door of the Student Union to find Pam sitting on the ledge to the side of the stairs. Her shirt is soaked through in places, stuck to her skin at the collarbones, deeply stained at her armpits.

"First," she says, "let's not say anything about the heat."

"Okay," Nora says, idling in neutral. "What's second?"

"Oh, man, I didn't have a second thing." Pam runs a hand over her damp, bristly hair.

Nora feels a drop land on her cheek. She loses track of what Pam is saying. It's not important. The hair is what's important, its dampness. Nora pushes an internal PAUSE button, freezing the little scene that pops up when she put a picture of Pam together with the concept "damp": they're in the bathroom of the railroad motel, and Nora is pulling a shower curtain aside, handing Pam a towel, then playfully reneging.

In the real world, on the steps of the Union, hoping she has only missed half a beat of real time, Nora tries to find some conversational analogue of throat-clearing, tie-straightening, cuff-tugging. "Well, then. I hope you enjoy your class. Have some fun."

"I'll make you an ashtray," Pam says, not joining in the straightening up. She's still in the motel room, lazy between the sheets.

"Oh, I quit smoking," Nora says.

"You might start again, though."

Night is falling. Nora pulls her car out of the lot behind the Administration Building. She hears on the radio that large patches of the North Side have had their power knocked out—payback for having sucked up all the available electricity with a few million air conditioners running on high. Everything looks normal and regular for a few blocks, then lapses into darkness. It's a little scary, also fascinating, to sail along a daily route made eerily unfamiliar by minor catastrophe. Nothing is quite itself. Block after unlit block, here and there a candle or flashlight visible in a window, on the street a sweep of headlights. Amateur anarchists splash in the water gushing from uncapped fire hydrants. Ancient beaters ghost by, heading toward the lake with their windows rolled down and mattresses strapped to their roofs. On the radio, she hears that the parks and beaches are filling up with a transient population looking for a cool spot to spend the night.

Sailing through all this, it occurs to Nora that if anything were to happen between her and this woman, they would already have this little piece of history in place, something to refer back to, a meteorological marker of their beginning.

Travels with Charley

Brian Bouldrey

In the fall of 2001, in a month that will live in infamy, I returned to Chicago after being away from it for sixteen years. I had been living in San Francisco. What was I—they wanted to know, there and here—out of my goddamn mind?

But San Francisco is like the domed city in "Logan's Run"; when you turn thirty, your hand crystal starts blinking red, and you have two choices: turn yourself in, believing that you will be reborn during the flameout at Carousel, or run like hell, hoping Michael York is your hunka-hunka Sandman when it comes time to be shot down like a rabid dog. I am exaggerating, but there is something deeply transient about San Francisco, the City of Thirty-Year-Olds. People say things like "The next town I live in will be Boston." For homos, San Francisco is certainly not Kansas, but people do come and go so quickly.

When I returned to Chicago, my best friend and her family came to my flat to celebrate the ninth birthday of their daughter, Miranda (horoscope: Pony-Crazy on the cusp of "My little sisters can have my Barbies now no they can't yes they can no they can't"). Miranda walked dreamily through my flat, one decorated by a gay man who has sacked Europe of its bric-brac thirty times over. "Hand over your precious tchotchkes, or my checkbook gets it!" Breakable Delft gewgaws, sofa-sized but challenging art on the walls, rare books, baby hybrid veggies in the icebox. Miranda picked up a horseshoe I was using as a paperweight, and sighed. "I like Brian," she decided. "He's *fancy*." While they incinerate you in San Francisco if you're over thirty, in Chicago, though you don't get to be gay anymore, you can be *fancy* for the rest of your natural life.

I am not saying Chicago is without its quirks. In the nearly ten years since my return, I have learned that the phrase "nearly legal" is a term used as a great compliment. "This parking place is nearly legal" or "When Yellow Cab was told it could have no more taxis in Chicago in order to avoid monopolies, starting a second company called 'Wolley' ("yellow," spelled backward) was nearly legal" or "What Mayor Daly did to Meigs Field with those bulldozers was nearly legal." Middle American idiosyncrasies and hypocrisies I not only understand but in some ways perpetuate; I had grown up in Michigan, after all, and went to college in Chicago, and maintained my level-headed Midwestern-ness in flaky California, where showing up for the job was rewarded by continuous employment. ("Ohio," said a pedantic would-be employer. "Here, we pronounce that Iowa." No, my dear. "Ohio" is the word Native Americans use for "yawn.")

Back in Chicago, I was delighted—delighted!—to find freshwater aquariums in high-end restaurants with carp and pike patrolling where I expected to see clown fish and lion fish. Native grasslands in the park—weeds as flowers! And there was that Lincoln Square neighbor (a woman I annually assumed died each winter because I never saw her come or go from her house until late spring), who, having surrounded her bungalow with an English-style garden full of long spiky flowers, mossy rockeries, and tomato plants and corn stalks lovingly trellised as ornamental plants, installed a little bench just off the sidewalk and stabbed into the lawn a little jigsaw-cut and painted image of a fat lady gardener, bent over, with the words "Welcome to My Garden!" scrawled on her ass. Not a foot away from that message, on a decal in the bungalow window, was the sign "We Call Police!" If there is any image emblematic of the Windy City Way, I would choose that. That, or the place in Andersonville where a parking meter was installed right next to a fire hydrant. (Nearly legal.)

When I saw the welcome/unwelcome signs, when I saw that the little pigs in Chicago built their houses of wolf-proof bricks rather than the feckless houses of sticks in San Francisco, when I bought my first hot dog at Al's Fun in the Bun ("Yo, Rogaine, yer wiener is ready!"), when I had learned that the peculiar mix of dust from city park baseball diamonds and early December snow had a name ("snirt") and those summer rain squalls that only brought down the temperature for a moment before bringing it up even higher were called "freshets"—though there is nothing refreshing about them—when all the guys I met at gay bars bragged about almost being picked up by Jeffrey Dahmer back in the day (a number of men roughly equivalent to the number of churches in the middle ages that claimed to have a splinter of the One True Cross), when I heard the glorious recorded announcement on the El, "This is Grand!" (meaning the stop's street name, but more useful as an appraisal of disposition when you're heading downtown), when I learned that chocolate pudding counts as a salad in the steak restaurants and that there are in fact two Damen El stops in two entirely different parts of town, the thing I thought was: *home*.

But I had lived in the town of transients for too long. I didn't know how to *be* at home.

Despite what I had pieced together from the details above, I kept challenging my own instinct. What *is* home? I remember that in Mary Lee Settle's novel *Celebration*, a Jesuit priest says that it is a place where you can die. That's nice. My problem was this: my job wasn't permanent. It was a four-year non-renewable teaching appointment, and I saw it as a crowbar that could wrench me out of California and set me free again, to roam the earth, like that devil guy in the Book of Job. I treated Chicago the same way I treated San Francisco, and my entire life: as if each day were my last. Nothing but parties. Serious was a four-letter word. If guys asked me on dates, they could expect no more sex from me.

Despite the fact that I can't, apparently, spell "serious," my employer decided to offer me a permanent position. Have you ever unexpectedly gotten serious about somebody who was supposed to be a summer fling? I felt like I was in a Chekhov story, that one with the Casanova and the lap-dog lady. I accepted the position with the same trepidation with which those two acknowledged their very problematic love. Chicago, by the way, was my love, not any particular Casanova. The human Casanovas and I were still "serious-ing up," if you catch my drift.

And now we come to the part of the story where I want to skip the gory details, because Susan Sontag says (and what Susan Sontag says, goes) if you write about something in nonfiction, you are essentially performing an exorcism, and if you write about it in fiction, you intend to let it inform your writing for the rest of your life. I choose fiction for this skipped part here—and you have to admit, it's pretty clever of me to stick an advertisement for my own novels in the middle of an essay. Unless—cue spooky music—this is actually fiction. I skip a part here, but let me tell you about the consequences of the skipped part so I can get on with my love letter to Chicago.

After nonstop parties and then the skipped part, I found myself stepping out of Lakeshore Rehabilitation Center ("The Unexpected Vacation!"), a newly minted proponent of the 12-step program. I have nothing but gratitude to the staff of that, uh, vacationland, to the Friends of Bill, to my fellow vacationers, and, most of all, to a certain gentleman I will call Charley, for that really is his name.

Charley became my sponsor. Charley is selfless, project-oriented, and, in his own words, "Serene? Serene like a hurricane!" Charley laughs at my jokes, tells jokes that make me laugh, and has a heart as big as the Heart of Chicago Hotel. Charley has saved my life, and that's all you really need to know.

Except the part where he has this land yacht, the Crown Vic, a former police cruiser that gets about four miles to the gallon and boasts operating windshield wipers so long as you turn the ignition off when you want the wipers to stop wiping, which can be tough when you're on the Dan Ryan, but can be done. Charley has stuffed the seats with empty McDonald's apple pie cartons and Diet Coke cups. Air-conditioning and heating are provided by the Ford Discomfortron System ("Are You Discomfortable Yet?"), and on any given Sunday, there are a handful of new halfway-heard books on CD with titles like "Obama-Nation," "Why God Hates Government," and "Franco Got a Bum Rap." Yes, Charley is that rare thing: the Gay Conservative.

I know, I know. But if you knew Charley like I know Charley, you'd think twice about dismissing him, because I'm not being clear. Charley is a libertarian. While he has some very rigid rules for himself and likes to pretend he's a crazed tea-party kook, he's got a lot more integrity than most of the hippies I encountered in my San Francisco days, and did I mention he laughs at my jokes?

Who knows how friendships grow, really. Have you ever unexpectedly gotten serious about somebody who was supposed to be a summer fling? I was sure my addiction was a summer fling. I was sure my recovery from addiction was a summer fling. I was sure my relationship to my sponsor was a summer fling. But you know what the real summer fling was? While I was able to keep my job safe from my new and terrible love, and my home, and most of my friendships, let's just say this fool and his money were soon parted. I spent all my money on goofballs. I'm that kind of guy. If there were a goofball bar, and we were in it, I'd have a goofball, and then I'd open up my wallet and say, "I love you guys! Goofballs all around!" I'm that kind of goofball addict.

There was a time in my life when I pulled down six figures, and would fly to Paris for a weekend with nothing but my passport and the clothes on my back, and make a necessity of luxury: I needed that pair of Italian loafers, or I'd look like a peasant. At home, even after what I refer to as "The Unpleasantness," you would never know I was financially set back by my goofball problem, because I am *fancy*. But for nearly two years, I was grounded. No more running with the bulls in Spain, no more backpacking across Corsica, and no more touching Jean Paul Gaultier's penis in that little bar in the Marais, which is a story for another time.

But Charley, being project-oriented, had a new project: we were going into business. Through a company called Orion, Charley was going to be a broker for people who run small stores and restaurants and—get this—bars who wanted to sell their business, and find a person who wanted to buy the business. His brother was making money hand over fist out in Orange County doing this sort of work, and we were going to get in on the Golden Age of Mom and Pop.

This is how it worked: Charley would have printed up some fancy (not *gay*, mind you: *fancy*) cards that read: "Are you looking to sell your business? We can find a buyer for you. Call Orion Incorporated at 773.555.5555." Cream-colored stock. Embossing. No expense wasted, because we were a class act. Class up the ass.

On any given Thursday, Charley would drop off three big boxes of cards and three big boxes of envelopes. On Friday, after a meeting, I stuffed the cards, ran them across a dedicated sponge, and bundled them in groups of twenty-five, tallied them, and put them back into the boxes, ready to go.

And on the following Saturday and usually Sunday morning, no later than 4:30 a.m., come snow, snirt, or freshet, I would get a call: "I'm out front." With a pat on the dog's head and three boxes of cards in my hands, I'd step out the front gate and find Charley madly consolidating apple pie cartons to make room for me. If I dawdled, he'd be studying a map of the greater Chicago area. Not just Chicago: ChicagoLAND. Like, you know, Disneyland. "Welcome to Chicagoland!" it says as you leave O'Hare airport. "You're Nearly Legal Now!" We wouldn't move from that spot until Charley had circled a neighborhood or community—Harvey, Chicago Heights, Rock Island, Belmont, or, cringingly, Aurora—and plotted our course.

"I demand to know where you're taking me," I would say, which is both the title of a really creepy Dan Chaon story and my own care for my fate that morning. Would there be a Starbuck's on the way? Would we stop for an architectural tour? Would it be a nice neighborhood or a bad neighborhood?

None of this really mattered. He would tell me where we were going, but most of the places he named were as meaningless to me as libertarian political candidates. Harwood Heights, Hickory Hills, Worth, Maywood. And at 4:30 in the morning, bad and good neighborhoods really are just about the same.

People, I have seen stores and warehouses and salons and derelict ideas for stores; I've seen bars that are still going strong at five in the morning and cinderblock bunker-style bars airing out in the dawn; you can feel the air inside cooler or hotter than the air I walked in with my packets of note cards, carrying the smell of cigarette butts, stale beer, and broken dreams. I have seen walks of shame that will make you feel good about your walk of shame.

We'd often come with a second helper, another recovering goofball addict. I have fondest memories of Tony, may he rest in peace, who liked to do imitations of people in the 12-step meeting from the night before. Tony cut my hair and cleaned my house and showed how my dog, too, with the right kind and amount of food, could inflate rapidly like Kirstie Allie, and got my car towed ("The car got towed," he wrote in an e-mail from the delirium of a relapse, the way Nixon said, "Mistakes were made") and watched Ultimate Fighting in the same spirit I watched it. He had been high since he was sixteen, and now he was approaching forty and just learning about normal human emotions. I am glad he figured some things out; I am sorry he is gone.

Anyhoo, Tony would take the west side of the street, and I would take the east. If it was cold, we'd put on disposable gloves with the fingers cut for good tactile sense. Each and every store, shop, gas station, day care facility, Thai restaurant, and bakery (oh, the bakeries—oh, the smell of donuts at 5 a.m. when it's cold and your fingertips are numb and you don't have money—it's like frickin' *Oliver Twist*) got a card.

There is an official law in Chicagoland that states that you must not put such cards or mail into an official U.S. Post Office mailbox. So we had to slip these cards under doors, fold them neatly and let them expand in the space between double doors, toss them through those accordion gates that get padlocked. My favorite game was to slip my hand through those accordion thingies and toss the card and make it land face up, leaning against the inner door. I called this move "Yahtzee!" I also do this when shaking my HIV pills out of a jar, and I get the correct cocktail combination on the table.

We were put out on the street with about four bundles of twenty-five cards, and we walked along while Charley idled in the police cruiser. If I were Oliver Twist and Tony were the Artful Dodger, Charley had no problem playing Fagin. "You missed one," he'd point to some decrepit, sketchy "art gallery." Nobody got back in the car until all the cards were gone.

Once the cards were gone, he would unlock the automatic-lock doors and allow Tony and me to warm up or cool down. We knew he was happy with our work when he did his imitation of that little exorcist lady from *Poltergeist*: "This block is clean," he would say, and pass his hand over the street we'd just worked.

This seems as good a place as any to say that Charley is not just a big-hearted man. Charley is also generous. He'd slip me twenties under the table at restaurants where fellow 12-steppers dined before meetings, so I wouldn't be ashamed. He'd pay me way too well for writing up website text for his various businesses and proofreading his letters. (He's a lawyer by day, a bankruptcy lawyer, who often dropped a handful of cards on folding chairs at Debtors Anonymous meetings.) My favorite trademark phrase in Charley's threatening collection letters is "Govern yourselves accordingly." I intend to have this put on my gravestone. For now, it is only my Facebook status.

I tell you all this regarding his free and easy way with money because he is not a rich man—he carries a wad of bills he calls the "Chicago roll," which I'm sure is "nearly legal," and shows his thrift in the oddest corners of life: the abovementioned windshield wiper system, for example, or the way he snatched rubber bands from me after I had distributed the twenty-five fancy cards in my hand.

He was right to be stingy with the rubber bands. They were as vital as Robinson Crusoe's knife—I remember saying to the rubber band as I felt the envelopes slip from my numb fingers, as I'm sure Crusoe did to his blade, "Please don't break, please don't break." It is amazing how, when you are reduced to the shelter of your own body and very little else, how little you need, and how the strength of a rubber band can be your lifeline. Rubber bands were also used to tally—one rubber band around Charley's wrist equaled twenty-five cards. At the end, it was fun, and sometimes shocking, to find we had dropped cards in over 500 stores by the time most normal human beings were crawling out of bed.

I came to love what we called "shitty little strip malls." "Let's go to Maywood," Charley would promise, if I was grumpy about something, like his turning the ignition off on the Dan Ryan. "It's full of shitty little strip malls." I liked them because the stores were close together, and I could drop more cards per hour.

I came to understand the health of neighborhoods by the sturdiness of the doors, the number of empty shops in a shitty little strip mall, the friendliness or ferociousness of the hostess in the local pancake diner. I was fascinated by "hybrid" stores that sold Indian food and pizza, auto tires and porn, waffles and bait. When I dropped a note at any number of day care facilities, we would "fix" the name on the card from "Tiny Tots Play Time" to "Tiny Tots Play Time and Rendering Factory." Charley and I are in love with the nearly legal history of Chicago, a Chicago built by robber barons and child labor and rerouted rivers and rendering factories. Nearly legal, at best. All of this, with the endless quips and color commentary, was my Chicago education. I know, as the song goes, every engineer on every train, all of their children, and all of their names, and every handout in every town, and every lock that ain't locked when no one's around.

I know where you can find a plaque on a corner that reads "All Belgians Are Equal." I know where the neo-Nazis hang out in Harwood Heights. I know a beauty salon called "Sardonyx," where you really have to wonder when somebody in the shop says, "Nice hairdo." I know a lighting store called "Sybarano" that sells lighting fixtures that would make Liberace puke. And basically, I have walked hundreds of miles in Chicago, when you were all asleep. Who knew you could travel so much when you're grounded?

If I got lost on those long walks, Charley was always nearby in the Crown Vic, a former police vehicle, which does not so much drive as patrol, like a barracuda. I watched sketchy young men duck behind bushes as we approached, and had to laugh, because we often had to explain ourselves to lily-white suburban police who wanted to know what we were up to. And Charley, who had lived in a halfway house and became its primary organizer, would sometimes frown in sadness as he recognized somebody from that place "still out there," as they say in 12-step meetings.

Was this all, then, a search for those still out there? How many walks of shame did I brush past, how many sleazy strip joints were just letting out in the dawn, or tire-and-porn store operations? I have often said that travel on foot is the only real travel, because you meet the road in real time—you have a strong understanding of distances and difficulties, borders and geography. And people. And what people call home.

There are many kinds of maps, most depicted from a bird's-eye view. Bird's-eye-view maps are just fine, but I am always haunted by a bird's-eye-view story of Mussolini's son, bombing Ethiopia in World War II, who looked out his cockpit and saw his own exploding bombs as "come fiori"—like beautiful flowers. Distance lends enchantment, and prettifies things that aren't very pretty. You have to get your feet dirty to really know what the land looks like.

There is, however, another kind of map, not so much in favor any more, but of great use to sailors. It's called a "periplum," and if you have ever seen that *New Yorker* point of view map where New York City is the center of the universe and everything else in the world rises out of the sea like lumps of stone, you have a pretty good idea of what a periplum is. Sailors used them to find safe harbor when getting close to land. I can think of no more useful map. Especially when looking for the way home.

Somewhere in my travels with Charley, though the get-rich enterprise didn't really pan out, so much of the bigger project, that of making friends with Charley, Chicago, and myself, was a huge success. Serious is no longer a four-letter word. Charley bought a giant house in Iowa, and though I miss our outings, I still text him, "From the train stop in Medina, MN: Angst Auto Services," and he responds immediately, "They only service Fords." We crack me up. I have a friend for life. I, too, have returned to my fancy ways. And I was able to construct a map of Chicago that is my own personal periplum. If I have not found a home in Chicago, I certainly have found a way to it. I can get lost and always know how to make my way on foot. And if the walk is too long, soon, Charley will be sliding up in the Crown Vic, a bundle of cards in his hands, and an apple pie from McDonald's, half eaten.

Forgiv: A Queer Call for Survival in the City

Yasmin Nair

Every late evening, for weeks, it appeared like a sign. It was, in fact, a sign. I would step out for my evening walk, or for a grocery run, and there it would be, a large white sheet with only one black spray-painted word, "FORGIV." It was affixed in a makeshift way to the wire fence in front of the lot surrounding the half-abandoned auto service store opposite the building where I live. The lettering was not inartistic or haphazard. In fact, it showed deliberate form, with the letters styled simply but energetically, with a retro look. The "R" was long and lean, with its bowl poised on the end of a long stem and the right leg extended not too far away, with casual, bell-bottomed ease, as if leaning against an open door on a warm summer evening. The mid-stroke on the "G" echoed the fanciful inward stroke on the top of the right hand of the "V" and was at the same height as that of the "F," which tilted away from the rest, toward the left. The remaining letters gradually straightened up until the "G" stood erect, after which they began to lean slightly toward the right, stopped only by the final "V." All in all, it was a beautifully balanced and elegant sign, which led me to believe that the "E" had not been left out because the artist suddenly ran out of space. It was all deliberate. A decision had been made: only six letters were necessary to achieve perfect balance, and the "E" was deemed redundant. Indeed, after all, its meaning was quite clear, an admonition to all who saw it: FORGIVE, even if you don't see an "E."

I kept reminding myself to take my camera to photograph the sign, and kept forgetting. Matters were complicated by the fact that the sign would disappear every morning. I told J. about it, and his eyes lit up at the strangeness of it all, a disappearing sign that only appeared at night with such a simple message. He lived around the corner from me but had never seen it. Years ago, I had told J. about a rooster wandering around the cemetery, "my" cemetery, whose view I enjoyed from my second-floor window. He was disbelieving: "A rooster? Really, come on. Are you sure it wasn't just a large pigeon?" And finally, one day, he came with me, and there it was: a lovely, red rooster with shiny plumage indicating it had perhaps once been a well-tended, perhaps even a well-loved, pet before being abandoned to the wilds of an urban cemetery.

Since then, J. knew better than not to believe me, and after I told him about the sign we met up one early evening for a walk before turning back to my place. And there it was, magically and mysteriously having reappeared after sundown. We walked like pilgrims toward a famous shrine, down Ainslie and to the corner on Clark. I had my camera this time, and began clicking away. Every time I was about to snap, a car zoomed by and drops of impending rain spotted the viewfinder. I clicked away, and finally got a few shots that weren't marred by either rain or a vehicle blocking the view. A few weeks later, the sign permanently disappeared; the auto-service shop was taken over by new owners, and there was no longer a call to forgive.

I never asked anyone at the store about the sign—that helped me retain my sense of mystery about it. J. speculated that the sign was put up by people whose cars were still locked in because of non-payments, and that this was their way of asking for clemency. But then why only post the sign at night? We never found out.

After that, I began to see the call to forgive in various parts of Uptown, Chicago. In Dollop café, the word was scratched onto the upper-right-hand corner of a bathroom mirror. I had by then learned to carry my camera everywhere I went, and I took a quick photograph. Walking down Broadway, it appeared on the barricaded door of a crumbling building like so many, poised among the hopes of developers, the anguish of residents pushed out of the neighborhood they had lived in all their lives, and the chasm of a recession that began the long nightmare of the end of upward mobility.

It turns out that "forgive" is a popular graffiti word; there's even a website devoted to it, and it sometimes appears with "yourself," as in "Forgive Yourself," a quasi-Biblical message. Still, the word appearing as it did in parts of Uptown had a particular and different resonance for me.

I moved to Uptown in 1997, when the area was still considered grungy enough that rents were relatively low. The building in which I still live faces a few auto repair shops with each, it seems, catering to a different ethnic clientele, including Africans and Indians. This is typical of Chicago, where racial and ethnic segregation has been honed to a fine point and where the resulting racism is disguised in narratives about cultural ownership. The Korean repair store, which stood exactly opposite where I live, was wiped out in a fire one night. I walked out of my building the next morning to be faced with its blackened shell, the roofs caved in, and the few cars in its lot burnt out and twisted.

That happened in the first few months of the housing crisis, and J., who is an expert on Chicago, has speculated that the fire may not have been accidental. Chicago's history is rife with blazes that occur with frequency during economic downturns, the result of desperate business and home owners looking for a way out of mortgages.

During the time I have lived here, I have worked as a writer and engaged in activism of the left variety, beginning with various campaigns against the gentrification of Uptown. In 1999 I was part of a large number of activists who banded together to fight for low-cost and affordable housing in Uptown's Wilson Yard Project. On the other side was a group of virulent "Orange Shirts," pro-gentrifiers who wore orange (my favorite color, alas) and who showed up at community meetings literally screaming about the potential threat to them by youth (read: black teens) should the neighborhood dare to concern itself with housing that was not aimed at potential waves of middle-to upper-class residents. In the end, no one felt they had gained a victory. Our side lost the Goldblatt's building that now houses Borders, which we had hoped to see transformed into cheap housing and community-based businesses. I refused to go into the Borders for two years after it opened until J., who had fought by my side, coaxed me in. I did notice that the staff was not quick to throw out the homeless who wandered in and stayed for relief from either the heat or the cold. (Chicago really only has two kinds of weather, with an unofficial third: construction.)

In the meantime, the various businesses in the Borders building have opened and closed with regularity; even the bookstore chain went bankrupt in 2010. A cell phone store becomes a yogurt store becomes a record store becomes a tailor's store becomes, becomes, becomes . . . The hair braiding store down the street has closed but another opens not far away. Meanwhile, on Clark, a few doors down from my building, the Kinetic Condominium complex finally opened its doors in 2002. To build it, developers razed the old and much-venerated Rainbow Skating Rink; the space had been there since the 1920s in various avatars. At one point, it was the Kinetic music club where Janis Joplin played a few times. It has always pleased me to know that. But in 2002 I was livid about losing a skating rink that I had never frequented—it just seemed wrong to me that a neighborhood treasure should be erased; memories that were not my own were stung. When they dug into the basement, they found a skeleton.

Well, actually, at first, they found seventeen skeletons. Or so the story went, buzzing around the neighborhood, into my local bodega and out into the streets, over to the corner outside Man's Country, our local bathhouse. Eventually, it became a story about just one body. They were able to tell its age from the sneakers it was wearing, from the 1970s. Forensic science can do wonders, but it can always be superseded by an acute sense of fashion.

Around the same time, in 2000 to be precise, the old BC Tap Bar, a working-class dive bar that was never divey enough to be hip amongst hipsters (who had, anyway, not yet begun to move into the neighborhood in droves) closed down. Distraught neighbors put up signs everywhere: "Save BC Tap!" These days, it's even hard to find an Andersonville resident who remembers the bar. In its place stands A Taste of Heaven, a café that moved down from its original location further south on Foster. The establishment bears the unique sign on its door that created so much controversy in 2005, when it was catapulted to national fame and infamy: "Children of all ages have to behave and use their indoor voices when coming to A Taste of Heaven." The owner, Dan McCauley, claimed that this was to make sure parents controlled children who tended to run wild and disturb adult customers. The story made it to the *New York Times*, surprisingly igniting a national conversation about how parents should raise their children—or if they were even doing so in an age of "child-centered" policies and places. And occasionally, as the story wound its way through national and local news outlets and the blogosphere, it became one about the differences between parents and non-parents. McCauley is an out gay man, so, to be specific, the story became one about straight people—"normal" child-rearing types—versus queers, who supposedly don't have children to take care of.

It is tempting to turn this story into one about yuppies taking over neighborhoods like Andersonville, which have seen queers migrating northward from places like Boystown after having been gentrified out (news: they won, we lost). The popular myth about queers and gentrification is that we move into broken-down houses in equally broken-down neighborhoods and fix them up, making it possible for wealthier yuppies to eventually relocate into "our" neighborhoods, pushing us out in the process. This narrative erases the reality that marginal and "undesirable" neighborhoods are usually first inhabited by a city's migrant workers and its poorest (who may or may not be queer—but nobody cares to run surveys among them) before being "discovered" by queers. And it ignores the fact that yuppies and suburbanites, the ones so many of us love to loathe, are in fact often wealthy gay men and women.

The Taste of Heaven story exemplifies traditional conflicts over ownership of a changing neighborhood. But at the end of the day, it's really only about who in the neighborhood gets to pay for the privilege of paying about or over ten dollars for soup and a sandwich at a café—and nearly twenty dollars if you include dessert and a drink. Despite all the talk about styles of parenting, of battles between yuppie gentrifiers and "original" residents, capitalists vs. bohemian artists—it all comes down to people fighting over the right to pay the kind of money that most of us living in the city can't shell out too often.

My point is that gentrification is cast in the light of ownership (cultural and material) and sentimental memories of the "old days." But, in the end, it's about who can pay to live in a neighborhood and whose tax dollars count the most.

Which brings me back to the issue of forgiveness. In my random encounters with the word all over Uptown and its surrounding area, I have sometimes been tempted to assume that there is this one person wandering around the neighborhood and inscribing the word into any medium necessary in order to provoke us all into some plan of action. What, exactly, is unclear, and the import of the message shifts with each sedimentation of memory that comes in and wipes out yet another era, however brief, of nostalgia and memory. Today I tell myself that the word admonishes us to forgive both debt and foreclosure, the sort that leaves the Kinetic desperately pleading that people please, please come in and check out its half-empty and grandiosely envisioned interiors, with the artificial plants and unused patio furniture set up to make us believe that people actually live in the units (they always forget to turn on the lights at night, a dead giveaway). I imagine that the word allows some forgiveness for my own entrance into the neighborhood. The irony is that even as I fought against gentrification, I was also part of the force that "cleaned up" the neighborhood, by sheer dint of my class status (however ambiguously positioned in the economic hierarchy) as a creative professional. I am fond of railing against hipsters and yuppies (and will do so till my dying day). But there are times, as I scour the thrift store for the next vintage find or eye the bottle of expensive olive oil in the seventeenth olive oil store within three blocks, that I wonder how I might be different from either group.

There is the difference in income level, of course. And the consciousness of not wanting to push out people who have the right to live in a clean and safe neighborhood without paying an exorbitant rent or being forced into mortgages they cannot afford. I tell myself that every day as I walk around a neighborhood that is constantly on the verge of shifting and, sometimes, collapsing. Yet another carefully haphazard store, with precious knick-knacks and an assiduously cultivated image of independent spirit, falls into disarray and begins to hawk its wares—20, no, 30, no, 50 percent off! On the last day, just take what you can, give us what you can.

I look for the word "forgive," for forgiveness, and I wonder: is the hidden message still out there? Are we to forgive and forget? Neighborhoods have bad memories. Gordono's Pharmacy, opposite the Jewel on Bryn Mawr, was once just that and then, about five years ago, revamped itself into a deli-cum-soda-fountain-cum-pharmacy and plastered signs all over that said, "The neighborhood's only Jewish deli." Which would be lovely, except . . . they boast of selling Manny's potato pancakes, but the ones in the case look like they were harvested from the back of Manny's freezer. Meanwhile, a local review website features enthusiastic testimonials from readers who write about how they step back in time in this "traditional" deli. Nostalgia is a funny thing. It makes you forgive and forget a multitude of sins.

Duped in Grit

Mark Zubro

As I lay face down in the alley, the four-hundred-pound blues singer stepped on the back of my head. I felt the grit of urban detritus as skin scraped off my nose. When her left foot finally left the back of my head, I muttered, "I don't like you."

The sneer in her laugh added no comfort to my condition.

I bit my lip. Tasted blood. Tried to move. I only got groans for my effort. I opened my eyes and got an image of blurry mud and cement. I managed to turn my head far enough to look up. My eyes had trouble focusing. At least that's what I hoped it was as I looked up between the legs at the interior portions of my gargantuan nemesis. A short skirt that would have fit a rhinoceros hid this view from the lucky. The sight of her ill-clad nether regions almost elicited more nausea than the punches from her goons earlier. Did I just see a garment a female impersonator might wear? But this was a woman.

With my left elbow and right hand, I levered myself onto my left side.

Mistake.

Pain. Vertigo.

Then she kicked me. Hard. In my nuts.

My groans of pain accompanied her rumble of the tune "Sweet Home Chicago" as she heaved her bulk toward the far end of the alley.

I lifted my head. Dizziness. I rested my head on my left ear. The grit scratched its surface. I watched her minions drift in and out of focus as they followed her. At the end of the alley, she and they climbed into two cars, one black, one maroon. Maybe a Cadillac and a Buick. They drove away.

I'm Mike King. Gritty. Urban. I'd been inside Club Blues, Chicago's hottest blues night club.

I ached. Everywhere. The stomping I got before Josephine Chiakparé added her tonnage to my misery had been thorough, messy, and deliberate.

It started to rain. November in Chicago. Gray skies. Cold wind. I saw a lump of scattered plastic nine inches from my left eye. I reached for it. My cell phone wasn't going to blip into service any time soon.

I felt for my gun. Gone. They hadn't used it on me. Good. I hadn't been able to use it on them. Bad. The attack had been too sudden.

I tried standing. No luck. My head throbbed. Jabs of pain protested throughout my body. I rested on the cold, damp ground. Something solid to rely on. I figured I'd give crawling a shot. Grit rubbed my hands raw as I used hands, elbows, torso, knees, and feet to attempt movement toward the street and my car.

I heard city noises: passing traffic, distant sirens, a car alarm not happy with itself or the world.

I tried calling for help. I got out a few rasps. Mostly my throat gurgled.

My jeans and jacket ripped and tore at whatever points they merged with the corrugated and corrupted pavement. I wished the streetlight would stop drifting in and out of focus. I heard someone give a harsh laugh. Me.

I shivered in the rain and wind-riven darkness.

Some time before an Ice Age set in, I made the end of the alley.

But I'd seen something significant. Somewhere. On the blues queen. In the alley. On the muddled minions. On, around, or about the cars. In the Club. Somewhere. Something.

Why the hell did Josephine Chiakparé have to sing the blues only at three in the morning and then only on the fourth Saturday of every month? Why couldn't the idiot who'd hired me have picked someone else?

Tough. Gritty. And I whine a lot.

At the end of the alley I paused, looked around for help. No pedestrians. Which meant no bad guys. No good guys, either.

I heaved myself to my knees. The evil minions didn't seem to have broken any significant bones. I checked for blood. Some. Mixed with alley crap that was best not analyzed under a microscope.

I used the building for support. Found my legs would keep me upright as long as I wasn't too demanding. I looked at my reflection in the first window I passed. Wasn't pretty.

All four tires on my car were flat. I was not surprised.

The mailbox at the corner provided welcome leverage. A bus on Twenty-Second Street. Going west toward Halsted. I could get to the office.

Maybe. I huddled deeper into my black leather jacket. I got a peculiar look from the bus driver, but I had exact change, and I didn't point a gun at him. I guess he thought he was doing good for the moment. I got a transfer at Halsted Street and waited for the next bus north.

After twenty minutes of trying to hunch myself away from the rain and wind, I was back on a bus. If I held myself very still, the pain was only excruciating. Made it to Diversey and dragged myself west two blocks to the office. It was closer than my place, and Malvina, my upstairs neighbor, would make sure my dog was fed, watered, and walked.

I don't remember if eternity or the top of the stairs arrived first. Staggering up each six-inch tread awoke dormant stabs of agony from my bones and muscles. Through the front door and outer office, into the inner office and onto the couch, cracked leather and oozing stuffing. Sleep.

Sounds of crunching metal that were not coming from someone battering my skull with an aluminum baseball bat woke me. Seconds later, loud thumps ascended the stairs. The inner office door slammed back against the wall. Harold Beal, the Club Blues client and Chicago alderman, staggered into my office.

He clutched at his throat with one hand. Gushes of blood fountained around his fingers. With the other hand, he pointed at me and gasped, "You're a dead man."

Beal collapsed. I grabbed the box of tissues on my desk, rushed to him, jammed a fistful of tissue to his neck, and applied pressure to the wound. With the other hand I fumbled for the phone on the desk and dialed 911.

The paramedics arrived in seven and a half minutes. He was dead seven minutes and fifteen seconds before that.

They worked on him anyway, as they always do. My adrenaline rush continued as I followed the sprays of blood down the stairs to his car. His vehicle was halfway through the front window of my downstairs neighbor, a deli.

Dark red splotches decorated the driver's seat and steering wheel. It was a maroon sedan. Like one of the cars that the assorted minions had gotten into earlier this morning. I heard sirens.

Cops. Detectives. Crap.

Detective Drew Molton arrived. He was tall, African American, and about as happy as a right wing religious nut at the Folsom Street Fair in San Francisco. We talked in the outer office. Crime scene folks swarmed the inner office. The cops aren't fond of me, but Molton at least tolerates me.

Molton said, "The mayor doesn't like dead aldermen."

I said, "That's so like him."

"What I can't figure out is, he's shot. He's dying. He doesn't dial 911. He doesn't rush to a hospital. He comes up here. Why? And why did he come to you with his problem yesterday? He's got enough connections to steal any election by a landslide. And he's dead." Molton eyed my tattered clothes and my bruises, cuts, and abrasions. "And you're not."

"Some days I get lucky."

"Did you find out anything?"

I'm suspicious when a powerful alderman comes to me for help. So, I'd called Molton.

I said, "I learned a couple of things. First, Josephine Chiakparé is a great blues singer. She's got this breathy voice that makes you yearn for slow, sultry days and long, tropical nights on remote islands crawling with intrigue and danger. Nights filled with languid kisses and passionate romance. She's also mean. Second, it hurts to have a fifth of a ton balanced on the back of your head. Third, Club Blues is dangerous. It was crowded beyond the legal limit. The fire-code violations would send Smokey the Bear into rehab. I don't care if someone else does drug deals, enjoys a prostitute, or gets in a fight, as long as I'm intact, but I do tend to avoid potential firetraps. Why hasn't it been closed down?"

Molton replied, "Maybe they're just lucky."

"In this city?"

Molton said, "I warned you about going there."

"They took my gun."

"You report it?"

"I just did."

"We found a gun." He had a smirk on his face that was disconcerting. "You own a .38 Smith & Wesson?"

"Yeah."

"There's one wedged under the brake pedal of the car."

I said, "I was passed out here in agony. With no witnesses."

He said, "And it's a dead alderman."

I said, "One more or less of them, I mean, who really cares?"

Molton said, "It's my job to care."

I said, "I was to case Club Blues. Sniff around. Talk to a few people. Beal showed me the books he had. Deeds to the place and contracts. All kinds of paperwork involving the ownership."

"You're an accountant?"

"I suggested he hire one. He said he wanted my help. He'd heard I could keep my mouth shut. He said the building was part of a family trust. He feared someone was stealing money from the club. Or making bad investments. Or cheating him. He feared there were more recent trust documents or maybe forged documents. The key, he claimed, was the Club. Most importantly, he didn't want to involve the police, since that could get the press interested. He said his whole family has been after him and his mother since his father died. I asked him if the Mob or gangs were involved. He insisted they weren't."

Molton raised an eyebrow.

I said, "Beal introduced people he said it was safe to talk to. I spoke with the bartender, who is a stepbrother. Another was one of the front-door bouncers, a sister."

"Did you learn anything from them?"

"Nope."

Molton asked, "How'd you get beaten up?"

"Beal left me about two. I didn't see him after that. I was to meet Chiakparé in her dressing room after her set. I spoke with her for all of two minutes before I got hustled out the door by her goons. They pinned my arms, dragged me to the alley, and started stomping. I think the car downstairs here is one of those that I saw Chiakparé and the crew getting into this morning."

"You must have said or done something to somebody that really pissed them off."

"Gotta be." I thought about the threat Beal had managed to blurt out before keeling over on my carpet. I thought about my notion that I'd seen something. I said, "Other than reaffirming my previous belief that pain hurts, I got nothing."

"The car downstairs is the alderman's own car." Molton let the silence drift for several beats, then said, "You were set up."

I shook my head. "If I was set up, I'd be dead."

The door to the inner office opened. A crime scene tech said, "We're done in here."

"Cause of death?" Molton asked.

"Gunshot wound to the throat. Fired from ten to twenty feet, give or take. With the amount of blood lost, it must have happened just before the crash." The techs left with the corpse.

Molton said, "We'll do forensics on your gun. Don't expect it back. Ever. Forget about involving yourself in this except as a suspect desperate to be cleared. They could have killed you last night. They didn't. They still might." On that cheery note, he left.

I switched on the coffeemaker. Found some aspirin in the minuscule washroom. The tablets were long past the expiration date on the label. I took three. I cleaned myself up some, then threw on an old sweatshirt. I'd used it to mop up rusty water when the radiator burst during the first cold spell this October. At least now it was dry.

I heard heavy steps thudding up the stairs. More cops? Instant death? My back-up gun was at home.

Four men trailed a woman. I thought her handbag and boots were Prada. Her Burberry coat hid a figure of some heft. This woman was in her late seventies or early eighties. The men with her might have been last night's minions. Or not. The assault had been too fast at the beginning, my vision too blurry at the end.

Breathing heavily, she reached the top of the steps. "You!" she pointed a finger adorned with a diamond of elegant simplicity. More heavy breathing. Then she gestured to the minions. "Wait here." She stepped into the office and closed the door on them. She said, "I'm Mary Lou Beal." She walked to the crime scene tape. "Is this where my son died?" she asked.

"Inside."

"I'd like to see."

I slipped off the tape. How'd she know so quickly to come here? She was the mother of a Chicago alderman. Someone would have found a way to tell her. She took a deep breath and eased herself to within two feet of the pools of blood. She tottered. I held out a hand. She said, "Thank you."

I said, "Perhaps we should sit in the outer office, or even step out for a cup of coffee."

She replied, "No. I want to stay here. I want to stay near where he was last alive." She accepted my arm to a chair. She sat in silence, taking in large gulps of air. I sat.

I said, "I'm sorry for your loss."

She glared at me. "He was a fool. Alderman! Pah! He was my son, but he was a fool."

"Why do you say that?" I asked.

"They're all fools. My family has been involved in that building in all its incarnations since the '40s and hip deep in politics in this town since before prohibition. We own the building. My parents fought about it. My son and daughters fight with me about it. My children do nothing but fight, about everything, including how much money there is and who is going to get it when I die. My nieces, nephews, grandchildren, all of them are at each other's throats. I don't trust the so-called friends of my late son. I don't trust the police or the politicians. I need to know who killed him and why. I know it was someone in the family. I know it. I want you to find out. I want them punished."

"I got beaten up last night by, I believe, some of the men who came with you here."

"If it was them, they won't touch you again." Spoken with toughness and assurance. I wasn't ready to break out the I-trust-you-now champagne.

I said, "Fine. I want the whole family at the club by three o'clock. I need to question all of them."

She said, "Done."

"And the employees by two."

"Yes."

"Why come to me?"

"You aren't dead and my son is. I need to know why. You are part of this. It's fair to you. It's fair to me. It'll answer some family questions that need answering. Such as who is willing to commit murder."

I held her gaze. She met it unblinking.

"Do you know if anyone in the family needed money?"

"They all did. They're lazy-ass sons of bitches who think they're going to be able to live off my money when I die."

"Why did he hire me?"

"He was suspicious of the rest of us. Not as suspicious as I am of the rest of them."

As she and the minions thumped back down the stairs, Duncan, my part-time secretary, and Georgia, a part-time operative, came in. Duncan was very muscular and very bright. A grad student at the University of Chicago who should be indulging in nuclear physics, not keeping my filing and accounts in order. He says he likes the work.

Georgia, full name Georgia De'Jungle (with an e), was the most accomplished drag queen on the North American continent. Her ability to disguise herself was unknown. That's how good she was. If she was legendary or unrivaled, that would mean people would know what she was up to.

Duncan took one look at me and said, "Have you been to a doctor?"

I responded, "No."

He said, "You might want to try that one of these times." He flipped on his computer and set to work.

Georgia was thin and the epitome of elegance. She wore a beige caftan over a pink pantsuit. She looked at me and said, "You've got more grit ground into your face than any three PI's on a cheap cable show."

"I had an accident."

Georgia said, "No, dear, being hit by a car is an accident. Grit and you are like gravity and everything. You are so drawn to each other. Add this to breaking up with your boyfriend last month. That was gritty, too."

"It was not gritty. He threw his drink at me. Wet. No grit."

Georgia said, "I still don't understand that. He was cheating on you with his wife. Why did you get the drink thrown at you?"

"He didn't think it was important to mention to me that he had a wife. I mentioned it to him."

Duncan said, "How did you find out he was a philandering boob?"

Georgia said, "Everybody our boss dates is a philandering boob."

I said, "No more discussion of my love life, such as it is, or more likely, isn't." I switched topics. "Do you have the pictures of the reverend from the case you've been working on?"

She replied, "I came to borrow Duncan's digital camera. His has more features than mine."

He handed her said instrument. She left.

Hours later, I headed back to Club Blues. The bits of the cold, gray November afternoon light that managed to leak into the bar did little to enhance the gloom inside.

Twenty of the employees sat at the tables. None of them looked happy. Mary Lou Beal introduced me and then said, "Cooperate with him. I've got a ten-thousand-dollar reward out for whoever can tell the most about what happened to my son."

At the mention of the reward the group turned from sullen to a little less sullen. Progress. Here's what I got from them. Beal had spoken to lots of people, worked in his office, had no quarrels with patrons, staff, or family. No one claimed to know where he'd gone after the bar closed. They said Chiakparé did as she always did: came in, sang, and left.

Mrs. Beal's guards claimed they didn't beat me up and knew nothing about Chiakparé's movements.

The family consisted of twelve: Mrs. Beal's two daughters and assorted nieces, nephews, and grandchildren.

They tended to be a hefty bunch. None were as big as Chiakparé. Most claimed to know as little as the hired help.

I interviewed the two daughters separately. Beatrice was the only one in the entire family who had avoided the plus-size curse. She said, "I can't imagine why my idiot brother hired you. I can't imagine why my senile mother is making us talk to you."

"I could tell her you're uncooperative."

"Screw you, asshole."

"What was going on with the club or the finances and the building?"

"What did my brother tell you?"

"That you and your sister were trying to cheat him out of his inheritance."

"Cheat him? Ha. He's the one who's trying to get his name on all the accounts."

"Has he succeeded?"

"Not for lack of trying. Every time he meets with my mother, I have to run over here to convince her not to invest in his crazy, harebrained schemes. He always has some stupid deal that he wants her to invest in. Sometimes he gets my idiot sister to go along, and I have to put my foot down."

"Did he have any enemies?"

"He was always paranoid. Always rushing off to hire another lawyer about some bull. It was all in his mind."

I said, "What do you know about Chiakparé?"

"Nothing."

She claimed to have gone home straight after the club closed and had been on her way to church this morning.

The other sister, Veronica, the bouncer from the night before, was a woman of some heft. She said, "Talking to you is stupid. I've already talked to the police. Mother has lost her mind."

I said, "Your brother thought you and your sister were trying to cheat him and your mother."

"I'm sorry he's dead." She sniffed. "But he was an idiot. He could never save money. Didn't know how to run a club. My sister is as big a fool. I have to watch her constantly. I've been afraid she'd form an alliance with him to cheat my mother. They rob this place blind. If it wasn't for Chiakparé, this place would have gone bust years ago."

"Do you know how I can get in touch with her?"

"No. No one does. She comes to work that one night a month. She gets paid in cash. She leaves. She's been singing here since dirt. The crowd loves her."

"No one's tried to find her?"

"Nobody's ever come back to report they've found her." She gazed at my more prominent bruises. "I heard what happened to you."

I said, "Good news travels fast. Your mother is Chiakparé's age."

"She hates Chiakparé."

"Why?"

"An old, old feud. Chiakparé had an affair with my father and in the deed to this place or in her contract, or in his will, somewhere, he stipulated that she got to continue singing the fourth Saturday of every month."

"Did your brother have any enemies?"

"He was a politician in this town. What does that mean to you?"

I didn't think there was much of a political angle here. Assassinate a Chicago alderman? What was the point?

As had her sister, she claimed to have gone straight home after the club closed and was on her way to church this morning.

I found Mrs. Beal in an elegant suite on the third floor above the club. I said, "Your kids don't like each other."

"That isn't news."

"Was your son trying to cheat you out of your money?"

"He was a fool."

"You didn't invest in his schemes?"

"We still own the club."

I said, "This isn't making sense. Your son is the alderman, and people are going to want to know what happened."

"I don't care about politics. I care that he's dead. I want to know who did it."

I said, "I heard you didn't like Chiakparé?"

"I haven't talked to that woman in years. Her presence is an offense."

"Why don't you like her?"

"It has no relevance to this case."

"I got beat up by her minions."

"That was your mistake."

I left.

I stopped at the office. Duncan had gone home.

Molton strode in as the bleak afternoon was leaking into evening misery.

"You catch who did it?" I asked.

"You get any information out of them?"

I said, "You'll be the first one on your block to know when I find the killer."

I took my throbbing head and aching body home. Fed my dog, Caesar, a basset hound. His droopy face matched my mood.

Why the hell had I been beaten up? The family all hated each other. And I'd seen something.

Mid-morning the next day, Georgia strode in. She wore a leather miniskirt under a leather coat. Both of which left a lot to keep warm. She dumped an envelope on my desk and said, "At least one of the right reverends in our beloved Illinois wishes to indulge in too much fun. Those are the pictures."

I replied, "The client is going to be pissed." The client was the reverend's untrusting wife.

Georgia sat in the client chair and draped a long leg over the other, and I knew what I'd seen in the alley.

She said, "You've never looked at my legs like that before."

"I'm not looking at them like that now. I gotta go."

I hurried to the club. I met a minion at the door. I said, "I need to get into Chiakparé's dressing room."

Still under the cooperate-with-him rubric from Beal's mother, I was permitted entrance. In the room I spotted vats of blush, tubs of rouge, trays of eyelashes, pots of cream, enough transforming substances to last Georgia for a lifetime. I found costumes. Mounds of heavily padded costumes. Chiakparé was a fraud. What I'd seen that night in Chiakparé's nether regions had been a thong straining to cover revealing excess. It was the kind of thong male dancers wear if they wish to hide obvious bulges in tight costumes. The kind of garment Georgia would have to be wearing under such a short miniskirt. I knew this because I'd dated a dancer when I was a senior in high school.

Who would have the nerve to pull off such a switch? Hefty sister? Heavy alderman? Elderly mother? Using a lot of the padding, slender sister could make it work. I examined the padding, found a pair of small scissors, and began ripping open seams. Half a mountain later, I found papers. Family trust papers, dated later than the ones the alderman had shown me on Saturday. I glanced at the inheritorship page. His mother was no longer the owner of the trust.

The door burst open.

Hefty sister Veronica said, "What are you doing here?"

I responded, "Trying to figure out if you or your mother killed your brother." I pointed to all the padding I'd unearthed. "Chiakparé is a fraud."

"My brother has sung the role for years. So what? He and my father cooked up the scandalous background to make it more alluring. It was a money maker for the club. That doesn't add up to murder."

I said, "Why did he/she grind my nose into the ground and have her minions work me over?"

"I have no idea."

"Your mother goes along with the sham?"

"It helps us make money."

"Who's going to own the club now that he's dead?"

"He didn't own it. My mother's name is on the trust."

I said, "Not on the papers he showed me and not on these." I held up the papers I'd just uncovered.

"Where'd you get those?"

I pointed to the padding and replied, "I didn't understand a lot of it, but the way I read the inheritorship names, the trust passes to your kids. Your mother is broke."

Mrs. Beal banged open the door.

I turned to her. "Were you aware these copies of the family trust were hidden in the padding of Chiakparé's outfit?"

Mrs. Beal whipped through the papers to the inheritorship page. She glanced at it for a moment, then glared at her daughter. Then each pointed a finger at the other and screamed, "Murderer!"

Nasty minions flooded the room. My last view was of the two hefty women snarling at each other. Then I was in the street. I found a pay phone and called Molton.

I sat in Molton's office late that afternoon. "Which one did it?" I asked.

"My money's on Veronica: her kids get the money. Mother and daughter haven't stopped accusing each other."

"Did you look at the books?"

"We've got forensic accountants going over them as we speak. Their preliminary notion is that someone's been cooking the books."

"Who's the owner?"

"Mrs. Beal isn't."

Molton's deputy, Jeanne D'Amato, walked in. She said, "We told Mrs. Beal she didn't own the place and that she's broke. She said, and I quote, 'I should have killed her not him.'"

I said, "Veronica had to be the one who hid the papers in the costume. She's the one who benefits."

"She says she didn't know about them."

I replied, "It's a terrific hiding place. Sister was duping mother and brother?"

"One or both," Molton said.

I remarked, "He hired me because he thought he was being cheated. Turns out he was right, but why beat me up?"

Molton said, "My theory is that he figures he gets the best of both worlds. If you stop snooping around, Chiakparé gets blamed. If you keep working, and you find something out that saves the family trust, then he's a saint."

"Why did the alderman come threaten me this morning?"

The deputy responded, "Mother and sisters had a huge fight when the alderman reappeared as himself after the show."

"They didn't go home like they told me?"

"Nope. Veronica got the alderman to believe you knew something and were planning to betray him."

"I was played for a fool."

"Yep, you were duped."

"Why did Mrs. Beal hire me?"

D'Amato replied, "She didn't know about the papers. Mrs. Beal wasn't sure who was cheating her, but she was suspicious. Veronica egged her on for her own nefarious reasons, pushing her over the edge, so that Mrs. Beal thought her son had cheated her. Mrs. Beal went nuts."

Molton explained, "Veronica gets her mom to kill her brother or gets her to order it done. Veronica's kids get the club, and she doesn't get a murder rap."

I crawled home. At the station, Molton had managed to keep the words "thanks for your help" from escaping his lips. About what I expected.

Basset hounds don't look happy to do much of anything ever, but at least Caesar wagged his tail.

5

Family Matters

The Mudroom

Nadine C. Warner

I vaguely remember what sex feels like. Sometime around 2006, just after my son Nick arrived, my partner, Lori, and I slipped into what I thought was only an urban legend—*lesbian bed death.*

Initially, it was the exhaustion from waking up every two hours to feed a newborn, followed by the nonstop upkeep on an aging Victorian and the frequent trips to fix "whatever" at Lori's mom's place. We thought that things would settle down by the toddler years, so we could squeeze in a little loving, but the combination of entertaining a "spirited" three-year-old—as people in the park have labeled him—coupled with entering our 40s, which I thought were supposed to be our cougar years, has left us too tired to do anything other than deliver a perfunctory kiss as we sink into sleep, which may or may not be interrupted by Nick asking, "I sleep in your bed?"

We did *not* sign up for a Boston Marriage.

The first time I laid eyes on Lori, my heart actually skipped a beat.

We're in the only dance bar in "Chambana," and I'm up on the speakers shaking my ass in biking shorts, matching blazer, and a black sports bra. Yeah, I looked good. The bass is pumping through my feet, then up my legs as I rock from side to side, scanning the crowd. Too butch, too femme, too . . . whoah—

It's like someone tripped a cord. The music stops—I can see everyone else dancing, but I'm frozen. The whirling disco lights fade, and all I can see are these almond brown eyes that meet mine, look away, then peek back, the faintest smile tugging at the corners of her mouth.

I climb down to the dance floor, push my way through grinding bodies, tiptoeing to see over sweaty chests.

I lay a tentative hand on her shoulder as her jet black bob swings back and forth to the beat—

"Hey?"

"Hey."
"Nadine."
"Lori."
"Law school."
"Theater."
"Wanna dance?"
"Sure."

Now the only dancing we do is to *Elmo's Sing-Along-Dance-Along* DVD.

Clearly, we need help.

I dust off the *bagua*—a tool from my days as a feng shui consultant—and overlay its grid onto the blueprints of our house. Nine sectors, nine areas of your life. All our sectors are looking good—Family, Health, Knowledge, Creativity—then I get to the Romance sector and immediately see the problem. The area of our home that should be a celebration of our lives together lands squarely in the mudroom, an uninsulated overflow space for tools, toys, groceries and *1,500 pairs of shoes.*

It's the *shit room*—and as any feng shui consultant knows, as goes the room, so goes the sector. We need to pump up the chi.

And since Lori—my Chinese American partner—humors this African American feng shui junkie, we purge. Three weeks, five Salvation Army drops, and seven craigslist ads later, we've cleared enough space to actually decorate. We're going to install shelves, spruce up the paint, and fix the broken stairs. As we cart out boxes of shrink-wrapped memories—plastic speculums and syringes from unsuccessful attempts to get pregnant, "We're Everywhere" pride necklaces from college when defining ourselves was part of finding ourselves—we uncover unspoken hurts as well, both real and imagined, that are a part of every relationship. From under a pile of aged Polaroids I unfold a creased newspaper ad for a three-bedroom apartment in Uptown—ah yes, the infamous "January" incident.

"So, I found a place at Lawrence and Broadway. We could totally swing 600 bucks."

(I'm sitting on the floor of the room I "rent" in my parents' basement, which is temporary, of course, until I pass the bar and shack up with my girlfriend in the city.)

Lori is silent on the other end of the line. "I . . . need time to think." In the background, I hear her mother's broken English calling her for dinner. "Look," she says, "I'm not telling you to drop off the face of the earth, I just—I can't do this right now."

"Oh," I respond. "Are you going to see Sam again tomorrow?"

"Yeah, just as friends. There's a lot of history."

"But we're meant *to be together."*

She gets impatient, as she always does, when I talk about frou-frou things like karma and destiny. "How do you even know that?"

"Because I wrote it in my journal."

"I gotta go. I'll call you in a few days or something."

The abrupt dial tone catches me off guard. I had been waiting for some reassurance to buttress my now-waning faith. Careful not to disturb my dad in the study next door, I cry softly into my pillow—

"What'd you find?" Lori asks as she walks by, tool belt slung low on her hips, jeans ripped at the knees.

"Nothing," I reply, carefully slipping the piece of newspaper into my pocket. Time may heal all wounds, but splinters it merely conceals.

She leans over and rubs her nose against mine. "I know you're hiding something, and you'll just tell me later," she says, then continues down the stairs. She's right, of course. After sixteen years, she's become an expert at decoding my one-word answers.

I check my Blackberry for missed calls from my mom. Two. Maybe she can wait till tomorrow. Then I click the radio on—"*Music from the '70s, '80s, and today*"—and press the paint roller against the wall. Cameo white gives the room a lightness it hasn't seen since we first moved in, when everything was still new and exciting. From the corner of my eye, I see Lori lift the handle of her circular saw. She's deep in concentration, a pencil perched on her lip as she calculates how much wood she'll need to replace the splintered stair tread. The safety goggles have left a red mark around her eyes, and her pushed-back hair stands up in random tufts.

I think she looks beautiful.

"You almost ready?" Lori nuzzles the back of my neck as I apply the final strokes of blush. Her mouth tickles the edge of my hairline, nibbling softly on the outer edge of my ear, before whispering, "How much time do we have?"

"Sweetie, they're going to be here in five minutes."

She grins smugly. "I only need three."

"Is that so?" I challenge, yet I shimmy onto the sink, giggling at her brashness, and drape my arms around her shoulders, completely losing myself in her kisses.

When I'm still trying to catch my breath, two and a half minutes later, the door buzzer sounds and Lori delivers a triumphant peck on my lips. "Told ya." As she saunters down the hallway to welcome our friends to the new condo, I shake my head in disbelief. It's always the quiet ones . . .

"Is that paint on your face?" She's taken a break from the saw to stretch out her back. I stop painting to look in the mirror and finger the twist of grey at my temple.

"No, just age. And there's more . . . down under."

"Really?" she quips. "I wouldn't know. We should remedy that." A teasing peck becomes two, then three, then I lose count as our kisses grow longer and more intense. This is *so* going to happen. Yeah, feng shui! But when I open my eyes and catch a glimpse of the clock, I realize we're too close to Nick's pickup time. We could squeeze in a quickie, but I want this to last—plus, *I don't want the paint to dry out in the pan.*

"Let's rain check till tonight," I finally say, twisting away to gently push her down the stairs with a quick swat to her rear. "I'll make it worth your while," I add, with what I think is a lascivious eyebrow waggle.

She rolls her eyes in response. "You . . . are such a dork."

We continue to work a little longer, in the same space, but separate—a bit like our relationship. I have visions of our celebration—maybe we'll shower, or maybe we'll take a long soak in the bath before our long-overdue marathon make-out session.

What happens is that Nick has "one of his days"—the kind that drives parents to drink. The bathtub holds a brown ring of sand, dirt, and God-knows-what-else from school, and the bedtime story is an extended remix of every Dr. Seuss book ever written. Yet at 8:30 I still hold out hope as I feel the slow and steady rise of his breathing. Downstairs, Lori loads the last of the dishes into the dishwasher, and I think, we still have time.

The phone rings. "Hi, Mommy . . . what do you mean your thermostat doesn't work?" This can still be okay if she handles it right and convinces her mom she doesn't have to go over till tomorrow . . .

Then my cell goes off—Incoming Call, Mom. *Shit.* If I don't answer this time she'll assume that I'm dead. As my mom explains her legal woes at work, I watch the digital clock in our bedroom slip into the next hour. Maybe skip the bath, and just take a shower?

At 10:30 I say goodbye to my mom as Lori comes up the stairs, bleary eyed, voice hoarse, a finger stretching out her ear.

"Wanna kick it?"

"Sure," she says as she stifles a yawn. "Just let me take out this splinter first." She walks down the hallway, flicks on a light, and rummages for the tweezers. She returns a few minutes later, holding an open safety pin, the tip of her finger, a burst of dug-out skin. "I seriously need to get my eyes checked. Can you?" she asks, holding the safety pin out to me.

I squint a couple of times, my eyes going in and out of focus. A few picks and pokes later, the splinter is gone.

And when I'm done, I press my lips to her finger, then slide her hand up to my cheek. I inhale deeply, taking in the sharp tang of her soap as I rub my top lip against the callused pads. She draws me close; I nuzzle into the space between her neck and shoulder.

"I love you, stinky."

"I love you too, sweets."

Together we sway to music heard only in our heads. There'll be no sex tonight, but right now, I'm okay with that.

At least we're still dancing.

I Am My Daughter's Dad

Coya Paz

I am my daughter's dad.

Now . . . there's a lot of things this doesn't mean.

It doesn't mean I'm trans-identified, unless you count my deep passion for drag queens, Dolly Parton, and drag queens that look like Dolly Parton.

And it doesn't mean that my daughter calls me Dad.

She calls me Mama, Hey, Coya, or Hey Mama Coya Mama Hey . . . depending on her mood.

As for Dad, it isn't even really a word she knows yet. I don't buy her books that feature fathers, and if one slips by me, I suggest the man is an uncle, like Uncle Raymond, or a grandpa, of which she has three. She knows people who have dads, of course, but I work hard to present that as just one of many options, not the default normal. By working hard, I mean I fast forward past the segments on *Yo Gabba Gabba* that feature two-parent heteronormative families and play *Sesame Street* on repeat.

On my daughter's birth certificate, I'm listed as parent.

So is my partner.

That's thanks to Illinois. Illinois is a great place to be gay.

The United States, however . . . that's another story.

Now . . . I'm no America hater, okay.

I love milk shakes, reality TV, and grocery stores.

I don't especially appreciate war or globalization, unless said globalization results in cute and affordable outfits.

And I have huge problems with the fact that one of the few growth industries in this country is the prison system.

And I really hate the accelerated rate of deportation in the past two years. When Obama talked about Change and Yes, We Can . . . I didn't realize he was talking to ICE!

And yeah . . . this is a country with a federal government that persists in acting like there are no gay people here.

Which is how I came to be my daughter's dad.

Because when I went to fill out her passport application, there was a space for a mother and a space for a father. When I say I filled out the application, I mean my partner did it and handed it to me to sign, so by the time I got my hands on it, she had already snagged the mother spot.

I filled in my name: Coya Paz, father, and started laughing.

I don't know how much you know about filling out a passport application for minors, but you have to do it in front of a passport application acceptance agent, usually found in a post office.

Our passport acceptance agent was a very nice lady who didn't really seem fazed by my daughter and her two moms until one of them started laughing hysterically about suddenly becoming a dad. And when she handed back our passports and accidentally said, "Here you go, Father," I really lost it.

This happens to me sometimes.

My friend Ricky says I have a flatline personality. I don't think he means I'm boring, just that I never seem too excited or upset about anything. I do have a spike in enthusiasm when CVS or Walgreen's has one of those buy-one-get-one-of-equal-or-lesser-value-free sales on Revlon cosmetics, or when I hear the song "A Puro Dolor," which is my favorite song on the whole planet, especially the mariachi version by America. I told you—I don't hate America!

But sometimes . . . rarely . . . I crack. I'm prone to horrible, horrible road rage—I'm talking a LOT of pendejos and idiotas and go-fuck-yourself dickwads, plus some old-fashioned screaming while I try to squeeze the steering wheel into something else altogether—and I'm also prone to hysterical, can't-stop-even-to-breathe-and-sometimes-I-pee-my-pants-just-a-little laughter.

I don't know why I found this situation so funny except to say that I really don't find it funny at all.

I don't want to be my daughter's father.

I want to be her Mama, Coya, Mama, Hey.

And I know . . . whether or not the federal government has the capacity to acknowledge a child with two moms doesn't change the fact that my daughter wakes up in the morning, turns to me, and says, "Mama kiss hug?" And then turns to Nina and does the same thing: "Mama kiss hug?"

But when is this country going to get it together?

Teach whatever you want in church or at home about gays being the downfall of modern society, and if you hate gay marriage, don't marry a gay.

Simple. As. That.

Okay, not really but c'mon. My partner and I have been together for ten years. I know straight couples who got divorced after ten days!

For me, it's not about marriage. I don't really give a fuck about marriage.

It's about expanding our capacity for naming lives, for making choices about the people we want to be; it's about creating a culture where people can maintain their sense of self and dignity without negotiating with forms and paperwork.

This isn't about being gay.

As Latinos, we feel it.

As women, we feel it.

As artists, we feel it.

The overwhelming pressure of always defining ourselves "counter."

No quiero ser counter-culture.

Solo quiero ser.

Porque no soy Father, Papi, or Dad.

I'm Coya,

Mama,

or Hey!

Waiting

Emma Vosicky

My tea cooled hours ago. I don't know why I arrived so early. It changes nothing. We scheduled our meeting for 10:00 a.m. He said that this would be more convenient. By "convenient," he meant that there would be the smallest number of people around—too early for the lunch crowd and too late for people needing their first cup of coffee and muffin.

Coffee shops abound in Oak Park, where our family had lived together in a now worn and heavily treed home. He chose, instead, a cookie cutter, strip-mall coffee shop in Schaumburg, nearly twenty miles away from our home and even further removed from Chicago's grittiness. His choice of location sends its own message.

Guilt about using these facilities without compensation finally drives me out of my chair. I delicately approach the counter. A young man with tri-colored hair and multiple facial piercings lounges, stooped against the back bar, supporting himself with crooked elbows, and staring into a point of space that eludes us all. Disturbing his comfort, I gently ask if I could have another cup of tea. With a kind grunt, he drawls out, "Sure." My appetite disappeared yesterday, but, in hopes of maintaining this young man's sales, I order two unyieldingly dense scones—maybe my son will share them with me.

I fidget my tea bag in its double-cupped container. Possibly, if I force the bag to spin faster in the cup, the water will transform itself sooner, not sit there as thin and meaningless as when it started. Nothing cooperates today—I can do everything I want to this water, but it refuses to change its pace. Impatiently, I dump in twice the amount of chemically contrived sweetener. From past errors, I know that I have now condemned my drink to a bitterly pleasant artificiality that will become progressively harder to swallow.

Returning to my table near the back of the shop, I reconsider my choices. When I had arrived, the room was bustling with people, causing me to search out a table in the back and nearly out of sight. One other table separates me from the deep corner. That table's occupant—a graying, solitary man with a raggedly aging beard—has elected to serve as my companion for the day. Laptop open, cell phone on, music rising and falling over his computer's speakers, he has established his residence with a rhythm that bespeaks repeated, empty visits. At one point he vanishes for ten minutes, his computer busily singing behind me, unaware of its abandonment. He returns from his "holiday" laden with papers and a cloth shopping bag, from which he removes, I swear, his lunch, all neatly wrapped in wax paper. He settles into the stiff-backed wooden chair, talks to himself and, sometimes distractedly, to his computer—this might be his only conversation for the day.

I find myself hoping this gray-bearded intruder will retreat to the lonely, unfurnished apartment that I picture him occupying along with hundreds of other people in similarly inhabited yet vacant buildings. Then I hear his increasingly testy conversation with an illusory figure. Their argument alternatively amps up and then ceases, after which the man knocks three times on the seat of the wooden chair immediately to his right. His pattern of arguing and knocking continues unabated for minutes on end, followed by almost equally absurd minutes of silence. Finally accepting the distraction, I silently bid my companion to stay as I slowly recognize that this behavior has seized him and directed his life, distancing him from those who have loved him.

Mid-January in Chicagoland is a hard season: any remaining holiday memories are pierced by the single-cloud, charcoal gray sky, extending from horizon to horizon. The snow even begins to look slightly used.

A blast of cold, dry air accompanies my son's arrival, rushing down the narrow alley-interior of the coffee shop as the door closes behind him. He peers down the length of the room, and then freezes as he glimpses me at the second table from the back. His hand grasps backward for the door. His body swivels slightly while pushing the door open a crack. Barely discernible crystals of snow swirl through the gap. Before the tri-colored clerk can finish looking up and asking him to choose a direction, Nathan releases the door; the cold wind shoves it closed.

My son has inherited my passion for extreme rationality. He has a doctorate in mathematics. He effortlessly reduces the world to clear, tidy, and defensible solutions. It engenders an admirable directness, and a not-so-admirable intolerance for those facets of life that refuse being reduced to obvious equations.

Nathan moves toward me in long, purposeful strides. Tall, he holds himself unflinchingly erect, never wavering once he has chosen a course of action. I remember how he always resisted our attempts to shorten his name to "Nate"—the informality made him uncomfortable. Since childhood, Nathan has always been a study in contrasts: while bluntly and honestly stating his positions, he has kept his emotional cards very, very close to the vest. His mouth is his only "tell." At this moment, his anger concentrates its energy into his upper and lower lip, which tighten, preventing his jaw from opening and then forcing his words to spill out in a near-mumble. I can still clearly understand his message through the mumble: "I already told you that I don't want to see you like this."

There is a segment of my existence that, in my family, lacks a proper noun. We prefer to allude to it through non-decipherable pronouns such as "this" or "that" or "it." We treat "transgender" as a magic term. We are fearful that speaking the word grants it legitimacy. We abstain from giving "it" voice or substance so that we don't invite unforeseeable consequences. The pronouns also ensure that there is a hint of tawdriness to the whole enterprise (for example, "Oh, you'll be doing *that* tonight").

We sustain a polite distance by seldom discussing "it." There will be the rare question from the kids. I will only mention "it" in intentionally measured servings so that we avoid the nitty-gritty of acknowledging that my gender—best summarized as bits and pieces of male and female—is a constant and central part of my life. Through thoughtfully controlled conversation, we have succeeded in downgrading a significant portion of my identity into a hobby, like golf (and how much detail does anyone want to hear about his dad's golf game?). To talk about the great sale I found on a sharp-looking black skirt would introduce an unpalatable level of detail into our lives. It would render my transgender existence too real, threatening the delicate balance of the charade in which we have invested such energy.

Nothing comes naturally. I pick and choose my moments to talk about "it," like an inspector in a minefield, vainly hoping that I do not disturb the untested ground and unleash an explosion. Quite content to join in the game, Nathan considers my reticence essential if I am to "respect" his discomfort at seeing me in any fashion that contradicts his image of his father. For seven years, I have "respected" the false image he has demanded. Today, I have broken the pact, as I sit here in a sweater and skirt and low-heeled boots.

Nathan and I are far too similar for our own good: I don't speak of my anger or my hurt over his words; instead, *my* anger pools around my eyes and forehead. The best I can do is to sheepishly challenge, "What do you mean by 'this'?"

His lips tighten further, if that is possible. He ignores my question. "What are you trying to do? Look, you can live your life however you want—just don't ask me to be involved in that part of it. I need something to drink." Unzipping his coat, he strips it off, like a befouled de-contamination suit, and tosses it onto the chair. "I'll be back," he half mutters.

As Nathan's back recedes, I touch the edge of the plate holding the scones. I could tell him that I bought one for him. I decide not to call out to him—he probably doesn't like scones anyway.

Nathan stares at the menu board for what feels like ten minutes. His indecision seems unrelated to the multiple drink options since he only likes coffee that is hot and unadulterated. I'm wondering if he wished that he had not left his coat with me. I won't ask.

The clerk and he engage in some friendly conversation. As he pays, Nathan glances briefly in my direction. Yes, I am still here.

My back-table companion springs out of his silence. He presses ahead with talk about stocks, and projects, and why someone didn't call. His agitation grows as his phantom dialogue sours. The intervals shorten between his conversations and his knocking. I cannot tell whether the knocking is intended to intensify or break the momentum of the exchange. I wish he would stop.

Nathan walks back. The man quiets behind me.

I stare as Nathan sets down a plastic plate, on which a scone rests. "I didn't know you liked scones," I offer.

"Mmm, yeah, my girlfriend from a couple of years ago got me into them. Seems you must like them too—you've got a couple of 'em there."

"Yeah, well, just in case I get hungry."

"Yeah, I hear ya, I seem to be losing my appetite too." Nathan studies the black pool of his coffee. "So what's this all about? I don't have a lot of time." He decides to give nothing up; instead, he pushes me onto the defensive, demanding that I explain my actions.

"What happened? You said on the phone that you could stay an hour or so," I begin.

Damn that guy behind me! I must have disturbed him, and now he's starting up his insane chatter again. Why doesn't he at least hold his cell phone to his ear and act like he is doing something useful rather than embarrassing himself?

"My schedule changed."

I want to ask him if the scheduling change has to do with seeing me, but there's nothing to be gained by asking the question since it would just make him leave sooner. He spares me the uncertainty. "What's the idea behind the clothes, Dad?" (heavily emphasizing the "Dad" part).

"It just seems so false."

"What?"

"Both of us acting like I don't exist."

"Going back there *again*?"

"Ah, come on, Nathan, cut me some slack, would you!"

Nathan's eyes toughen. "Cut *you* some slack? Whatever happened to respecting what I have to say? And I have already told you—how many times now?—that I don't want to see you when you look like this." Nathan's tone contains an end-of-discussion finality.

I have no idea where to go from here. I never do. A long time ago, I abdicated my role as a figure of some authority and power with my children. I so wish that I had not given up because, even though I'm not the sharpest knife in the drawer, I do have a little insight to pass along, some wisdom gained with age and experience. I also have an exceptionally distinct appreciation of bigotry. My knowledge, unfortunately, comes both from being the target of other people's disgust and from my targeting those people who are different from me. It wasn't so long ago that I would have smiled at the young man behind the counter while feeling offended by his piercings and peculiarities. I refused to see a human being unless he conformed to my standards. And then to further distance myself from anyone who might remind me of *my* differences, I made a sport out of judging the unworthiness of the transgender persons I met—picking out their deficiencies, calling them "men in dresses," ignoring their struggles to find out who they are. God help me, I've known bigotry and disgust, and I can hear its unseen scampering in myself and in my son. I don't know how to tell him that.

And Nathan will not talk with me. We've made this circuit so many times that he has stopped coming around. As he said in the past, he's not interested in my "haranguing" him. According to him, "It's always the same thing. If this is all we're going to talk about, then what's the point?" My response is to retreat from challenging him for several months or more, telling myself that I am giving him the time he needs. Seven miserable years have now passed since I gave "the talk" (as my family calls it) about being transgender. When I first told Nathan, he listened, absorbed the information until he had his fill. As far as he was concerned, there was nothing more that he really needed to see or know. I would ask if he had any questions, and he would answer, "Why?"

My friends keep telling me not to push it, give him more time, be patient.

I've waited. Shit, I've waited. I'm left feeling like a jerk for seeking recognition from someone I love. My anger is rising like a dark plume. I am tired. I am not putting up with this anymore. I HAVE HAD GOD-DAMNED FUCKING ENOUGH OF THIS SHIT! THIS COMES TO AN END RIGHT HERE AND NOW!

An irritating jabbering from behind me interferes with my internal soliloquy: he is still at it. Jesus Christ, does this guy ever stop? The endless talking. The knock, knock, knocking. More and more talking; more and more knocking. Talking/knocking, talking/knocking. Talking/knocking. He is incessant. What does he think he is doing? You son of a bitch! That is it! I twist my anger straight at the man residing behind the last table. "Would you cut out that crap!" I blurt.

He's cowed. The fervor drains from his eyes. Looking slightly away with an imperceptible twitching of his neck, he apologizes to me: "Lady, sorry." *He* apologizes to *me*. What is wrong with me? He twitches again. I soundlessly consider words to convey that I am the one who is out of line.

Nathan decides to come to his aid. "Dad, what is wrong with you? He wasn't doing a damned thing!"

"You haven't had to sit here listening to him for the last couple of hours!"

"So what? He has a right to exist. I don't see him hurting a soul. What's your problem?

"*My* problem?" I can barely contain myself. If I were constructed of glass, I would shatter into a million tiny shards. "You would defend *him*, but not *me*?!"

"Hey, not if you're going to act like an ass!"

"Don't try that with me. I'm not the only one who is acting like an ass!"

Nathan leaves his chair, his hand extending toward his coat.

"Leaving even sooner?" I ask, standing up.

"You didn't warn me."

"Of what?" I won't give him the satisfaction of leaving "it" unnamed.

"You know damned well."

"Doesn't matter. Say what you're thinking."

"*This* isn't my father."

"Oh no, you're wrong about that! This," I said as I gestured to myself, "is your father. You just want me to fit the image that works for you."

"And what's wrong with that? That's what parents are supposed to do for their children."

"What am I supposed to do?"

"Parents are supposed to compromise, sacrifice, do things for their kids."

"No, be specific! Say what you really mean: Dad, you should sacrifice for me."

"Well, I'm not asking you to compromise. I'm just letting you know that I won't be around when you're acting like this."

"You mean, acting like me?"

"Whatever you want to call it."

"It's not what I *want* to 'call it.' It's who I am. Jesus, Nathan, how can you be so brilliant and not see what you're saying? Of course you're asking me to compromise. Actually, you're not even 'asking'—you're telling me to compromise. You're telling me that you will leave me if I am not who you want me to be. You're using the continuation of our relationship as a tool to extort behavior that satisfies you."

"Oh, that is so much crap!"

"You really think so? You think you are entitled not to have your life disturbed, messed up, or challenged, at least not by me."

"I never said that."

"Get real! Whenever you think that I've complicated or burdened your life, you don't talk to me about it; you just get that tight-lipped anger you're showing right now." Nathan glares back. "And it's not like I'm making matters any better, because I don't have the guts to act like your parent, tell you that I won't put up with your ultimatums anymore, and warn you, from my experience, that living your life this way has trouble written all over it. It's sad that neither of us has shown the courage to break this stalemate."

"You really think *that* would've made something better?"

"Christ, Nathan I don't know. The only thing I know is that I didn't even know you liked scones."

"What?"

"I didn't even know you liked scones."

"Yeah, I heard that. But what are you talking about?"

"You're thirty-three, and we're keeping ourselves further and further away from each other. We don't talk. We just maintain our distance, like a couple of boxers dancing around each other to avoid contact."

"So this comes down to scones and boxers?"

I weakly smile. "Yes, it all comes down to scones and boxers." Like a million other times, my strength saps. Maybe in another two weeks or two months, he will think about this . . . and want to talk. Or maybe, this is the place where it all dies.

I hear it again: once more, the murmuring, then talking, increasing to chattering, loud, loud chattering. Then the knocking—knock, knock, knocking. More chattering, more knocking. Then more chattering, more knocking. The tempo increases; the knocking grows more forceful. Now, I want out of here. My right hand stretches for my coat and purse. Nathan looks relieved. Neither of us wants anymore of this. I lift my coat.

From nowhere, a hand grabs my forearm. The bearded man spins me around and then meets me halfway till we are eye to eye. I try to shake him off, but he's dogged, unyielding. He is desperate.

"Tell him," he says as he shakes me. "Tell him!"

"Tell him what?"

He only squeezes harder. "Tell him!"

"Damn you! Tell him what?

"All you tell him is the anger."

"Let go!"

"Tell him the pain!" Beneath the beard, his mouth contorts. It's been almost three hours since I first walked into this place, and I finally look in his eyes. I try to pull away, but he yanks me back. And I look again at his pale, blue eyes, as they turn red and wet.

I mumble, "You hurt . . ."

He shakes me harder. "Our time here is short. Say it before you repeat the same lessons."

The realization floods me: I'm the one who has shown Nathan how to avoid all of this. If change is going to come, it must come through me. I don't like going here. I don't like doing this. My time with Nathan grows tenuously short.

And then I look in the man's eyes as tears begin to wend their way down his cheeks, losing themselves inside his beard . . . and I feel it—a large bubble birthed in my guarded recesses and hastening its way up my throat. My ears are ringing. The room seems so still.

"Nathan, I love you. And your coldness is killing me. You are just tearing my heart out."

I can see my son closing his gates, arming his battlements. I have to break through. I can't live another seven years of famine. I speak what neither of us wants to hear. "You are embarrassed by me."

He begins to protest.

"Nathan, please, don't say that anymore. Don't lie. Don't tell me about needing more time. This isn't about time. Six months after I first told you, it probably stopped being about 'needing time.' It's about you being embarrassed by me. It's about you thinking that I am weird. It's about you not wanting to *see* that I am transgender, as if that makes it disappear. Can you conceive how much it hurts to have someone you love say that they don't want to see you anymore?"

"I never said that I didn't want to see you."

"Ah, Nathan, let's bring these word games to an end. I am your dad—your *transgender* dad. You will not see me if I look like your transgender dad because that's not who you want. If I were a wolf, I would be howling right now in solitary pain at a cold, distant moon because *you don't want me*. It hurts so much that I want to scream in pain. Think about it—what if you walked into our house someday, looking like the kid behind the counter, and I told you to get out of my house and stay out because I refuse to see you like that."

"That situation is different."

"No, it's not. It's just a different set of differences—my 'differences' are ones with which you don't want to be associated. You don't want a girlfriend or an employer to know we are related. You feel no pride in me finally finding myself and being whole or good. You're ashamed to be seen with me. You don't take pride in defending me against ignorance or bigotry; instead, you mourn any 'losses' or inconveniences you might incur in the face of other people's bigotry. Rather than gladly stand up for me, you regret that I have forced your hand. I know—believe me, I know—it is so easy to talk about being accepting and open of other people when it's not part of your family, your universe. Your bigotry, my bigotry, often hides behind grand gestures that cost us nothing, but, now, I've upended your universe, put you to the test. In response, you hide me from others, from you."

Nathan's back straightens as he plays his hole card—the one that trumps me every time. "You don't respect me even though I've told you how far I can go with this."

I start folding, yet I know I can't. I can't do this again. I love my son too much to watch this die. And then, after seven years, I finally hear the irony of it all.

"Nathan, this isn't about respect; this has never been about respect. Respect comes from honoring something of value in another. You want me to honor your bigotry."

Nathan's shoulders pull back so tightly they could snap. "How dare you say that!"

"How dare I not. And damn me for not having dared to say this sooner. How could I have not seen this? What if you showed up tomorrow with a fiancée whom you loved, but whose race or ethnicity differed from our family's? What if I told you that, out of respect for me and our family, I didn't want you to bring her around? What if I told you that you must respect my wishes and not marry her? What if I told you that I would only see you when she was not present? What if I refused to defend your choice if the rest of the family wanted to criticize you or attack your decision?"

"It's not the same thing."

"You bet it's not the same thing. In that situation, *you* are the person being mistreated, which means *you* feel the injustice. It's much harder to see when you are not on the receiving end, and especially when you are the person mistreating someone. Plus, while children want parents to respect the children's differences, they are not always as quick to respect their parents' differences.

"You would have every right to demand my support even if it meant that I lost family and friends. Here, though, the tables are turned: you would have to face your discomfort and possibly pay some price for standing up for me. You and I have allowed you to twist the meaning of 'respect' in order to generate guilt. You are not loving or respecting someone when you tell him that he can't live his life in a way that brings him joy. Loving someone is about welcoming the person regardless of her differences. You and I have conspired to disrespect me, but then characterize our behavior as 'respect' so that we never have to question it.

"Nathan, the scones are just a symbol. I don't need detailed knowledge of your pastry choices . . ."

"That's good."

". . . It just reminds me that I don't know you any longer. And the thought of losing you hurts as much as your embarrassment about my differences. Life moves too fast. I don't want either of us separated from the people we love. I hope that one day, soon, you will *want* to see me because this *is* who I am."

Nathan bends, but won't break.

Looking straight at me, while picking up his coat, he responds, "I need a little more time, Dad."

"Nathan, not another seven years."

"Okay."

"I'll call you in a week."

"Maybe I'll try to get ahold of you before that." He slides his arms into his coat sleeves.

Does he really mean it this time? "I'd appreciate it, Nathan."

"See ya."

"Hope so."

He pushes his chair back under the table, steps into the aisle leading toward the front of the store. He is leaving, once more. I am spent, once more. I console myself that, this time, I've said it. Nathan has answered that he'll get back to me. Surely, this is different. I have changed our script. But he is leaving, again.

The bearded guy says nothing. Still, I can hear it: knock, knock, knocking. I ask the sound to stop. I've done my best. What more do you want? Nathan's thirty-three. What right do I have? Can't you see the progress I've made? I've never pushed it this far with him before. Stop the knocking; just stop the knocking!

His interminable knocking rumbles inside me, bangs on my walls, knocks over my furniture, disturbs my pleasant vistas, disrupts my years of excuses . . . and then illuminates me for what I have become.

Oh my God, what kind of parent have I become? What has happened to me?

"No!" I shout.

Like everyone else in the shop, Nathan turns. His face flares with disbelief . . . and the barest hint of hatred.

"No. No. No!" I repeat, my voice remaining loud and, for a rare moment, firm. "No, you do not leave like this. It doesn't end this way anymore. This is wrong—you, me, this dance we do. Look what we've done! This is insane!"

"Speaking of insane, you . . ."

"No! You don't get to do that. You don't get to call me names. For once in my life, I won't back down to you."

"So this is all about who will back down?" Nathan asks, almost with a sneer.

"No. This is about both of us having the courage to stand in here and talk until we can find a healthy resolution. If you're angry with me, then you stay here and talk about it."

"What good does that do? You're still going to do whatever you want."

I want to waver. It comes so easily to me. I scour for the strength to continue. It would be nice if I could do this for me, but I'm not quite ready to draw from those reserves. Rather than crumble, though, I impel myself forward by remembering my obligation, as a parent, to state the truth for my children.

"Here's the deal, Nathan: if your anger with me is about something I've done to hurt you, then talk about it so that I have a chance to apologize; if your anger isn't about my hurting you, then we better start talking about it because it's wrong to blame me for something I didn't do. I've made more than enough mistakes, but that sure as hell doesn't give you the right to dump your shit on me. And dammit, Nathan, nothing you've said so far about my being transgender suggests that I have ever intended to hurt you—that is, unless, you're saying that I chose to be transgender so I could hurt you."

"Don't be ridiculous. I'm not saying you chose to be transgender."

"And yet, you want me to pay a price for it."

"I'm just saying, keep it away from me."

"That's one hell of a price, Nathan—telling me to stay away from you."

Nathan hesitates for a moment, looking around the room, probably for an exit. I am grateful that his stubbornness keeps him from leaving; I am pissed off that his stubbornness keeps him from seeing possibilities. I want to run, maybe even more than my son does. I pray for strength and am rewarded with anger—the good kind of anger that drives us to change our world. I plunge.

"You know what? I am not an ax-murderer. I'm a human being with the right to be who I happen to be as long as I am compassionate, caring, and ethical. I have spilled sweat and blood for you, but that's not good enough, is it?"

The ice wall melts as Nathan's anger finally sparks. Facing me, he grabs the top of the chair before him, strangling the wood. "Oh, come on!"

Nathan would have snarled this at me but his body still restrains most expression. "Don't try shifting your guilt onto me."

"Oh, don't worry. I'm not shifting guilt anymore. I'm releasing it. I spent a lot of my life doing things for all of you kids, and I would gladly do most of them again because I love you. But it was never enough, for either you or me. I kept believing that I should have done something more for all of you, and, in small, subtle ways, you reminded me that you expected as much.

"I've wanted your childhood, your life, to be perfect, painless, and unencumbered. I've wanted to protect you and to never cause any disruption or disturbance in your life. I couldn't give you all of the 'things' so many other kids had, and, even though you are actually a better person for it, I still believe that I let you down."

Nathan, not feeling the need to choke his chair any longer, throws his hands up in the air. "Well, don't look at me. That's your problem. I never said you should feel that way."

It's my turn to grapple with the top of a chair. "Don't give me that! We're both happy to reinforce my guilt. Whenever you kids tell stories about growing up, there is never any conversation about what I did for you or how I was there for you. The only stories are always about how I didn't do enough, about how I wasn't there enough. And now, you are asking me to compromise *my identity* to make your life easier. You avoid feeling empathy for me out of concern for what people might think about you."

Years of silence shatter under the surge of long-imprisoned feelings. "Here are some facts. I have, without hesitation, loved you since the day you came into existence. I changed diapers, fed you, walked you in the middle of many long nights, cared for you when you were sick, spent many sleepless nights watching over your crib, moved heaven and earth to keep you healthy, played with you, read to you, timed you out, kissed you goodnight, told you I loved you, gave you oatmeal baths when you had chicken pox, took you to your doctors' appointments, bought groceries, made dinners, cleaned house, held a demanding job, went upside-down in debt to keep a roof over your head, sweated out bills, drove you to school, and was present for nearly every open house, parent-teacher conference, baseball game, football game, basketball game, concert, play, and recital."

I feel myself dropping over a cliff to a place where I have been too proud to go. "Nathan, I have been there for you because I love you. Now I need you to be there for me. My ego is screaming at me not to admit it—but I need you."

As words pour out of my mouth, my brain departs my body. I see myself standing there, skirt, boots, sweater, and blouse, an outcropping of breasts where I am usually flat and straight. I hear my voice in tones I've never before heard: strong and feminine. Nearly six decades passed before I came of age. In my wholeness, I'm finally remembering what it means to act like the parent. I want him to hear me—this time.

"I need to feel the excitement of finally coming home. I need to feel the peace. I need to feel your love and support just as you need to feel mine. It hurts so badly when you threaten to leave me, rather than see me. I need you . . ."

It's a shame that I waited this long to call us both out. "I love you, Nathan. I don't want our relationship to remain broken. I don't want your emotions checked so tightly that your display of feelings consists of that vise-like tightening of your lips."

Nathan brushes his hand up across his face.

"We've got to deal with this stuff! Now."

Like an old steam engine easing into the station, my voice slows to a natural stop.

For the first time today, Nathan looks at me. He considers. I pray. He absentmindedly taps his chair, three times. I receive a gift: Nathan's humanity, which has always resided near the surface, replaces the hardness in his eyes.

"This hasn't been easy," he says.

"I know."

"You're different . . ."

". . . Than either of us expected, but the universe doesn't spin according to our expectations."

Nathan sighs. His face softens, and, for the first time today, he relaxes his shoulders so they can gently fall into place. "You wanna go talk? I actually don't have any appointments for a few hours."

"Thanks for the honesty."

Nathan shrugs.

I gesture toward the door. "Should we get out of here? I think we've distracted everyone long enough."

A small smile appears. "Yeah, they can go home and work things out with their families. Where do you want to go for lunch?"

"How about somewhere a little closer to home?"

"I can deal." Pushing in his chair, he asks, "Ready to go?"

"Yeah, let's. Hey, Nate?"

"Yeah, Dad."

"I'll meet you out by the cars. Just something I need to do before I leave."

"Want me to wait?"

"Nah, I think we're done with the waiting. I'll be right behind you."

"Okay." With a slight, questioning tilt of his head, Nathan zips his coat and walks the narrow length of the store, until he sweeps open the door. An electronic beep says goodbye.

I pick up the plates with the three, untouched scones. I can't take them home; I can't waste them. I turn toward the steady droning behind me. There he is, hunched back over his laptop, scrolling and scrolling hurriedly so that he never stays on anything too long. I try to catch his attention, but he appears deep in some burbling conversation with his phantom guest. I slide the plates with the three scones onto his table, near his laptop, without infringing on his space. He never looks up.

In a moment, I slowly put my arms into my coat sleeves, button the coat against the cold, and sling my purse over my shoulder. I walk past the counter, where the tri-colored kid says, "Have a nice day!" I think he means it.

It seems wrong to leave this way. I return to the empty counter while opening my purse. I smile at the kid, who continues to rest against the back counter, waiting for something to do. Glancing toward the back of the room, I ask the kid, "Is he here a lot?"

"Yeah, every day: same table, same time."

I hand the kid a twenty. "For as long as there's any money left, use it to pay for his charges."

The kid says, "I'll take care of it, ma'am."

He could be blowing smoke—pocketing the money after I leave—but, when I look below the tri-colored hair, I see eyes that speak of integrity and that seem to understand the raggedly bearded guy.

"Thanks." I throw some extra cash in the tip jar.

As I reach into my purse for my keys, the kid says, "Hey, lady!"

"What?" I answer, curious.

"You know, 'different' can be honorable."

I study him and smile. "Yeah, I noticed," I reply as I nod in his direction.

I follow my son's path out the door.

The air feels warmer.

6

Hooking Up

The True Story of S/Him and Femme

C.C. Carter

Ours is a story of fairy tales come true, like Romeo and Juliet *and* Westside Story *but with both parties still alive at the end and both main characters girls.*

We lived in the middle-class section of Roseland—South Side of Chicago—back in the day when parents, both Dad and Mom, broke their backs to be first-generation home owners and who wanted to be able to raise their families in safe "It Takes a Village" type neighborhoods.

I was the girl with the s-curve shape whom boys chased when they played "catch a girl kiss a girl" but would rather let the cute tomboy who played on the boys' side catch me and sneak kisses while the other girls "Yucked!!!" and pretended to mock puking. *Her* was the girl who played on the boys' side that chased the s-curved She except they played this game on different blocks with different Them's. Even though we lived in the same four-block radius as kids, we wouldn't meet until twenty years later, when Her became S/Him and I became Femme.

Her went to Fenger High School, played basketball, and stole kisses from closeted girls in the locker room after everyone had left and only the curious ones remained—those losing to a game of "Truth or Dare" on purpose at lunchtime, or lingering a little too long after gym class, showing off their white bras and panties.

I was a missionary brat, moved every five years for most of my young life until the family settled in New York during my teens. By then I had been kissed by too many neighborhood tomboys to be a part of the love-struck girls' clique, necking and petting boys in after-school basement parties while somebody's parents were at work. I missed Chicago always.

Her went to Northern and majored in criminal justice, refused to join a sorority but left a white towel on her outside door and a light on in the window that sent a message to the curious sorors that she was one whom they could cuddle up with when no one was looking and, if a roommate came in, pretend that they were just two girl friends studying.

I went to Spelman, an all-girls school, home to the black elite pageant queens back then, except even though I looked liked one and eventually became one, I would have rather been escorted by a more grown-up tomboy girl in a suit then the pretty boy KAY who ended up being my date for the homecoming dance that year.

Her would sneak back into Chicago on weekends with a fake ID, while her family thought she was downstate working, and party hardy at CK's, meet older women who would inform her identity and call her Butch or Stud, but she preferred S/Him. Accepting the fate that God made her female, but having every thought and biological desire that a man has for a woman.

I had a boyfriend in college who knew I was different and allowed me to have girlfriends on the side, although eventually he got jealous. I didn't like girls like myself and began to prefer the company of Hers who looked liked Hims but not quite understanding why I had feelings for women like that. Finally somebody labeled me Femme.

For ten years after that, S/Him and Femme each wandered from woman to woman and place to state searching for the ideal mate. Until one day, Femme met a Her while visiting her longtime, back-in-the-day tomboy friend who was one of the Hers who used to chase She. Femme moved back to Chicago, Chatham neighborhood, right off Michigan, and Femme's new Her took them to a party. S/Him was there. It was love at first sight, except neither S/Him nor Femme was single.

But in the middle of the party I heard the familiar whispers of warning, "Danger, danger, Will Robinson"; not a sign for danger but that attraction was overwhelming and to stay calm. I knew this whisper but was not able to ward off the voice that said, "You must be new in town, because I've never seen you before, and I know pretty much all of the fine women around here." S/Him was arrogant and cocky like I liked them, "bad boys" and the badder the better. But I was nothing but loyal to the Her who had brought me to the party, so I made conversation short and sweet and excused myself. We would not see each other again for three years.

I had become known on the Chicago underground spoken-word circuit, had been discovered at an open mic at Paris Noir night at the now defunct Paris Dance Bar on Montrose. It was one of the few girl bars that featured "colored" girl night. I was recruited off that stage and launched onto another with a performance company called A Real Read, the first LGBTQ African American performance ensemble in Chicago. Together, we performed in front of (largely white) sold-out audiences at the Bailiwick and some of Chicago's other well-known small theater houses and soon became recognized.

But not before my mentors, who eventually became my family, hosted me at Mountain Moving Coffeehouse. Mountain Moving wasn't really a coffeehouse, but a Unitarian Church with a stage and some folding chairs. The women who ran the space bought coffee and tea to brew and sold it for additional funds, all the while presenting women artists, musicians, and performers in Chicago's first "woman-born-woman," pay-what-you-can performance venue for women.

After that performance, I was asked to perform my signature piece at the first Black Bra party held at a northwest nightclub, down the street from the late-night after-hours house music club, the Generator, a little way down under the El tracks, on Lake Street, past what used to be called Club Reunion. Five hundred women crowded into the three-hundred-capacity space with flying aerialists, bombshell cocktail waitresses, tequila-shot girls, and techno music blasting, barely any black girls, and me, the only one on the bill that night to perform. Nonetheless, this was Chicago girls' night out at its best. And when I walked out onto the stage—still s-curved, dressed in sequined black bra and deep V front black velour cat suit, an instrumental of Pink's "I'm Coming Out" blasting over the loud speaker, women screaming, whooping and hollering—it didn't matter what came out of my mouth. The noise level said that I had arrived.

After three minutes and forty seconds of pure hip-gyrating strutting across the floor, I bowed and made my way to the stage steps, grabbing the waiting hand of a stranger who helped me down so I wouldn't fall or break one of my five-inch pumps. I hear that whisper again, "Danger, danger . . ." and the voice interrupts to say, "We really need to stop meeting like this." This time I was single.

At home later that night after about four more shots of tequila, I turned over to S/Him's arms and body, forgetting how we got to my house and where my car was; had I left it on Lake Street, and "man, I know I have a ticket." I didn't even know S/Him's name and I don't think S/Him knew mine, either. And then, we would not see each other again for two more years, when Thursday night was the night to be a lesbian black girl who liked to party on the South Side of Chicago.

I, still single, needed to get my "dance on" and ventured down Stony Island—home of the used-to-be "Funtown, Funtown, for the kids and you, 95th and Stony Island Avenue, FUNTOWN!" It's a strip mall now, with a Jewel's grocery store; AJ Wright; Shoe Carnival; my favorite clothing store, Ashley Stewart; and the one-on-every-corner Korean nail shop that caused women to use PayDay Loan to purchase overpriced acrylic nails, pedicures, and false eyelashes, which was attached to the beauty supply store selling every kind of Remy weave hair and new collection of lace-front wigs.

I continued down Stony toward 87th Street and passed Uncle Joe's Jerk Chicken, and J&J's Fish. Harold's Chicken is closed and has been replaced with Pizza Hut, but BJ's Soul Food Restaurant is still open and thriving. Finally, I passed Jackson Hospital, parked in the 73rd Street Jewel's parking lot, checked myself in the rearview mirror, and headed across the street to Club Escape for the Thursday night Partners' Girl Party. "Danger, danger . . ." We hadn't seen each other since that drunken night and early morning when I made up an excuse so that S/Him would have to leave with no numbers or names exchanged, only cordial words of "I had a good time" and "thanks for getting me home okay." By now, I had moved from Chatham to Morgan Park, closer to Southwest Side than the then somewhat safer East Side.

To my embarrassment, S/Him greeted me at the door. It turned out S/Him was one half of the Partners promoting the party. S/Him let me in free, didn't check my ID, and pulled out a bar stool, which is boi code for "This is the one I'm taking home tonight." I was immediately sized up by the club members—the other bois who are part of this elite crew of butches and studs—until S/Him interrupted and took me into the middle of the crowded dance floor.

Beat and bass blared from the speakers and women started hollering, "Hey nahhhh, DJ you betta work" and the voice on the mic said, "That's what I'm talkin' about" as the music thumped, "deep down inside me, deep, deep inside me, deep down inside me." Sweat poured down my arms and back. S/Him guided my hips and kissed salt water from the nape of my neck. We never spoke but S/Him and I knew—we found a familiar rhythm like the night once two years prior, forgot about the dance floor packed with people curious to know "when did They happen?" This would get out for sure, but right then, music blared "deep down inside me" and it had me oblivious to the nosiness of the who and the whatevers.

Weeks and months pass of me finally knowing S/Him's name and her mine, and about how we grew up within a four-block radius but never met. How back then were the days of walking up to Roseland to buy art supplies and snow cones. Of hauling ass and praying not to get caught by the train at 112th Street right when the street lights came on 'cause "you better be on somebody's porch before dark hits." How if S/Him had been Her on my block I would have let S/Him catch me and kiss me for sure. How we wondered why we had never met back then. How we found old pictures of when I moved in with my ex-Her on 80th and Michigan and that S/Him actually came to one of our infamous backyard barbecue parties although we never remembered seeing each other there. How S/Him was in a relationship that S/Him felt responsible for, because the girlfriend had no other place to go, despite the fact that S/Him stayed over many nights and weekends without going home and without calling to check in. I was not comfortable being "the other woman."

So after six months of a heated love affair, S/Him and I broke up. S/Him let me go off with another Her who had come into the picture two months prior, and I had begun seeing both of them. S/Him couldn't commit even though I loved S/Him and I knew S/Him loved me. I went off with Her because I wanted a committed relationship. *New-Her* lived on the West Side, off the 290 expressway. In my whole time being in Chicago, I had never ventured there. But New-Her wooed me with promises of stability and I really liked New-Her and saw myself loving New-Her. I had the fairy-tale come true—prince charming, gold stallion, white picket fence in the heart of the West Side of Chicago. Eventually S/Him faded into memory of what could've been but wasn't, and New-Her and I set up house for happily ever after.

I traveled. Performed over two hundred days in a year over the first four years when New-Her and I were together. New-Her got tired and resentful. I refused to slow down. Once in a while I would see S/Him across a crowded room at a Pat and Vera, Executive Sweet party, or a Joeann Mack, Touch Bases party; back ally jook joints on 83rd Street, where you BYOB, and the ole skool girls wear matching colored stud and femme outfits—the old studs wear colorful zoot suits and the femmes are as fierce as any social elite, dressed in furs in the winter and strutting stilettos and minis in the summer. S/Him would be respectful, but not. S/Him let me know I was still the one. I would remember, then force myself to forget. S/Him let me go, so it must not have been meant to be.

I started POW-WOW at Lee's Unleaded Blues, home to some of Chicago's greatest blues notables before they became big names. Every Tuesday, from seven to midnight, over seventy-five women and male allies crowded into the historic "watering hole" on 74th Street and South Chicago Avenue, tucked in the corner of a dead-end street between the new Comer Center, home of the South Shore Drill Team, and the ETA Black Ensemble Theater, to hear queer poets "tell it like it is!"

I also joined Chicago Foundation for Women's Lesbian Leadership Council to help raise money for organizations owned and run by lesbians in Chicago. Every year CFW has an annual luncheon at the Hilton on Wacker in the Grand Ballroom. Over a thousand of Chicago's elite women corporate and not-for-profit executives and philanthropists attend the luncheon banquet, which features top women activists as speakers and presenters. On this particular year, the keynote speaker was Sarah Jones, and I had an extra ticket. S/Him called out of the blue one day to ask me to write a recommendation letter for a job, so I asked S/Him to meet me at the luncheon. Maybe S/Him could network there. We went out afterward for drinks. Reminisced and then tried hard to forget. We didn't talk to each other again for a year.

New-Her and I tried to work on our relationship; we had been seeing a therapist, had broken up one year prior. We worked on the relationship for our adopted son. I worked hard, paying attention to detail, and trying to be a dutiful wife and mother.

In the meantime, S/Him showed up at POW-WOW one day, and said she'd been single for over a year and was tired of running from bed to woman. S/Him never forgot us and shouldn't have let me go, but really thought New-Her had the better hand and " . . . what kind of boi would I be if I couldn't take care of you like I wanted but was selfish to keep you anyway?" Says if New-Her and I ever break up, call S/Him first to make things right like they should have been. I said okay and dismissed the statements as S/Him just being S/Him.

I came home from work one night three weeks after the last encounter with S/Him to New-Her saying, "This is not working for me, and there is someone else." I packed my clothes that night, taking everything I could to my car. I said goodbye to New-Her, now *ex New-Her*, kissed my son, made custody arrangements—I was not the signee on the adoption papers—submitting to be the other mom from now on. Got in my car, drove to the corner of the alley, out of sight of ex New-Her, and cried hysterically, but not enough to drown out the always blaring, always alarming ambulance sirens that serenade certain parts of the West Side where police conveniently never seem to be, not sure if I wasn't the emergency they were coming to rescue. Finally, after red, flashing lights sped past Madison Avenue, I calmed myself enough to hear a whisper say, "Call me first." I reached for my cell phone, hit speed dial four, not sure why the number was still in my phone. At one in the morning, S/Him answered my question, "Did you mean what you said, when you said call you first?" We finished the conversation while I drove to my old apartment that I kept for emergency situations. (I'd been letting another friend apartment sit while New-Her and I had tried to work things out.) At 10:27 the next morning I opened the door to S/Him, who had taken the red-eye flight from New Orleans.

Five years later, on the coldest day in Illinois; in the second largest queer community in the country, Oak Park; in the year of the newly elected president, Barack Obama, 2009; on the day before his inauguration and Dr. Martin Luther King Jr.'s birthday; at a small lesbian-owned bar called the Velvet Rope, one hundred and fifty people braved the winter storm, the Kennedy (90/94) traffic, 55 Eisenhower Expressway slow crawl, and 290 Interstate construction to join in the celebration as S/Him and Femme professed their love till death do they part.

The quaint restaurant is decorated with foil reflecting royal blue and silver snowflakes shimmering from the ceiling, royal blue linen on bar tables, blue champagne cocktails, an archway made of white and royal blue painted carnations, and a three-tiered half red velvet and half chocolate cake with white cream cheese frosting, decorated with royal blue flowers and two glass doves perched high on the top. S/Him and Best Butchman look dapper in black tuxes with royal blue long-sleeve shirts and ties, and Femme in long, royal blue gown, accentuating full figured, grown s-curves, and her godfather/mother walk up to the loft landing where Pastor Phyllis, decked out in her white robe and African kente cloth sash, proceeds with the ceremony.

With ex New-Her and Her *New-She* looking on, with our son standing next to his *New Step-S/him*, the two once-little girls, who lived in a four-block radius but never met, meet at the shoulders, turn to look into each other's eyes, and I, who was now Femme, allowed myself to be She for the Her who was now S/Him, to be caught in a final game of "catch a girl kiss a girl."

Lesbian Movie Night

April Newman

My seminal love tragedy was in college with this girl, Cole. She was the first out lesbian I knew, and also a writer—so it made sense that I would fall madly in love with her and she would instead choose my busty, plucky-lipped, straight roommate, Stacy. Cole had a "Xena for President" bumper sticker on her car and created wallpaper in her bathroom out of tampon boxes. I loved her not especially for these things but because she once wrote a story about a lady named Myrtle who froze lasagna trays in preparation for her own funeral. That seemed especially deep at nineteen.

Inserted love story cliché: *Couple meets in college over mutual admiration of author Lorrie Moore in their English class junior year. Postgraduate plans include: roadtrippin'. They settle down in an artist colony outside San Francisco sometime in their late twenties.* Fail.

I met Kara at a lesbian movie night three years ago. This evening was hosted by strangers—the upstairs neighbors of my closest friends. I'm not sure exactly how I got the invite, except that there certainly was a clandestine discussion, most likely in the laundry room, about my gayness. Despite the intense social anxiety, I decided to go because I had been unlucky in love.

When I stepped into the kitchen, I saw Kara first. Total slow mo, I strode in and she was leaning on the refrigerator, eyes down. She had dark hair with two streaks of blue, and then she looked up with these great big blue eyes, almond shaped. Creases formed around the edges, like she knew something and wasn't telling. Like she's sitting on the greatest secret. She dipped her chin to the side and smiled.

The two of us exchanged unremarkable pleasantries. I was in graduate school and insecure that I didn't work enough.

"So what do you *do*?" I asked.

"Chemistry!" Kara cheered.

"Good lord, are you a teacher, too?" I winced, thinking back to my troubles with teachers.

Kathy was the wrong-time-and-place love. Just when we were on the romantic verge, I moved to Chicago. But I couldn't help pining anyway and we spent a few months in a long-distance-call sort of relationship. The sexless kind. Kathy was sharp as a tack, an English teacher to boot; she was six years older and had these great wise eyes. Damn. There's just something electric about a cougar! Finally, I got it together for a visit and when we kissed it was super-charged, like a thunderstorm. She tasted like pear from the chardonnay. It felt like my shirt wouldn't fit anymore, my heart was so swollen with happiness. On the way to the airport I couldn't help but say, "I have feelings for you. And I thought if I moved to Chicago that they'd go away, but they're not—"

Kathy exhaled softly. "I'm sorry, but long distance just doesn't work for me."

Inserted love story cliché: *Budding intellectuals begin their courtship via letter writing across the nation. They settle in Paris and spend their summer sabbaticals in the countryside—growing fat on cheese and wine. They decorate exclusively in yellow and blue.* Fail.

I paraphrased the Kathy story for poor Kara in the kitchen that day.

"Dude—that's brutal," Kara said and poured me another glass of wine.

"I know, right?" I smiled and shook my head. In that light, thinking about Kathy didn't hurt as much as it did before.

"Enough about my sad, broken-hearted-girl stories, let's talk about something that matters. What do you do for fun?"

"I'm a reader," Kara beamed.

"Nice," I replied.

"I'm in a science book club!" she boasted proudly.

"Like science fiction?"

Kara tilted her head. "No. Like books about science," she said, authentic nerd all the way.

Authentic nerds are the shit. They designed Apple and all other sorts of gadgetry; they like Tolkien novels or *Battlestar Galactica*—and an authentic nerd won't hurt you, because under their big brains lie pretty sizable hearts. It's the folks who dress like nerds that you should beware.

My ex Amie was one of these. She wore cork-bottle black glasses, but it was all for show. I met Amie when I was living in Tampa. She was engaged when we met but also from the Midwest; there were all these midwestern cultural things that we shared, like Euchre and winter. Believe it or not, those things get swollen with nostalgia when you're a thousand miles from Chicago. Amie looked vaguely like a geeky Elizabeth Shue, and I hit on her because of this, but mostly because she was not available—as pathetic as it sounds, I was still caught up with the idea of Cole, who never even loved me anyway.

One night after whiskey drinks, Amie's fiancé, Chuck, passed out. She snuck into the living room and kissed me as I pretended to sleep.

I whispered, "What about Chuck?"

She said, "That's my problem." And kissed me harder—which somehow green-lit my body and we slept together on the futon.

Inserted love story cliché: *Couple begins a torrid affair in a restaurant. The drama heightens the passion until finally they can't take it anymore and elope in Ontario. They drink Super Tuscans at dinner. And sleep until eleven a.m. every day.* Success?

Nah. It's never that easy, right? This aside about Amie is longer than the rest. Amie was longer than the rest. Together three years after that one-night stand. I'll provide one highlight and one lowlight and get on with it.

Highlight: She crossed the room like a bull, but pulled my clothes off slow, a piece at a time. Shirt tossed over the wicker chair. Trail of shorts and sandals leading to the bed. When I struggled to flick off the lights, she caught my hand, eyes devouring me like I was a painting and she was art starved.

She said, "I just want to look at you tonight."

Better than drugs. A beautiful woman staring at my body like she'd been in a titless desert her whole life! Not touching, breathing over my skin, inhaling me. It was the first time in my life I ever felt beautiful, *really* beautiful. I was twenty-three.

Lowlight: Month three of the affair and Amie's man was onto it. Chuck took me aside at work. "Something's wrong. I think it's all the wedding planning. I'm gonna surprise Amie with a trip to Fort Myers, and we're gonna elope on the beach. I want you there 'cause you're our best friend." He looked like Opie, his hair and cheeks shiny.

What happens next felt like skydiving. That sick feeling while plummeting from any great distance when you're not sure it'll be okay in the end.

"Chuck," I said. "I'm not your friend. I'm sleeping with her."

His face was a gravestone.

"I'm sorry."

I watched Chuck's face twist. "Why? Amie and I had plans—we had a life together!"

I didn't tell Kara about Amie at that first movie night. I didn't tell her because twenty minutes later, buzzed with the possibly and maybe of our exchange—I discovered the hostess, Jenny, was dating Kara.

Instead I got drunk on red wine. Jenny asked me to move furniture to accommodate more seating, and a husky-voiced lesbian remarked, "You're so strong." Pleased as punch, I kissed my biceps. Then crushed a glass in my hand. Bah! To hell with it! At that point, the situation was so hopeless, I didn't even bother fantasizing.

I did what I was good at. Told stories and DMF (drank more faster). Stories about Cole: "The chick would drink forties and go running," I said.

The roomed bubbled into laughter. "What the fuck?"

"I know," I said.

Stories about Amie: "Crazy—threatened to mail naked pictures of me to my boss."

"*Ohmygod*, what did you do?" said a tiny-voiced lesbian.

"I was a teacher." The room exchanged confused glances. "I mean, I had to have a meeting with my principal," I finished.

I saved the Kathy story for last. It showed that I was romantic, heart-broken, but in a good way—due to circumstance as opposed to self-loathing.

The movie night thinned down. It was just Kara and Jenny and me.

"Let's go to the bar," Jenny yelled.

"Where?" I asked.

"Stargaze!"

"No way," I groaned. "That place has plastic glasses. Let's go to T's."

"But what about dancing?" Kara said, and shook her shoulders, rising like a bottle of seltzer.

Oh, to hell with it. And the three of us leapt into the night. I remember looking over at the couple, Kara happy and smiling and dancing on the sidewalk all the way up Foster. No knuckle dragging through life for this one! The way she swaggered was captivating, like she just ate up her life. Waiting for the light to change at the corner, I remember thinking, *Why can't I be with someone with energy? Someone cute like this? Didn't I deserve someone good like this?*

At Stargaze it was four rows thick to get to the bar on Latin Night. All the ladies were doing the salsa, and the sweat was boiling off, the AC blasting that frigid air. I bought three beers. All in plastic cups.

"Let's play a game," Kara said.

"Like what?"

"List every brand of shoe you know. Okay. GO."

Jenny rolled her eyes and went to the bathroom.

"Umm, Payless . . . ," I mustered.

With Jenny gone, Kara leaned over. "You have to give me your number."

I shot the beer out of my nose. "What? No way."

"I mean I want to hang out with you sometime. I like you," Kara said, like some brave soldier.

"You're not calling me."

"I'm totally calling you." she replied.

I narrowed my eyes and scribbled my number on a page of her journal.

I walked out of the bar with a bottle still in my fist, weaving in and out of the alleys between Bryn Mawr and Magnolia. Homo alone again.

Kara never called me. I like to joke that she lost my number under Jenny's bed. A few months passed and we randomly bumped into each other at a barbeque during Pride Fest. She was hanging out in the patio on Foster Avenue. And when I saw her face, I stopped dead in my tracks.

"I'm the patio daddy-o," she said and smiled. I pulled up next to her in the lawn chair. Come to find she and Jenny had broken up the month before.

Inserted love story cliché: *Couple meets at lesbian movie night and makes instant connection that's so powerful it warrants wine-glass crushing. Stalled by circumstance, they wait a month and rekindle their romance on a patio in Andersonville. They get married in Iowa and retire to a six-flat in Chicago, where they spend their days walking the dog, growing an organic garden, and, well, loving the hell out of each other.*

spilling over

Jeanne Theresa Newman

we're eating sushi, we're laughing i'm spilling water i'm spilling sake i spill a lot, i tell her not to worry, see, she spills, too i'm mopping the table with a napkin spitting ice on myself but i play it off i'm charming, i tell her (and myself). see, i'm nervous and we're laughing and laughing i tell her about the old town aquarium the frozen parking meters and my dad she tells me about indonesian take-out and her dad and a bum credit card we eat far too little drink a bit too much then we're in the tequila roadhouse i excuse myself to the bathroom come back, sit down with a flourish, hook the table with my flip-flop & dump two beers onto the ground the waitress, erica (with a shirt that says bada bing) bring us two more for free (she spills, too. she shares with us) and we're watching people do karaoke and we're watching one another out of the corners of sly eyes i go to the bathroom again i come back she says she'd like to kiss me she says she's nervous asks if that's okay I say it's okay to feel however you feel she leans in pecks my eyelid i go for her lips she swerves i hit her square on the cheek and there's people dancing to sir mix-a-lot, irene cara, dwight yoakam and marcy playground and she gets up to pee (the first time of the night, i notice) and i follow her into the bathroom and catch her by the sink (i didn't have to pee this time, but i went anyway. just in case. you know.) we make out next to the sinks girls come in we discuss george w. for a minute and return to each other's mouths this happens twice during the night and we kiss in the car on the seats, through the window on glenwood ave. my favorite street and where she lives as i peel out smiling all the way home.

The Liar

Sheree L. Greer

Opal was missing a finger. Well, not really missing it exactly. The pinky on her right hand was a nub. It stopped short, ended just at what would have been the second knuckle of her three-jointed appendage. Instead, she had a stump of bone, flesh, and skin—no nail—that ended in a smooth roundness that tingled when rubbed directly. As far as she knew, she was born that way. She remembers doctors, therapists, teachers, and foster mothers trying to get her to write with her left hand, but she refused. As a result, she only wrote with short, stubby pencils that she held like tiny pieces of chalk, with bunched fingertips; her thumb, index, middle, and ring fingers went pale in the fierceness of her grip. Her hand hovered directly over the paper, no slant, pencil tip straight against the pages of her journal as she wrote entries that would have a hard time becoming stories.

Opal never revealed the real story of her pinky—or lack thereof—to anyone. When asked about her finger or her mother, she always found it more interesting, and in the end much safer, to lie.

Opal told people her mother's name was Lillie, a name Opal chose after reading *The Temple of My Familiar* for the ninth time. The name was the first lie of many that would follow. In most versions, Lillie died when Opal was a baby. Opal was then "tolerated"—as she liked to say—across foster homes until she turned eighteen.

When Opal took lovers, which she did liberally, she told them different stories about her mother and about her finger. The lovers marveled at the story, trying not to look at the nub as Opal spoke. They stared directly into her large brown eyes that always seemed to be shiny with impending tears, a characteristic that complemented the storytelling because it made her look sincere. The listening lover, whether self-proclaimed or closeted freak, would take Opal's hand gently and kiss the soft round stump of her last digit, sending a lightning bolt of tingling arousal to flip and swirl and flutter between her legs. Some lovers, the more adventurous ones, begged Opal to pleasure them with her nub, hurriedly pushing her hand between their legs before she had even finished the story.

Opal told January, a journalism student at UIC, that she lost her pinky in an unfortunate door-slamming incident. The heavy, rusted passenger door of a 1985 Mercury Marquis clamped Opal's five-year-old finger like a bear trap, and in a panic of pain and surprise, she yanked away, jerking her hand up and out, the top portion of her pinky left inside the door. Yes, even as a child, Opal was that strong. She told Marisol, a woman who'd only dreamed of snow until arriving at the University of Chicago, that she lost her finger to frostbite, a wicked case that turned her finger tips from brown to red to yellow to white then blue to black. The doctors could save them all except one. Opal told Marisol, "Don't buy gloves. Always get mittens. The fingers need to be together to truly stay warm."

A single mother named Tomorrow, who was studying social work, got a story about a knife fight that went down at one of Opal's foster homes. For Mina, a factory accident working for a meatpacking company in Melrose Park. Kimora, a tale of a careless slicing accident from Opal's days working at a deli; "To this day, I don't fuck with pastrami," she had said. For Daesha, sweet, sweet Daesha, who was studying for her GED, Opal imparted a story about getting distracted by a fight that broke out in a high school wood-shop class and how the buster-ass shop teacher, Mr. Kuklah, gave her an F because she didn't finish her birdhouse, never mind the band saw that severed half her pinky in an even cut worthy of an A.

Unlike her lovers, Opal recycled her stories. She changed tiny details: the make and model of the car—'81 Cadillac Seville, '78 Olds Cutlass, '85 Buick Skylark; the name and location of the deli—Ada's on Wabash, the Riverside on Cortland, even the Subway out by Ford City Mall; the wood-shop project—spice rack, lazy susan, lamp. The only details that never changed were the hospital, Cook County Emergency, where she sat bleeding down her arm, shirt front, lap, and the floor until they finally called her name, and, of course, the imminent loss of half of her pinky finger.

The love affair would end shortly after the storytelling. Something about the woman asking about the finger coinciding with a shift in the lovemaking from the figurative to the presumed literal. And perhaps that's what made Cree different.

Cree and Opal met at the Checkerboard in Hyde Park. It was a blues club, at the time too big for its own good, the small, empty tables a reminder of better days. With tea lights as centerpieces, the dark club was like its own universe, candles like intermittent stars, lonely suns with no planets in orbit. There were a few regulars at the far end of the bar, sipping Hennessy or Crown Royal, bodies slumped on stools. A few couples hunched over the small tables near the stage, whispering and bouncing their legs under the white tablecloths. After a song or two from the band, at least one couple would courageously make their way to the shiny, wooden dance floor to two-step the night away. Opal always went on Thursday nights and sat to the right of the stage, or stage left as Cree would correct her, and watched the faces of everyone in the band. The bass player thumped his strings with his eyes closed, and the drummer held his bottom lip between his crooked teeth as he attacked the snare and the high-hat. The lead singer, Lizz, caressed the microphone as if stroking a lover and sang with the voices of women long gone, women that made Opal wish she was from another time: Bessie Smith, Ma Rainey, and Nina Simone. Then, there was Cree on guitar.

Cree's guitar, a hollow-body made for the blues, was the shiny, deep purple of a grape Jolly Rancher and just as sweet. It wailed, whispered, and whined as Cree's fingers slid up and down the frets. Opal was mesmerized by the way Cree's fingers moved. She fantasized about how they would feel on her skin, the rough, callused fingertips, short nails, and what she imagined to be soft, warm palms. Cree broke into a solo that twisted and turned so slowly on itself it forced Opal to cross her legs. She took Cree in from blown-out afro to thick-soled, scuffed, black leather boots. Cree held her guitar close to her, a swell of breast drooping over the curvature of the guitar's wide, glossy body. Opal imagined being on top of her and smirked at the thought of requesting, breath hot and voice husky in Cree's ear, that she keep her boots on.

Though Cree said she had noticed Opal from the first moment she saw her, it took them a month of Thursdays to finally speak to one another.

After the show, Opal made her way to the parking lot behind the club. Shivering from a light drizzle that made the air heavy with the threat of cold rain, she waited for Cree. Opal buttoned up her peacoat. The band members finally came ambling out the door and down the small steps, exchanging hugs before dashing from under the awning to their cars. Lizz and Cree came walking out together, arm in arm. Opal's heart popped and went dark, a blown light bulb. When Lizz and Cree reached the parking lot, Opal's new idea was to compliment the band and be on her way. Lizz slipped her arm from Cree's and twisted her lips at Opal.

"I enjoyed you tonight," Opal said to Lizz and Cree.

"Thank you," Cree said.

"Huh uh," Lizz grunted before whispering into Cree's ear. Cree said she was fine and kissed Lizz on the cheek. Lizz offered Opal a phony smile and turned on her heels, clicking toward her car.

"What's with her?" Opal asked.

"Lizz is cool. She's just a little overprotective of me sometimes. I usually get a ride home with her. And . . ." Cree shuffled her guitar case to her left hand, adding, "She's always suspicious of groupies."

"So, I'm a groupie?"

"I don't know yet." Cree narrowed her eyes. "You waited out here just to compliment the band?"

"Yeah," Opal said. "That, and I was hoping you'd take me home with you."

Cree's eyes widened. "You're bold."

"What kind of groupie would I be if I weren't?"

"What's your name?"

"Opal."

"Well, Opal, you caught me on a rare night. Come on."

Opal and Cree walked to the bus stop. They exchanged small talk as new acquaintances do, small silences filled with the crunching of gravel underfoot and the awkward chuckles of two people both anxious and nervous about the coming night. They compared zodiac signs: Cree's Ram to Opal's Virgin. They shared aspirations: Cree, record an album of original songs; Opal, finish a novel-in-stories. They sighed about the banality of making ends meet: Cree, part-time at the Wine Warehouse, and Opal, unemployed, living off school loans while barely attending classes at Columbia.

"We're both in the South Loop," they said in unison.

When the number 14 bus arrived, Opal stood back and let Cree board ahead of her. Slyly, she hoped, Opal smelled Cree's hair. Lilac and cigarettes.

The bus zoomed up Jeffery, the streets quiet and wet. And when they made it to South Shore, both pointed out the Jeffery Pub as they passed it. Thinking forward, they made a date to go there on Saturday. Cree pulled the cord for 75th Street.

Cree and Opal stepped off the bus and back into the cold, wet air. The bus revved, then hissed off, exhaust billowing where Opal and Cree stood.

They walked wordlessly to Cree's apartment, a foreboding, four-story brick building with creaking wooden stairs and no elevator. Over their hard, hollow footfalls, Opal could hear Cree's breath. She wanted to feel it, hot and wanting, hovering in the space between her lips before a kiss.

Once inside, Cree lit every candle she owned while Opal was in the bathroom. They sat on the floor in the living room, surrounded by pillows and waltzing shadows, and drank sherry. Cree played a song she had written, the electric guitar sounding metallic and stiff without the amp, and Opal, sliding a Sanchez book from a leaning stack of titles in front of a book shelf, read her favorite haikus aloud.

The sun was slowly pushing up from the horizon when Opal finally, and gently, pushed Cree down on the pillows that were gathered on the floor. They kissed, touched, and exchanged breath and sweat in ways so bold and rare, they came together in a burst of blinding purple light not caring if they ever saw each other again.

While Cree was sleeping, Opal crept out. It was just after noon. When she got home, she took a pencil stub and her journal into the kitchen. She wrote about a woman and her lover. She used the name Cree because after the morning's love-making, it seemed to be the only name her tongue ever knew.

Baptism

By Opal

Nearly every Sunday, Cree and I take a bath together. She picks the music and I run the water. In the kitchen, Cree makes cocktails, the sigh of the freezer, clink of ice, and her humming as she pours. I'm in the bathroom, testing the water. Dipping a toe, submerging a foot, the steam making the hair on my legs curl. Finally I lean back; the steaming water makes islands of my breasts.

Cree enters, naked. Passes me drinks and I place them on the window sill. Cree sits on the covered toilet, lights a cigarette, and smokes, the corners of her mouth curled into a grin.

"One day, you're going to boil the flesh right off your bones."

I love it when she's morbid. I laugh. She puts out her cigarette and comes close. Cree steps in between my legs. Her breath coming out in gasps, she folds down slowly between my legs. When I finally touch her, she is slippery and hot against the ridges of my fingertips. She makes me feel unique.

Cree came over to Opal's tiny Hyde Park apartment after working the Friday wine tasting. They made love on Opal's futon with an immediacy so severe there was no time to recline it. Upright and out of breath, they sat tickling each other's palms.

"Aren't you curious?" Opal asked, tracing Cree's life-line with her nub.

"I was," Cree said, grabbing Opal's hand and kissing the tip of each of her fingers and her stump of pinky, sending the tremors to where they were needed most. "At first."

"Then?"

"It passed."

Opal frowned. Stunned.

"You look disappointed. Do you want me to ask about it?"

"No." Opal shrugged. "I mean, yes."

"Why?"

"So I can have the opportunity to finally tell the truth."

"The truth doesn't need opportunity. It just is."

Opal felt a shift, and it scared her. She got up and grabbed her journal. She read "Baptism" to Cree. It was the first time she had ever shared anything from her journal with anyone.

Cree gave her a suggestion. "Mention something about the hiss of the bus rolling past. I like that sound. I can hear it in my apartment."

Opal smiled. "That's actually a good idea." Cree put her head in Opal's lap. Opal looked down at her. "My muse."

"I have a boyfriend," Cree said.

No opportunity needed.

Jeffery Pub looked small from the outside, easily missed even with the neon rainbow hanging in the first of two dark windows. Once inside, the place opened up, wide and deep, the mood dark and warm like walking inside a hungry mouth. There was something defiant yet desperate about Jeffery's Pub. It was proud, a firm fixture in the South Side for decades. The resiliency of having survived infused Opal with a sense of challenge as she settled on a stool scratchy with cracked vinyl. Opal looked over her shoulder at the sparse crowd, a private party clustered together in one corner, the shine of their Mylar balloons swallowed by shadows. There was a desolation to the place. It was too open, its mouth too hungry. As time pushed forward from the pub's staunch history, a longing trailed like the fleeting tail of a falling star.

Opal sipped her Guinness and watched the door. She had kicked Cree out after her announcement, but as she had watched her walking up the street, she fought the urge to raise the window and call after her.

As she hoped, Cree entered, unbuttoning her jacket and loosening a long, red and black scarf that wrapped around her neck more than twice.

Opal waited until Cree took a seat at the far end of the bar before going over to her.

"Dump him," Opal said.

Cree laughed. "Okay."

They ran the four blocks to Cree's apartment and kissed each other roughly, smashing lips and bumping teeth while clambering up the stairs. After making love on the floor in Cree's bedroom, they listened to the streets and laughed with each passing bus.

Cree's grandfather, who lived in Milwaukee, was dying.

"I need you," Cree said. "Can you come tomorrow morning? I'll wait for you at the train station."

"Yes," Opal said, her mind already someplace else.

Opal hung up the phone and finished sharpening her pencils. Sitting alone in the apartment, Opal thought about death, thinking maybe she could write a story about it. Her journal on her lap as she sat on the floor of her warm apartment, her tiny pencil gripped between her fingertips, she whispered the name "Jocelyn" before writing it on the top of her page.

Jocelyn, a girl Opal had gone to high school with, had been killed two weeks before Christmas break during her junior year. It had been a stray bullet, a searing point of destruction that moved quick and resolute, though it had no eyes, no ears, no mind. A drive-by was no surprise to the West Side. It was merely a case of "where" and "when," with little thought given to "who." Most people get uncomfortable when asked open-ended questions, especially ones that involved rival neighborhoods, Gresham versus Englewood for the title of . . . what exactly?

Opal drew a line under Jocelyn's name. She hadn't really known Jocelyn. She remembered Jocelyn always popping her gum and patting her braids to quell the itch of her scalp. Opal always saw her in the cafeteria, laughing a whopping laugh that always sounded too large for her small frame. She cussed just as big, "fuck that" and "fuck this" and "fuck you," and she ate a bag of Flaming Hot Cheetos for lunch every day.

After returning from Thanksgiving break, there was a candlelight vigil with singing and crying, the superintendent saying a few kind words before hugging Jocelyn's mother awkwardly. There was a white ribbon tied around every tree that lined the block between West Normal and South Normal, the irony of the intersection going ignored. The flag was lowered half-staff, and the rest of the week was solemn. The table she used to eat at with her friends was quiet for a few weeks. All of Jocelyn's friends ate their

Cheetos in slow motion, sucking them rather than munching, forcing swallows rather than smacking. By Christmas break, Opal felt a normalcy creeping back into the school routine and wondered if anyone else felt guilty.

Classes resumed in the New Year, and though something had definitely shifted, everything had settled into its new place. Opal still listened for Jocelyn's laugh and watched her lunch table like maybe one day she would show up, patting her braids and popping her gum.

Opal read over Jocelyn's name then put a line through it. She went to the next line and started writing. She wrote and wrote, her hand aching. She fell asleep mid-sentence and woke up to a dark apartment. It was a quarter after five.

Death

By Opal

~~*Jocelyn*~~

When people die, they're gone. You don't see them again. And there is a cold certainty that hardens and sharpens you, coal into diamond. What of people who abandon you? Are they dead?

I remember being born. The warmth of my mother, her body holding me, being inside her. Then, the violence of being expelled. I was squeezed, pushed, pulled, twisted, and turned. Metal clamping my head and skin tearing around me. Screaming. A familiar voice. Soft, hushed, muffled in layers of flesh and fluid. My mother's body moving against me, stretching against my face, shoulders, and I slid out into the world. A rush of air colliding with my skin so brutally, freezing and absolute, that it hurt. The darkness that was my solace burned into red. Body trembling against my will, frantic hands slipping against my skin. I was tender, felt the lines of their fingerprints; the ridges and lines of their palms scraped against me like claws. Fingers in my nose and mouth, I gagged and screamed. My voice a surprising horror to my own ears.

The warmth, the voice, gone.

I don't know what a father is and my mother is dead. I am cold. I am certain. I am a diamond and

Cree broke up with Opal for not coming to Milwaukee. She did it over the phone, saying she never wanted to see her again. She then paused, breathing heavy into the phone.

"I needed you," Cree said.

Opal knew it. Her throat tightened. Cree stifled a sob.

Three Words

By Opal

Body covered in diamond dust from the wearing down, the grinding, the carving. My skin catches light only to shoot it out of my pores. I touch and kiss and lick and bite and leave streaks of rainbow on my lovers' skin. I have nothing to say, only things to show you. Look at the colors that bleed through the sheets when we make love.

Opal read over all the journal entries she wrote while with Cree and decided her heart was just as stumped as her pinky. She wondered if being born a certain way—half-hearted, with an abbreviated appendage and stunted stories—had to be a permanent condition.

Itch

J. Adams Oaks

Ryley's hands reminded me of da Vinci's ideal. I procrastinated late, crammed for exams. He fiddled with clay in the campus studios, losing track of time, then stopped by my apartment above the Korean restaurant on his way home, slipping past the screen door to keep it from creaking. We were willing to be exhausted during classes in exchange for conversations till dawn while Chicago snored. He romanced me with his goodbyes—long handshakes turned to hugs turned to sighs on my neck turned to cheeks brushing turned to kisses against the screen door, creaking loudly against his back.

Marty had a boyfriend. He had a boyfriend. A boyfriend. We couldn't eat each other with our eyes over lunch on a crisp autumn Lincoln Square patio confettied in leaves, flustered with pigeons. We chewed on it between us, gnawed the rawhide of need. I brushed my hand over the nape of his fuzzy neck, turning away with my smile, respectfully.

Noel and I built a fort from the *Alice in Wonderland* set pieces we found in the rusted dumpster behind our elementary school. We wanted to undress each other. The structure took all day, but the janitor caught us before we could explore skin, making us put the giant cardboard mushrooms and playing cards back, he said, where they belonged.

Mike always smelled. So. Damn. Good. After inhaling, eyes shut, washed away by the beauty, I'd ask him, "What is it?" No cologne. No spritz or splash. He'd shrug, answer, "Just me." But it was grass from falling toward a Frisbee in Wicker Park and the lemon sliced for his iced tea, fabric softener and sawdust from fixing a windowsill, and City Farm peaches he'd picked. And I'd think, *Yes, yes, it is just you . . .*

I hadn't planned on Peter. But I was drunk, determined, indiscriminate. The Boystown dance floor beat helped. The liquor helped too. So much liquor I hoped I wouldn't heave out the window of the cab that flew down Western Ave. toward my place. His tongue tasted tangy, like coffee and smoke and a long-lost toothbrush. And I wished I'd been able to see him naked before we committed to the night. I didn't sleep, but my arms did, my single bed too small for both of us to pass out. He woke angry, asking why I didn't throw him out before dawn. And I understood why people got kicked out after the deed was done.

Ray kissed me on the corner of Rush and Division. Surrounded by straights. I dragged him down the street, down the El station stairs, asking him how . . . he knew? He smiled, slid his hand past my belt buckle, saying, "Finding out was worth the risk."

"Gay!" Spit dove off my lips. "You are gay!" Oliver had taken my truck from the sandbox. MY truck. We'd played around together in his basement before. The things he did, like taking my truck, made me madder than when other boys did. I wanted my truck back. So I used the worst word we knew. Recess was over. He handed me the toy. Then we stopped being friends.

The truth is hard to come by. Black and white. You are two colors, brown and peach. Others see this difference. They comment on it away from you. But in bed you roll around together with skin tinted by the TV gone blank, its light dyeing the moment, both of you just blue.

Too much attention gets mistaken for attraction. Those not interested need not apply effort. All others, please smile. At least. Just smile.

We slipped out of Barbara's Bookstore when the thunderstorm ended and stood on North Avenue with our chins straight out, watching furious clouds rearrange themselves, like tussled white sheets. Panicked, they dragged the pink and robin's egg blue away with them into the night. We stayed so long in that spot, both desperately searching our brains for a bed we could share, that passersby shook their heads, confused as to why two grown men would stare blankly into nothing.

At sleepovers, Wayne let me sleep in his bed, but drew a line with his hand over the sheet between us, dividing our space. His back to me all night, I watched the shadow of his eyelashes flutter on the wall and listened to his breathing never slow.

Jesus, the El train makes me crazy. I see him. He's fucking perfect. The one. Across the car. And careening toward The Loop, I dream our meeting (an accidental bump maybe; I pick up his dropped book), the first date, the dating, the discussions, the difficulties, the divorce. Shit, no! He hops out with the rest of the crowd, and I never see him again.

Just like the ones that pester you right in the middle of your back where only scraping against the sharp bark of an old oak will cure the delicious annoyance.

Paul never laughed at my missing a hoop, taught me badminton, soccer, golf, tennis, and occasionally missed the volley, his racket intentionally slicing air near the net to make me want to keep playing. His latte-tanned tummy, so taut, so casually exposed, distracting me as his shirt seam stretched to his sweat-shined, enviously acne-free face. Jealousy and need mixed in me so furiously I forced myself to hate him.

Jude broke up with his best friend for me, just for week six at summer camp, my glistening eyes mistaken for hero worship. Other guys liked to wrestle Jude. I didn't wrestle. I just watched him, bestfriends like boyfriends sometimes.

In the Marshall Field's bathroom, a finger wagged naked under the stall partition. The body part looked alien and got no answer, the question unsure.

Valentín could tickle me until I laughed. Before him, only my grandmother could. She reached behind my knee so lightly. I laughed until my stomach hurt, writhed, kicking and panting. He managed to unbutton my shirt while my elbows bruised on the hardwood floor. I heard my own voice echo into the hallway. I could barely open my eyes before they forced themselves shut, flashes of white wall, his ruddy dimples and grin. My belt buckle clacked against the floor.

I can't stand the way you like me. God, I fucking despise the way you pay attention to me, spend time with me, fit me, think about me enough when we're apart to bring me gifts. Not big or bought ones, but just right. Jesus, just stop. Oh, sure, an article in your *Tribune* about exactly what we were talking about, you thought I'd like it. I don't do that for you, do I? I just read the *Sun-Times* online and click close when I'm done. But you have to find your scissors, fold the sheet neatly, wait to see me again. And that blue shirt that didn't quite fit, so you thought I could give it a try. And it fit. Perfectly. Screw you. Now I have a You Shirt . . . And to top it off you take me on a date, the most romantic date of my life. You suck. Sure, to you it's just two friends hanging out, but you can't tell me that slipping in smooth Cuban jazz and sipping fancy martinis at your place, talking art and philosophy and world news and life and the future wasn't beautiful. All of it exquisite. After cocktails, you pick that new restaurant in Uptown—not me, *you*—and the corner table and the tasty wine. Even the server watches us with Date Eyes—*Isn't that cute*, she thinks, *two guys on a first date.* And we talk without pause, which is rare with another man. You keep up, you push me, teach me, let me teach you, before you ask me back to your place for a fragile crystal glass filled with peach liqueur your mother brought back from France. It's so lush that I lick my lips and avoid your eyes for my heart's sake. Even the walk back down Broadway had "The Bump," the one when you walk so close together your shoulders knock just before you veer away and come together again. Shit, and the air off the lake, ideal, that wet breeze misting the streetlights. I go back to your house and drink with you, peek at your bed through the doorway, picture climbing in, curling up while you talk at me about the girl you like. I did run my hand over your comforter while you busied yourself with the music. I know what your bed feels like. But, even liquored up, I know I'll never get in it, even if I wait. So I say I have to go. And, being the asshole you are, you walk me. I've never been walked before. I've never even thought about walking someone, and you had the nerve to do it to me, you goddamned gentleman, to make sure I was safe, to continue our discussion. You shake my hand, you fucker, because we are friends. You suck, you know that, right? No, probably not. Because I've said nothing.

Jamie broke into hysterics at the woman on Oak Street Beach tucking her poodle into a stroller. I would have also if at that same moment his long fingers hadn't suddenly, casually grazed mine to slip the burning cigarette from my fingers, the nonsmoker giving in to my vice, uninvited.

My best friend told me to get a work crush. "Otherwise, what do you have to look forward to?" she asked. So I got one.

The only one I still wonder about is dead, a clubbed-down tourist, caught in a Peruvian protest. We only touched accidentally. Nick treated me like a prince, gave me a ring inside the Jewel's automatic doors. From one of the gumball machines. A red spider. Its legs tickled my knuckles.

We hopped the fence to our high school pool and pulled back the thick plastic cover to the deep end, steam slithering over its surface. Curt was scared. Nervous, he said. He didn't know how to swim. I was on the swim team. I wanted to be reincarnated as a sea otter, loved sitting on the bottom until my lungs forced me to the top. I watched him undress, clothing piled quickly at his feet. We hugged our goose bumps, then climbed slowly down the ladder, surprised the water was warmer than the midnight air. Curt gripped the lowest rung. I showed him how to blow bubbles through his nose to keep the water out. After coaxing, he submerged, his hair seaweed on the surface. I wanted to be two sea otters. I supported Curt's stomach as he practiced, thinking that skin was the best thing I'd ever felt in my life. Before we snuck away, he torpedoed silently below the water by himself, as I held my breath for his return.

Whales

Rose Tully

My girlfriend wore a helmet. Well, she wasn't my girlfriend. We just acted like girlfriends. And my therapist said we were girlfriends. Or no, she didn't say that; she said, "You're in a relationship whether you like it or not."

My therapist was not really my therapist; I only saw her one time. Her name was Sarah, because lots of people from Naperville seemed to be named Sarah or Jessica. I imagined she liked to grab martinis in Lakeview after work.

I whined. I do that sometimes. I said, "I don't know if I'm really ready for a girlfriend right now, I don't know what I want, I just got out of a break-up. It feels overwhelming. I feel overwhelmed."

She said, "Whether you like it or not, you're in a relationship."

(Because I informed her that I'm always hanging out with this girl, I'm with her all the time, she tells me she loves me, I tell her I love her, and I do, I love her.)

"Does it feel good to be with her?" Sarah asked.

"Oh, yeah, she's so much fun to be with."

"How's the chemistry?"

"So good. It really is."

"It's very rare we get to have that."

And it made me all smiley, because then after therapy I met up with my girlfriend who was not my girlfriend, feeling so right about everything, not an indecisive hair on my head or cilia in my throat as it swallowed her warm, funked-up, late-afternoon saliva when we made out, right out in the middle of Grant Park, which was kind of tacky, and it made me feel uncomfortable and relatively skanky, but especially with her because she wasn't even really my girlfriend, and would I do that with just anyone?

About my girlfriend who was not my girlfriend:

1. Her name was Helmet. Her mother called her Jenny, but only her mother. I heard it once when Helmet was talking to her mom on her cell phone. "Jenny, huh?" I said, when Helmet hung up. Helmet tickled under my knees and in my pits until I couldn't breathe and I swore never to say "Jenny" again.

2. When she hadn't showered, she smelled like a salami sandwich that fell in some dirt.

3. She improvised odd noises to describe things. She would say, "There were kids on the bus today going to the farm in the zoo, screaming, 'Blagodebogledbla,' you know?"

4. She wore a helmet. It was a wrestling helmet. With a chin-strap. You could tell she didn't ride a bike or skateboard. It was painted metallic gold.

5. She walked with her helmeted head tilted to the right, which I learned in this community class I took in abnormal psychology might be an indicator that something is a little off. But they also told me not to self-diagnose in that class because eventually you'll think you have everything, so I guess that also means don't diagnose other people.

6. Kissing her was not boring. Sometimes when I kiss people, we're just moving our mouths around for what we consider to be a reasonable amount of time. Then whatever it is happens next: do it or go home or freak out or continue watching *Breakfast at Tiffany's* together. But Helmet was different because her big, puffy lips were soft and everything felt really soft. I finally felt like I caught up with myself, like my life wasn't running off in a million different directions without me.

Whales Invade the World

Everyone thought dolphins were going to evolve first, but whales beat 'em. Killer whales, sperm whales, humpback whales with their lovely gargantuan humps, beluga whales. So many whales. Walking sloppily upright.

Genius architect-city planners were raising electric lines and building whale-friendly service stations on the outsides of most buildings, which from the whale's point of view might have felt like a cashier's window in a box office.

Everyone thought we'd be dead by the time another species evolved, but it turned out we were off by a couple million years. Like forty.

And there was no time to talk about it. You couldn't really report, "Whales Invade the World" when you've got whales standing right there, saying, "I'd prefer not to be called a cetacean. While that is my classification, I'm a person, too. Now, please release my people from your aquariums."

The whales were very polite. I don't care if that's a stereotype. They were polite, every single one. Say what you will.

The only time I ever talked about the whales with anyone was with Helmet, because you couldn't really talk about most things with most people. When I brought up the subject of the whales, Helmet and I were at the Beach.

We called it the Beach, even though it was really just an elongated puddle at Minute Man Park next to the airport at Midway. The Beach pond was also known as the Rain That Wouldn't Drain, loaded with trash. The passengers flying in that day would have heard, "Welcome to Chicago. Temperature is 104 degrees."

We sat on the Beach, Helmet and I, every week, after a trip to Shop 'N Save for my mom, who wasn't good on her feet. We pushed cigarette butts aside so we could dig our palms in the sand and our feet right up on the edge of the brown water. Grounded in the water was a wet Reebok running shoe and a 2-liter bottle of Tab with the last swig of cola swimming around in there, looking warm. There were even waves. If you closed your eyes you could pretend you were at the ocean. This was where we talked about deep shit.

I said, "Sometimes I forget the whales have only been here a few weeks, I'm so used to them—I forget that they haven't been here all that long."

Helmet said, "They've been here longer than us."

"Yeah, but you know," I said, "I mean out of the water. What do you think about it?"

Helmet said, "About the whales? Better than cockroaches."

We both smiled the way we do when the other one says something funny, kind of without looking at each other. A plane landed with a scalding boom that ran for three full minutes. It felt like the plane was skimming our faces. Helmet never used to plug her ears until after the first few times she saw me plugging my ears. We plugged our ears together and watched the wheels rolling out, the plane hitting the ground.

When the noise mellowed out to a wheeze, I realized Helmet had been talking the whole time, but I only caught the last part of it:

". . . what I want to know is, how did humans make it this far?"

More Stuff about Helmet

1. She made me feel unique, even though none of us is unique, except when Mr. Rogers says it. Her and Mr. Rogers make it true. She didn't even do anything to make me feel that way; she did it by just hanging out with me so we could tickle each other to death. Out of anybody in the world, I only wanted to tickle the shit out of *her*.

One time I had my hand inside her, and she said, in her harsh, buzzing voice that would be terrible for radio but just right for the phone, "I love you, Elmer. Elizabeth. Elizabeth Marie. Elmer, I love you."

And I freaked out. Because when girls say that, you don't know if they meant it, or if it just slipped, because sometimes that kind of thing slips. We were at her house, on her brown floral sheets that were maybe just starting to turn a little. On top of it, the sun was cooking us through the windows. She didn't have curtains. The garbage truck outside was the only noise until she said that. Then it seemed to be the only noise that ever happened in the history of the universe.

2. I would reason to myself, "What does a helmet have to do with your place in life? What's the difference if you're ten years old and wearing a helmet or twenty-two and wearing a helmet? You're wearing a helmet and you're still you. It's just who she is. She likes to do stunts. It has nothing to do with being fucked up." For instance. Sometimes she jumped turnstiles. Or you might have found her rolling onto the hood of a car stopped at a stoplight, pointing and going, "Ohhh! Delayed hit! It was a delayed accident, you didn't see it coming 'cuz it was delayed!"

3. Sometimes she'd take the helmet off to shower. "So that I don't make the inside of it all squashy," she would tell me. She liked to talk in the shower if I went in to pee. I saw the helmet on the floor and asked her one time about it. She said, "My helmet? When it gets wet? Water gets stuck in the middle. Kinda like those clear cups with the palm trees inside. You think the cup is heavy because of the Kool-Aid, but there's hardly any Kool-Aid in those cups. Such a disappointment."

4. Helmet liked Kool-Aid.

5. She also had fake front teeth; they make her look kind of tough, and kind of make her look like a horse. But not really. More like a heavyweight champion.

I (Elmer) take thee (Helmet) to Gordita Palace

You know how you walk into a burrito place on the North Side, and there are all these generic people eating there? And somehow that makes the walls even more orangey-yellow and the fluorescents even more glaring? It sucks because you think, "This burrito really does taste good, this one I get with all the grilled vegetables in a spinach tortilla, but I don't want to be associated with all these generic people, with their generic piercings and their generic 'I'm going camping' look with their land/water shoes." I don't want to be like them, but I am, because I'm hungry, and as soon as I walk in there, we're all smelling the same smell that beans and melted cheese make when they combine; we're all waiting in the same line with the same "I don't wanna wait for our lives to be over" horseshit coming out of the speakers everywhere, and I sound exactly the same amount of generic as the guy ahead of me when I order using dangerous, loaded words like "fajita."

But it was okay because it was me and Helmet and I felt comfortable saying anything around her because I could say "fajita" eighteen times in a row, and Helmet would tell me I am super hot. We were five months into being in a relationship that was not a relationship, doing a thing that people in relationships do, which was: eating quietly together way in the back of Gordita Palace.

We ordered. We sat down.

"Oh God," Helmet said, "I'm sooo hungry. You can see it in my stomach. It's starting to talk again," she said, and threw her shirt up over her Buddha belly. She pinched it, turned it around all different ways, made it talk in a sock-puppet voice: "Eat Elmer's fingers! Eat Elmer's fingers!"

Then Helmet crept into my side of the booth and proceeded to come at me making a lawnmower sound, chomping in the direction of my fingers. She had a black bean skin stuck between one of her fake teeth and one of her real teeth. She was holding my wrists together, sometimes getting my knuckles. I almost choked on my chips, suppressing my laughter so hard I thought I might die without sound, trying not to make a scene, when this girl from one of my community classes, Bernie, appeared out of the floor, it seemed, smiling warmly, and not saying anything. How long had she been standing there?

"Hey," I said, still laughing, nervous, feeling displaced.

She said, "Hey," looking impossible, like she was.

Bernie was impossible because:

1. She had beautiful brown eyes and eyelashes that she could have tripped over, they were so long. The billions of freckles all over her face made her look like an androgynous model for classy cologne.

2. She had been doing photography for a long time; she just wanted a class for structure.

3. She had so many cameras, so many, many cameras. She was actually letting me borrow one of her cameras.

4. She was roommates with one of my friend's friends. I heard she thought I was cute.

Bernie was studying Helmet, the way all people studied this girl who wore a dirty gold helmet everywhere she went.

"Oh, hey, this is my friend, Jenny," I said.

"Call me Helmet," Helmet said, holding out her hand.

Bernie didn't want to take it, it looked like. You could hear the grip; like wet skin against wet skin, it rubbed. Then it was gotta go, okay, see you in class, goodbye, and Helmet and I finished eating without really talking much at all. She crumpled up her foil, then mine, threw it in the garbage, stacked our trays, grabbed my hand, and pulled me outside.

"What was that?" she said.

"What?"

"What *was* that? What *was* that, what *was* that?" She kept saying it, holding the sides of her helmet and pacing all over out in front of Gordita Palace, the neon lights from the Play Lotto sign next door making her helmet look green, then yellow, then green.

I didn't know what to say.

"*Jenny?*" she yelled. "You said *Jenny*? You don't call me Jenny. You don't call me that."

My mouth felt like one of those dreams where everything is in Jell-O. Oh God, I had to say something, I wanted to say something.

So I said, "I'm sorry, I won't call you Jenny anymore."

And nothing could have sounded bitchier.

"Do you *like* that girl?" said Helmet.

"Who?"

"Do you *like* her?"

"Bernie? No, I mean, as a person . . ."

"Goodbye, Elizabeth."

She started walking.

"Am I gonna see you at the Beach tomorrow?" I said after her, following her.

I said it again, "Am I going to *see* you?"

She didn't answer.

I fast-walked alongside her to the bus stop. The bus was coming right up. Before I knew it, she was getting on.

"Goodbye, Elizabeth," she said again, and the doors closed.

Whales Are People

1. They are mammals.
2. They have lungs.
3. Their babies drink milk from mammary glands.
4. They can live to be a hundred.
5. They are fat like us.
6. The only difference is that they hear through their jaw, and when they hear, they seem to listen.

The acute underwater hearing of whales taught them pretty much everything they knew about humanity, because of conversations on passing boats. There wasn't really a cruise ship culture, because all kinds of people take cruises. Newlyweds and old people. People with money and people who won a sweepstakes. Families, couples, people who want to pretend they're on a voyage by themselves. People from Tokyo, people from Houston.

And hearing conversations on the number 80 Irving just from that morning, which had double-deckers to accommodate whales, I learned there were:

1. Whales speaking seven languages.
2. Whales taking feng shui community classes and mastering the basic ins and outs of interior decorating.
3. Whales knowing all the words to "Shoop":

> Here I go, here I go, here I go again
> Girls, what's my weakness? Men!
> Okay then, chillin', chillin', mindin' my business
> Yo Salt, I looked around, and I couldn't believe this
> I swear, I stared, my niece my witness
> The brother had it goin' on with something kinda . . . uh
> Wicked, wicked—had to kick it
> I'm not shy so I asked for the digits . . .

That morning on the way to work I decided to go up to the top of that double-decker bus to see a whale. There weren't any whales working with me at the camera store; I never really got to see them up close, I guess, not even really on the streets, because most of them only took the bigger streets, and you couldn't really stare up at them because that would be rude, and they were photographed a lot, I supposed, but only under the guise of just photographing people in the city all together.

I went up there, real quick. I didn't think humans were really banned from being up there, but decided it was maybe frowned upon, because it didn't exactly free up very much space. There he was, a humpback, looking like he was dead, there was so much dead weight, sitting by himself. He didn't see me right away, at least I thought, even though his right eye was looking dead at me. His left was scanning out and over the side rail at all the things passing by: two liquor stores, the medical clinic, the Golden Nugget, a parking lot, the same old *elote* cart. I could study the charcoal grooves of the edges of his flippers, dried out like old toes.

That night, just before I went to sleep, I could hear a million different sounds, some like clocks, some like screaming, and I knew—whale songs. Altogether it sounded so familiar. The only other time I heard sounds like that was in my old neighborhood at Midway, because it was industrial and you could hear aliens, whistling. When I was little, that's what I thought they were. My mom told me they were the freight trains screeching their wheels against the tracks. I couldn't get it out of my head that it was aliens. This whale song sounded like those whistling aliens, and it sounded underwater, even though the whales were done with that water.

tattoo

avery r. young

aint ever enuf air   bofe of us   heavy on me   if i
sleepin   if i walkin   if i thinkin i thought i
imagined knowin we laid night to mornin bent
in each other   somethin bout de word *never*
becomes genesis 1st chapter / 2nd verse

is it i be real-est dark naked   is it i be buck-ed-toof talkin   is it i be crook-ed-foot-ed dancin   is it i be too hard to comb / notty ghetto geek to ever *nee-gro* sheen yo hood sunday mornin juke-joint-like   aint i got enuf nazareth in me to lay down & resurrect wif

it always comes down to how biblical we gon be
whenever i wonder if de devil ever gonna show
up to work him post   trick us into fig leaves
atop our shame   *baby*   i be luvin u so hard my
skin scripts yo name underneath itself   i break
into a wall dat jericho wish it knew to keep u
out / side of me   cause *no* found yo lip bone
quicker den a second cud set itself inside a
minute   de day i ax u to be mine   *baby*
sometimes i feel like mama's dumbest chile i be
wantin u to be permanent

7

Winter

At the Rosehill Cemetery, Chicago, 2001

Richard Fox

I hate your death—
not its foreignness
& not your dying
of it, but the fact
of it—the no-moreness
of you. Your tree's
still here—occupying
space over the sun-packed
fence next to the broken-
into mausoleum—
its tree-breath
outlasting yours:
the only birch
in Rosehill. You loved
looking at it through
the wavy art glass window
from your perch,
turning tricks as you did
in some rich bastard's
death museum.

I love being here
when the snow comes,
when everything
gets a lesson in

humility, but I hate
your death. And
I've come to talk,
to come here for
the *other* gay experience—
it's where Suki's come at 32

& Frank's brother
at 27, but most—like you—
just past young
& on the cusp
of becoming interesting.

I've come here
between the markers
where you've come
into the palimpsest
of earth
(*life's rust*   *body's rust*)
& where words like
fag & *AIDS* have
also come to rest,
closed tight in your grave.
You lie beneath
Chicago, where I've come
to live & where life
streams by like
it does on the coasts
& in between,
but once inside either
grave or church,
you must invest
in silence, but
you neither
want it nor possess it:
I must tell it to you
or bring it with me here,
where you no longer
have to self-suffice.

Grief—like farming—
is bitter work.
Stranded, I will cry;
stranded again, I will cry.

But I've come to talk,
& now I will let string
& tin can slip between
the clay & gravel,
down into your grave—

old tech telephony—
to catch you up on things
that have happened
since you died
in the fight against
the Plague,
& how we still doff
responsibility
as we flip between
the binaries of
natural cause & genocide
as easily as taking off
our Sunday finery.
It was your kind of fight:

oh, to have lived your
life bookended by
the span of the twentieth
century. Oh my liege,
my queen, my queer,
I would dig you up
with the souvenir
spoon you brought me
from your last trip
to Cancún.
But out of spite,
I want you to break
up through the earth

like a swimmer who breaches
the surface, where
you become an anti-
spadeful, pushing up
from the ground
like you've dedicated
a construction site
before the builders
come; before the rabble
come in their over-
extended reach.

I will quilt the patterns
of your long hours'
watch over
the eighty-something
birch tree—rings
uncountable as Saturn's—
into swaddling
to cover you
against the dearth
of your last days—
the dizzy wig of
your last minutes doffed—
when you were
taken away so some-
one else could birth
in your place.
What did you mean
when you said
My words are meant to mean
or when you said
Bury me in my mother's wedding gown
as if by then you'd be
thin enough to fit into it?
Of all the raw
deals, explanations
abound: pick one
from the gee & haw

& boo-hooing
above-ground.

I shall miss your tree
& your eye-stare
through the glare-bound
squares of mortuary glass.
My bad eyes,
your rotten death:
I've come here to say
goodbye to all that.

Everything You Always Wanted to Know

Goldie Goldbloom

Marvelous Limonjello sits in a café in Paris, France, with his long-term partner, Andy Melrose. It has been raining steadily all morning but now the sun has come out. Marvel lifts his camera, preparing to shoot his lover. Andy hunches over the tiny white cup of espresso, his blond hair covering his face. Marvel no longer has hair. A surfeit, he is told, of testosterone. His barber encouraged him to completely shave his head when the bald patch resembled the Soviet Union. His head gets cold now, and even in spring he has to wear a dorky knit cap. Like an old man. Which he absolutely isn't. Fifty-four is middle aged. Andy just had his thirty-fifth birthday. This trip is—in fact—the birthday gift.

Marvel reaches into his pocket and slides from his chair to kneel on the filthy flagstones at Andy's feet.

"Not here!" hisses Andy, panicking. He hates when Marvel makes it obvious they are a couple. What do the young people call it these days? PDAs. Public Displays of Affection.

"Andy," says Marvel, plopping a jewelry box on Andy's knee, "will you marry me?"

Andy folds his arms across his chest and looks away. He snaps his fingers under cover of his cashmere-covered elbows.

This gesture goes through Marvel like a circular saw, spitting out bone and gristle, little bits of his brain and heart and bowels hitting the pressed-tin ceiling like shot, landing in other patrons' cups of cappuccino. *Plink plink.*

He is older than Andy, and dare he say it, wiser too. Wealthier. More masculine. He has more cats. That alone ought to count for something.

He's always wanted to be the one who asked, who snuck out to get the ring, the guy down on his knees in a puddle of coffee and emotion, madly in love, in Paris, in a chic little café, on a delicate, light-filled spring morning. He knows it's a bit late for all that, but he *wants* it to be true.

A street-cleaning truck roars by and a fish skeleton flies up from under the brushes and hits the wooden door frame of the café with a sharp *tchack*, and then hangs there, trembling, somehow suspended from two splinters of bone that are jammed into the wood.

He shudders and his left eye twitches.

"Excuse," says the waiter, returning with the check. "Is your Papa okay?" he says to Andy.

Marvel tugs at Andy's hand and tries to slide the ring onto his finger. It doesn't fit. Of course. Marvel has always been terrible at details. When Andy jerks his hand away, the waiter asks, "Is this gentleman bothering you?"

"No," says Andy, but then he turns to Marvel. "Not here! Can't you get *anything* right?"

Marvel stands. "This is such bullshit," he says. Snaps the box shut. Remembers again the photograph of the old man at the Pride parade. He leans down and kisses Andy hard, on the lips, mouth open. PDA. Public Display of Aggression. "I'm going home." He knows he does not mean the boutique hotel on the left bank, or even his apartment in Boystown, but his mother's house in Avalanche, Wisconsin. Where there are mice and manure and people who will love him forever. He vomits a little defeat into his mouth and swallows it down.

Marvel's been waiting all these years for Andy to grow into the mature partner he needs. He's endured hundreds, no, *thousands*, of people saying, "Is this your son?" He's patiently sat through the barhopping phase, the alternate piercings phase, and the open relationship phase, waiting, waiting, waiting for when Andy could officially be declared old enough for him. Friends had made jokes about NAMBLA, and Marvel had flinched.

Now, on Marvel's way out of the café, he turns to inspect the fish skeleton hanging on the doorframe. It stinks. Marvel can't believe no one else notices the odor. He wants to cry. But truthfully, he isn't really into Public Displays of Anything. Including tears.

Marvelous Limonjello crouches under the dining room table, a book tucked between his legs. *Everything You Always Wanted to*

Know About Sex, but Were Afraid to Ask. He's almost worn out the chapter on homosexuality. Large parts of it dart through his mind at inopportune times. He is thirteen. He has a hard-on every afternoon at four o'clock.

Twenty-nine years later, he finds a copy of the book on a table at the Brandeis Used Book Fair. The book smells faintly of lube and, turning it over, he sees again the doctor, the *professional* who wrote it. What, exactly, is under that trench coat? Trench coats are like kilts. They make him curious.

He glances right and left, then opens the book to the chapter he was obsessed with as a teenage boy, completely unable to remember a word of it.

"Couldn't homosexuals just be born that way? A lot of homosexuals would like to think so. They prefer to consider their problem the equivalent of a club foot or a birthmark; just something to struggle through life with."

What the fuck? The man, Marvelous Limonjello, overcertified art therapy professional and concert harmonicist, forty-two years old, thrusts the book from him, angry and blushing, thirteen years old again. No wonder there is a whole generation of gay men dragging their sorry-assed selves to his practice. He sees now that all those forgotten passages have been dripping into his veins like a life-long transfusion of toxic shame. *Clubfoot.*

Fuck. No wonder he can't get a boyfriend.

The Sunday before he met Andy for the first time, Marvelous visited his friend Apricot. She rented a run-down Victorian in Roger's Park. The dusty windows let in a little drugged light that slurred and staggered all over Apricot as she lay on the couch with her lover, Squishy. They were rubbing each other's feet with an eroticism that seemed entirely misguided. It was indecent, but who was he to say? Marvel dropped into a straight-backed chair near a dead geranium.

"Do you know if you can use Botox on places other than your face?" he asked. "I mean, does the 'tox' mean it's toxic?" He clutched his hands tightly together so he would not inadvertently give away the location he had in mind.

"The person who you end up living with for the rest of your life isn't going to love you for your body, Marvelo," said Apricot. "He's going to love you for your mind. Your heart. You have such a big aura. Someone has *got* to notice that."

Squishy sat up a little and said, "They'll probably love you for that ass of yours, too. Someone's *got* to notice that. You should buy tighter jeans, Marv."

Apricot stopped rubbing. "Shut up, Squishy. Marvelo needs to be philosophical about this. He needs some healing around the whole age thing." Her skin, at forty, looked plowed by a drunken Amish man.

"Can we not talk about this with Squishy here? It's . . ." Marvel squirmed in his chair. He ripped off some of the dead leaves from the geranium and waved them in the air. " . . . embarrassing. I'm not remotely interested in the way either of you views my ass."

"Go make some tea, Squishy. Go." Apricot shoved her lover's legs off the couch. "You know what, Marvelo? I saw an ad in the personals yesterday that you might be interested in."

"Oh, God. I hate gay men."

"Sure you do, sugar butt."

"You're *not* funny."

"Aw, Marvel. You've lost your sense of humor. Ever since your fortieth birthday, everything is too serious to laugh at. Here. I got the ad from the *Windy City Times*. It's funny. Really." She threw him the paper.

"Jesus, this has got to be the *most* depressing bible of human loneliness on the planet."

"Not to mention kinkiness. Check out the fourth one from the top. *White-out!* That's what I call imaginative!" Suddenly she was the expert on what was kinky. He frowned. Where had his friend gone, the one who made tasteless British food and wore a chunky hand-knit sweater that looked like a llama had died on her shoulders?

"Here it is . . . 'I would like to dedicate this ad to my mother (narcissistic burlesque dancer, 78) who is responsible for me being an anal-retentive, straight-acting, self-hating gay man at 42. Man. 42. Almost single. You too? Join me.' Isn't that great? He sounds just like you!"

Marvel didn't move or respond. There was a long silence.

"Jesus! It *is* you!"

That night, after he'd cried for an hour or so in his bathroom, he'd spotted on Yahoo the review for a new bar.

Ramrod, Halsted St., Chicago

I agree with the other reviewers, that Ramrod has some serious flaws. The crowd tends to be fat and middle aged. Their speakers are tinny pieces of crap and the music is smooth rock, if you can believe that. The shirtless bartenders should spare us the gory vision. Those hypocrites made their patio non-smoking. They sell alcohol and I've bought weed there almost every weekend. I personally think the manager, a former smoker, is just being a dick.

It had sounded like his kind of crowd.

So the next Friday night, Marvelous tries out the new bar. In one corner there's a writers' group going on. A guy with a small waist and a ponytail and Levi 501s looks his way and then looks again.

Marvelous checks the man out in the mirror several times before heading for the pool table. Ponytail hands a sheaf of papers to the guy he's standing next to and walks toward Marvelous, not exactly looking at him, but not looking away either. Marvelous mimes sliding a pool cue between his fingers. Despite his strong instinct to run, run, as fast as he can, Marvel summons his muscles to smile. The overhead lights flicker.

"Manhattan?" Marvelous asks his new friend later, after completely routing him at pool.

"Jack Daniels, straight up," the man replies, all trailer-park butch. Andy. His name is Andy. Their hips bump in the crowd. The first time accidentally. Andy runs his hand back through his hair and tightens the rubber around his ponytail. Marvel gets a whiff of Irish Spring, clean sweat, something yeasty and delicious drifting from Andy's armpits.

"Uh," Marvelous says. His stomach rumbles. "I'm working on some Debussy. Would you like to come back and hear it?" He doesn't mention that he plays Debussy on harmonica.

"I have perfect pitch, you know," says Andy as they walk toward Marvel's apartment. Marvel would like to take Andy's hand, but he thinks it might be too forward. He hasn't held a man's hand in years. They pass the park where only last night a man sprang from the swing and groped Marvel, panting, "I want to have my way with you."

"Get off me," Marvel had said then, shoving the man away. "I need to get to know you *a little*, you know. Haven't you ever heard of a *relationship*?"

"Jee-sus!" the man had said. "You old queens make me puke. Listen man, I seen you walking home alone for about two years now. Can't you tell a mercy fuck when you see one?"

Old queen? Forty-two isn't old. But these days, standing in a bar, hardly anyone looks his way. *Look at me look at me look at me for godsakes look at me.* "I'm a human being!" he wants to shout. "Deserving of love!"

"What's wrong?" asks Andy, squeezing Marvel's hand. "Don't you believe me?"

Marvel can't remember what it was that he was supposed to believe. "Of course I do," he says.

Although it turns out that Andy doesn't, after all, have perfect pitch.

Sometimes Marvelous secretly wondered if he was a lesbian. It would certainly make things a lot easier. Unlike most of his friends, he wanted a relationship that lasted for forty years, or until he died and his lover came on Sundays to cover his grave with red roses. He'd wanted Andy to move in right away and told him the joke that Apricot had told him: What do lesbians bring on the second date? A U-Haul. It wasn't funny. It was true. At least for him. He still couldn't believe his good fortune that this wonderful man, Andy, young, beautiful, witty, wanted to live with him. The night that Andy actually came round with a U-Haul, and they carried the boxes in and lined them up against the dining room wall, was one of the best nights of his life. Andy sat on the edge of the bed, their shared bed now, and bounced gently. "I never thought I'd find someone like you," he said. And Marvelous thought he meant someone kind and gentle and clever and handsome, but now, sometimes, in his worst moods, he thought maybe Andy had simply meant wealthy.

They worked from his home for years, him painting with clients in his sun-filled front office, Andy creating huge canvasses on the glassed-in back porch, so that the smell of turpentine lingered all through the apartment, and he could taste it in the back of his throat when he ate Andy's rice and tofu stir-fries. Sometimes, new clients asked him about the monumental murals on his walls, and he smiled to think that they didn't know Andy. Who could not know Andy? His slender neck bent over his work, pale and tender, like a bean sprout, inviting caresses. The huffs and puffs as he maneuvered bigger pieces of work down the back stairs. The way they washed dishes together after supper, Andy snapping the wet towel at his legs, moving closer and closer to him, leaning against him, so that all their movements moved the other man too.

How they laughed when, one day, Marvel said, "If I find out there's a heaven after I die, and all my friends who got AIDS are in it having a gay old time, I'm going to kill myself." It became their inside joke. *If I find out there's a heaven.* The truth was something he'd never said to Andy. He'd felt, all these years, that he'd somehow stumbled into heaven and the door to his earlier, lonely days had closed quietly behind him.

"We can't be late," Andy says, the night before the Pride parade. It's a month until his thirty-fifth birthday and a couple of days before their twelfth anniversary. Andy's been rootling through the cupboards in search of hidden presents. But unlike in previous years, Marvel feels uninspired, present-wise.

"Why not? It's not like *I'm* getting the lifetime achievement award."

"We're not talking about you here, Marvel."

Sometimes Andy drives Marvel crazy: he's a stickler for protocol, always worrying what people will think. That he ever agreed to go out with Marvel is one of the wonders of the modern world. "There's a rule," he'd said, "for how old a person has to be in order to date them. It's half your age plus seven." Marvel had done the math. Andy had been, was still, too young for him to date.

"You have the tiniest hands, you know," says Andy now. It was one of the first compliments Andy had ever said to him and still had the power to evoke that earlier, intense phase of their relationship, when people they knew avoided them because they'd been embarrassing to watch. He smiles to hear it now. "Hands like a woman." *Like a woman.* Marvel knows it's a sentence from that bloody book. *Everything You Always Wanted to Know.* He knows it and yet he's completely defenseless.

"I meant it as a compliment," says Andy later, to the icy car. "Your skin is so soft."

Marvelous drives without blinking. If he closes his eyes even once, even for a moment, he's going to cry. Will his eyes get so dry that his eyelids get stuck open, like sometimes happens to his top lip when his teeth dry out? Would that warrant a trip to the emergency room? What do desiccated eyeballs look like? Will prune eyes make his twitch worse? Who will put roses on his grave?

Andy lays his hand on Marvel's arm. "You're beautiful, you know. Just the way you are." As if all this is about is their age difference, Marvel's wrinkles and gray hairs and love handles. Andy offers up this comment whenever he thinks Marvel is feeling decrepit. It used to make Marvel feel better for a day or two, but now it's passed into the realm of meaningless comments like "Have a nice day" and "I love you." His left eye twitches again, and he glances in the rearview mirror to make sure that his sclera isn't dehydrating. Andy's face is turned away. He mutters "I meant it as a compliment" and something that sounds like "oversensitive."

At the awards dinner, they sit near the front, masticating the Chicken Kiev in silence even though it's absolutely not part of their macrobiotic diet. When the MC stands up to announce Shepsel Lunkowicz, pioneer gay activist, they lay down their forks and look around. An old man, Shepsel, probably, pushes his walker down the central aisle. The hind legs of the walker are covered with split tennis balls. Someone drops his spoon and the clink as it hits his plate sounds abnormally loud.

Shepsel reaches the dais and frowns at the three steps. He can't quite lift his foot as high as the first step and his shoe hits the edge repeatedly, with a sound like a head hitting a wooden beam. There are snickers from the back of the room. A fly falls into Marvel's wine glass and drowns.

There's no railing. Shepsel kneels briefly to steady himself. Breathy sounds of exertion break the absolute and appalling silence. There are two dirty streaks on the knees of his white dress pants and he bats at them with his paws and staggers a little. The MC puts out his hand to catch the honoree and as he does so, glances quickly but obviously at his own watch, and then there are outright laughs and a shudder of applause.

It is only later that Marvel wonders why no one in that huge crowd stood to help the old man. It is only then that he wonders why *he* didn't stand.

The next day, at the Pride parade, which Marvelous always wants to boycott but which Andy insists they attend, Andy takes photos of horrified farm parents standing abandoned in the crowd, their gray faces slack with shock. Andy holds his camera, watching for the precise moment when the float bearing Taj Mahal passes by, trailing clouds of glory and expensive perfume, for the moment when the spackled old man and his haggard wife see their son in feathers and rainbow glitter and a bra, and he presses the shutter exactly then.

"You've got to stop that," says Marvel. "It's abusive."

"It's art."

"It's hateful. Drag queens aren't who we are."

Andy looks at him and his lip rises so that the brittle light hits his canine teeth. "The world is bigger than when you came out, Marvel. There's all types of folks under the queer umbrella now."

"Oh, so now I'm some old fogey who had a lobotomy back in the fifties."

"That's not what I was saying."

"What *were* you saying then?"

"It doesn't matter. Whatever it was, you'll turn it into a criticism of you."

Andy lifts the camera and aims it at Marvelous. "You have such an odd look on your face right now. Hold still. No one ever need know you aren't here for your son."

"Yes," says Marvelous Limonjello, as the flash explodes in his face. "You're right."

The photo in the gallery is labeled *Old Man in Chinos.*

When Marvelous manages to get Andy off to one side, he asks, "Who makes up the titles for your photos?" and Andy, a little drunk on the free wine and the success of his show, says, "Me. Why?"

Old Man in Chinos. Marvel is wearing those same chinos now and he wipes his hands on them. "I'm going home," he says. "I'm not feeling so well."

At home, on the computer, he looks up airfares to Paris, romantic hotels, wedding rings. He pulls out his credit card without thought, even as he browses Manhunt, the sad pickings, mostly straight men. His cat jumps up onto his shoulder, her claws seeming to hook right under his scapular. It's 2:00 a.m. Andy must have forgotten where he lives with this *old man in chinos.* Marvelous wanders the apartment, shutting windows, pushing the cat away from his feet. The proposal, he thinks, will be beautiful.

Tiny Moon Notebook

David Trinidad

for Tony Trigilio

A perfect half
moon. Walking
Byron. Hot
breezy night.

*

Above the roof of
the building across
the street: a bright
gibbous moon in a
nest of silvery clouds.

*

Corner of Hollywood
and Glenwood.
Above trees: moon,
just about full, obscured
by small puffy clouds.
First hint of fall.

*

Full moon, moonlit-
clouds—through
trees.

*

Clouds moving
across the round

moon. The night
Jim died.

*

Walking down Clark
St. with Doug. The
moon, waning, against
a black backdrop,
above Alamo Shoes.

*

Leaving Jim's place
with Priscilla: a
gibbous moon, lightly
smeared, between
telephone wires.

*

Doug and I walking
out of Whole Foods in
Evanston: gibbous moon
on a clean blackboard.
Doug eating a cookie;
me, a Rice Krispies treat.

*

The moon, almost full,
glowing a little, but alone
in the sky. A yellow
leaf fell in front of me.

*

Radiant and
full, the moon,
alone in the
sky.

*

Walking Byron
(with Doug) on

Hollywood Ave.—
whiteness through
the trees.

*

Hollywood and Ridge:
waning gibbous,
out of focus.
Beneath it: a
bluish wisp.

*

Outside Ebenezer Church:
the moon, shy of
half, and fast-moving
gray streaks.

*

Glenwood and Hollywood.
Everything pointing up:
steeple of Edgewater Baptist
Church, trees—one stripped
clean, one hanging on to half
its yellow leaves. The tip
of the latter touching the sharp
point of the half moon.
It looked like a blade.

*

Half moon on its
back, quickly enveloped
by orangish-gray gauze,
through wind-tossed
trees.

*

Gibbous moon in
the thicket of an
almost bare tree.
Halloween.

*

Day moon over
the Art Institute.
How did it get
so big?

*

Moon—removing
her gray veil.

*

Not yet dark, the moon,
nearly full, with nimbus,
in a net of bare branches.

*

Gibbous moon
in black branches,
burning through
swiftly moving mist.

*

Hopping out of a
cab at Hollywood
and Clark: gibbous
moon in a cloudless
sky.

*

First Christmas
lights. No moon
for the longest time.

*

Crescent moon.
Then: a low plane.

*

Half moon, hazy,
directly over
the clock tower
at Dearborn Station.

*

Half moon, white
as a tooth, through
a mass of bare
swaying branches.
Shroud-like clouds
moving across.

*

Clear, icy
night. Gibbous
moon—white
and gleaming.

*

Byron sniffing
shoveled snow.
The moon, not
quite full, free
of branches by
the end of the block.

*

Same moon,
high in the sky,
lighting the ice-
tipped branches.

*

The moon—as full
as it can be and not
be full. Do the craters
make any shapes?

*

Full, horror film
moon, complete
with clinging branches,
shredded clouds.

*

A small faint dot,
barely burning through.

*

Waning, bright
and white.
Wintery.

*

Morning moon
in a slate blue sky.
Some of it was
eaten away
in the night.

*

Moon over
Manhattan.
It too is
far from home.

*

Quarter after midnight,
with Jeffery and Soraya,
corner of 9th St. and 6th Ave.,
the moon, its top
sheared off, above the building
where Balducci's used to be.

*

2:30 a.m., in Marcie's
kitchen window:

a crescent Cheshire
cat grin, rising
fast, above Denver's
twinkling lights.

*

I thought it was
the moon, but it
was a clock at the top
of a cell phone
tower.

*

The day after
Christmas. Home
from O'Hare.
Hello Byron!
Hello (half) moon!

*

Through the overcast:
a wedge of light
glowing, then dimming,
almost disappearing, then
glowing again.

*

A waxing, afternoon
moon.

January

cin salach

Everything whipping
by me and me slow in the
middle, wondering

if she might want to kiss me
when my mouth thaws into spring.

Afterword

E. Patrick Johnson

Before I moved to Chicago over a decade ago, what I knew of it I had learned from African American literature and black popular culture. Books like Richard Wright's *Native Son* and plays like Lorraine Hansberry's *A Raisin in the Sun*, both of which offered a bleak commentary on the status of new black immigrants from the American South to Chicago's South Side, and television shows like *Good Times*, which also portrayed Chicago as one big urban jungle where blacks struggled to make ends meet, ingrained images of poverty, crime, and racism in my head. The "ghetto" seemed to be the common theme that marked both the physical landscape of the city and the places where blacks were forced to live. The flip side was representations through the works of Gwendolyn Brooks, whose poetry depicted a somewhat more diverse black life and geographical landscape than what I had experienced in *Native Son*, *Raisin*, and *Good Times*. And yet, what was still missing were representations of queer life in Chicago.

Now that I live in Chicago, and on the South Side specifically, I know much more about the vibrant queer community that existed "back in the day" and still exists. But just as my early exposure to depictions of Chicago was absent of queers, one might also believe that to be true of neighborhoods on the South Side in general. That is, until you look closely. After attending a party at a neighbor's home just one block away from my house, I discovered that my entire neighborhood is peppered with queer residents. Unlike the North Side in neighborhoods like Lakeview or Andersonville, where queerness is explicitly marked by rainbow pylons and flags, many neighborhoods on the South Side are just as densely populated with LGBTQ folks, but the expression of sexuality is not so much clandestine as much as it is hidden in plain sight.

We might think of this notion of hidden in plain sight as a metaphor for the city of Chicago and queer Chicago writers in relation to the coastal cities of New York, San Francisco, and Los Angeles. East coast queers may not think of Chicago as a vibrant queer town or about the importance of queer Chicago writing; and yet, the city and the work of its queer writers are ever present and lurking in places not always obvious. Midwesterners' general "no drama" way of being in the world owes much to the influence of Southern gentility brought by southern immigrants and the hard work of farming that required focus and fortitude as opposed to frivolity. That is what residing "in the middle" allows—a space in between that does not lock one in, but provides options to move about openly and sometimes surreptitiously. The writing collected in this volume reflects this in-betweeness through poetry, short fiction, and personal reverie. Indeed, *Windy City Queer* is an archive of the ways in which queer Chicago writers represent not only queer life in Chicago but also the ways in which the ebb and flow of the queer waters on this "third coast" are felt on the shores of Lake Michigan and beyond.

Contributors

Aldo Alvarez is the author of *Interesting Monsters: Fictions.* He teaches English full time at Wilbur Wright College and, on occasion, creative writing in Northwestern University's MFA program. He has a PhD in English from SUNY Binghamton and an MFA in creative writing from Columbia University.

Carol Anshaw is the author of the novels *Aquamarine, Seven Moves, Lucky in the Corner,* and the forthcoming *Carry the One.* Her books have won the Carl Sandburg Award, the Ferro-Grumley Award, and the Society of Midland Authors Award. Her stories have appeared in *Story* magazine, *Tin House, The Best American Stories,* and most recently in *Do Me: Tales of Sex and Love from Tin House.* Anshaw is a past fellow of the National Endowment for the Arts. For her book criticism, she was awarded the National Book Critics Circle Citation for Excellence in Reviewing. She is an adjunct professor in the MFA in Writing Program at the School of the Art Institute of Chicago.

kay ulanday barrett, a Campus Pride 2009 Hot List artist, is a poet, performer, educator, and martial artist navigating life as a pin@y-amerikan trans/queer with struggle, resistance, and laughter. Currently based in NY/NJ, with roots in Chicago, kay's work is the perfect mix of gritty city flex and Midwest open sky grounded in homeland soil. In Mango Tribe and in solo work, kay has been featured in colleges and on stages nationally and internationally. From the NJ Performing Arts Center to Chicago's Hot House, the Brooklyn Museum to the Loft in Minneapolis to Musée Juste pour Rire in Montreal, kay's bold work continues to excite and challenge audiences. Honors include a being a finalist for the Gwendolyn Brooks Open-Mic Awards and Windy City Times Pride Literary Poetry Prize 2009. Publications include contributions to *Mother Tongues, Kicked Out, make/shift,* and, most recently, *Filipino American Psychology: A Collection of Personal Narratives.* See more of kay's swerve online at www.kaybarrett.net and brownroundboi.tumblr.com.

Brian Bouldrey, described by the San Francisco Bay Guardian as "our cheeriest bard of sorrow," is the author of three novels and three works of nonfiction, including *The Boom Economy* and *Honorable Bandit: A Walk across Corsica.* He recently published the novella *The Sorrow of the Elves.* He is the editor of Open Door North America, a fiction series for adults learning to read, and teaches literature and writing at Northwestern University.

Sharon Bridgforth, a resident playwright at New Dramatists since 2009, is a writer working in the Theatrical Jazz Aesthetic. The 2010–11 Visiting Multicultural Faculty member at DePaul University's Theatre School, she was the 2009 Mellon Artist in Residence in the Performance Studies Department at Northwestern University. Her piece *blood pudding* was presented in the 2010 New York SummerStage Festival. Bridgforth has received support from the National Endowment for the Arts/Theatre Communications Group Playwright in Residence Program and the National Performance Network Commissioning Fund. She is the author of *love conjure/blues* and the Lambda Literary Award-winning *the bull-jean stories*. Bridgforth is the coeditor of *Experiments in a Jazz Aesthetic: Art, Activism, Academia, and the Austin Project.*

C.C. Carter is a Chicagoan with national prominence on the performance poetry scene. A graduate of Spelman College who received her MA in creative writing from Queens College, SUNY, C.C. was nominated for a 2003 Lambda Literary Award for her collection of poetry, *Body Language*. She is the winner of a host of poetry slams around the country and is the founder of Performers or Writers for Women on Women's Issues (POW-WOW, Inc.), a weekly spoken-word venue that showcases women artists. She has received numerous awards and honors, including induction into the Chicago Gay and Lesbian Hall of Fame. C.C.'s work is currently anthologized in more than twelve collections of poetry and prose, including *Word Warriors: 35 Women Leaders in the Spoken Word Revolution.*

Barrie Cole is the author of numerous plays, performance monologues, and short stories that have been widely produced throughout Chicago. Nina Metz of the Chicago *Tribune* called her most recent play, *Fruit Tree Backpack*, "Terribly smart and engrossing." Her story "Yearners" was originally presented at the Prop Theater as part of the 2010 Rhinoceros Theatre Festival. Currently, Cole is working on a short story collection tentatively titled "Fascinating Mistakes." She holds an MFA in creative writing from Columbia College and lives in the Chicago neighborhood of West Logan Square with her two young children and a throng of books.

Carina Gia Farrero, writer and interdisciplinary performer, earned an MFA in writing from the School of the Art Institute of Chicago and a BFA from the University of California at Berkeley. She is currently a PhD candidate in English at the University of Wisconsin at Milwaukee, and teaches at the Illinois Institute of Art. She was a cofounder of the dance theater company The Turnbuckles and of the poetry collective Poetry for the People, and she has toured nationally with Sister Spit. One of her plays was produced as part of Performing Arts Chicago, and she was a principal actor in the feature-length film *By Hook or By Crook*. Her poems were most recently published in *Verse Daily*,

Arsenic Lobster, and *The Encyclopedia Project*. In 2008, two of her poems were nominated for the Pushcart Prize.

Byron Flitsch is a professional freelance writer living in Chicago with his incredible partner and adorable dog. He's been featured in *Advocate*, *TimeOut Chicago*, *Toasted Cheese*, and is a travel editor for *Night & Day Travel Guide*. He's the publisher of *eg: Examples for the Everyday Gay*, an online magazine that can be found at www.theeverydaygay.com. He can also be found online at www.byronflitsch.com.

Richard Fox, whose first book of poetry was *Swagger & Remorse*, has contributed work to many literary journals. He received a full fellowship for poetry from the Illinois Arts Council. He holds a BFA in photography from Tyler School of Art, Philadelphia, and lives in Chicago.

Goldie Goldbloom's novel *The Paperbark Shoe* won the 2008 AWP Novel Award and the Great Lakes College Association's New Writers Award. Goldie's short fiction has appeared in *StoryQuarterly*, *Narrative Magazine*, and *Prairie Schooner*, and her recently published story collection is *You Lose These*. Several anthologies have included Goldie's fiction and nonfiction, including the groundbreaking *Keep Your Wives Away From Them: Orthodox Women, Unorthodox Desires*. Goldie lives in Chicago with her eight children. She adds, "That last bit isn't a joke. And there's a cat involved too. A really, really crazy cat."

Sheree L. Greer, a native of Milwaukee, Wisconsin, has been a featured reader with Serendipity Theater 2nd Story Collective, at Women and Children First Bookstore, Affinity Community Services, and The Center on Halsted, and, most recently, hosted Oral Fixation for Tampa Black Pride. She won Honorable Mention in the Union League of Chicago Civic and Arts Foundation Writing Competition. She worked as a research assistant for the Institute for the Study of Women and Gender in the Arts and Media and completed freelance projects for the Hands Off Assata! Campaign. Her work has been seen in the *Story Week Reader*, *Hair Trigger*, the *Windy City Times*, *Reservoir*, and *Fictionary Magazine*. Greer received her MFA from Columbia College Chicago and teaches writing at St. Petersburg College.

Allison Gruber is a playwright, poet, and essayist. She holds a BA in English from Carthage College and an MFA in writing from the School of the Art Institute of Chicago. Her plays have been performed onstage in Chicago and Milwaukee, and her prose and poetry have appeared in *Pindeldyboz*, *Flashquake*, *The Stickman Poetry Review*, and *580 Split*, among others. A Chicago native, Gruber now lives in Milwaukee, where she teaches college courses in composition, literature, and creative writing.

E. Patrick Johnson is a professor and chair in the Department of Performance Studies and a professor in the Department of African American Studies at Northwestern University.

He is also a fellow at the ESB Institute for the Study of Women and Gender in the Arts and Media at Columbia College. A scholar/artist, Johnson has performed nationally and internationally and has published widely in the area of race, gender, sexuality and performance. He is the author of *Appropriating Blackness: Performance and the Politics of Authenticity* and the coeditor (with Mae G. Henderson) of *Black Queer Studies: A Critical Anthology*. His most recent book is *Sweet Tea: Black Gay Men of the South—An Oral History*.

Owen Keehnen is the author of the novels *Doorway Unto Darkness* and most recently *The Sand Bar*, as well as the interview collection *We're Here We're Queer: The Gay 90s and Beyond*. He coauthored (with Tracy Baim) *Leatherman: The Urban Legend of Chuck Renslow*, coedited *Nothing Personal: Chronicles of Chicago's LGBTQ Community 1977–1997*, contributed many of the essays for *Out and Proud in Chicago*, authored the online humorous gay novel *I May Not Be Much But I'm All I Think About*, the "Starz" book series, and is on the founding committee of The Legacy Project (www.legacyprojectchicago.org). He lives in Rogers Park with his partner, Carl, and his two ridiculously spoiled dogs, Flannery and Fitzgerald.

David Kodeski is the creator of *David Kodeski's True Life Tales*, an ongoing series of critically acclaimed solo performances. His *Niagara! (you should have been Yosemite)* inspired an episode of National Public Radio's *This American Life*, and an award-winning radio version of *Another Lousy Day* was heard on *All Things Considered*. Kodeski has been an ensemble member of the Neo-Futurists, cohost and creator of the Pansy Kings' Cotillion, and is founding member of BoyGirlBoyGirl. He has performed his work at the Perth International Fringe Festival, the Perth International Arts Festival, and the Dublin Gay Theatre Festival. In 2011, "Suitcase, an Opera," his libretto based on a collection of found letters written by a young gay man in 1940s New York with a score by composer Eric Reda, was performed in Chicago and Belfast.

Deb R. Lewis's work has appeared in many journals, including Cellstories.net, *Criminal Class Review*, IsGreaterThan.net, *Gertrude*, *Susurrus*, Invisible Cities Wiki (a collaborative wiki-novel), *Outsider Ink* (Artist Spotlight), *Velvet Mafia*, *Blithe House Quarterly*, *Sleepwalk*, *Dyversity* (UK), and *Hair Trigger*. Her unpublished novel, *Hades Son*, was a Project Queer Lit Top Three Finalist. She was awarded the Windy City Times Pride Literary Supplement 2009 Prose Prize and has been a two-time feature on the Printer's Row After Dark stage. As a 2nd Story company member she tells stories and assists with story development. She received her MFA in creative writing from Columbia College Chicago and her BA in English rhetoric from the University of Illinois at Urbana-Champaign. Her website is DebRLewis.com.

ert McDonald is a longtime resident of Chicago, hunkered down in the north side ndersonville neighborhood. His poetry has appeared in many literary journals, including *Court Green*, *Columbia Poetry Review*, *New York Quarterly*, *La Petite Zine*, *The Prose-Poem Project*, and *Boxcar Poetry Review*. He is the coauthor of the book *A Field Guide to Gay Chicago*.

Yasmin Nair is a writer, activist, academic, and commentator who lives in Uptown, Chicago. The bastard child of queer theory and deconstruction, Nair has numerous critical essays, book reviews, and op-eds to her credit, and has also produced an extensive amount of investigative journalism and photography. Her work has appeared in such publications as *GLQ*, *make/shift*, *The Bilerico Project*, *Windy City Times*, *Bitch*, *Maximum Rock'n'Roll*, and *No More Potlucks*. She is part of the editorial collective Against Equality and wrote the introduction and contributed to their first volume, *Against Equality: Queer Critiques of Gay Marriage*, and is a member of the Chicago grassroots organization Gender JUST (Justice United for Societal Transformation). She was, from 1999 to 2003, a member of the now-defunct Queer to the Left, and opposed the Borders store in Uptown. Her activist work includes gentrification, immigration, public education, and youth at risk. Nair's work is archived at http://www.yasminnair.net/.

April Newman is an adjunct professor and writer. Her published work has appeared in *The Iowa Review*, *Hair Trigger*, and *Swell*. It has not appeared in *National Geographic* or *The New Yorker*. She lives in Chicago with her wife.

Jeanne Theresa Newman is a poet, prose writer, videomaker, and performance artist. As an artist with a multidisciplinary focus, Newman has performed as poet and writer, has shown video work and installation pieces throughout the country, and has performed for the last seven years primarily as her burlesque alter-ego, Ms. Bea Haven. Jeanne is also the former curator and host of Dyke Mic, one of Chicago's best-loved queer girl open mics. She holds an MFA in interdisciplinary arts and media (with a focus on performance and video/new media) from Columbia College Chicago.

J. Adams Oaks is author of the Booklist-starred novel *Why I Fight*, which won the National Society of Arts and Letters regional competition, the juvenile award from Friends of American Writers, an Illinois Arts Council Fellowship Award, and has been included in the 2010 ALA Best Books for Young Adults and Texas Tayshas Reading List. His short fiction has appeared in *River Oak Review*, *Cellstories*, *Sleepwalk*, *No Touching*, and *The Madison Review*, and has been featured on Chicago Public Radio. He lives in Chicago, where he is a curator and editor for the Serendipity Theatre Collective's 2nd Story storytelling series, and is at work on his second novel.

Achy Obejas received Lambda Literary Awards for her novels *Days of Awe* and *Memory Mambo*. She is also author of the critically acclaimed novel *Ruins*, the story collection *We Came All the Way from Cuba So You Could Dress Like This?*, and a collection of poetry titled *This Is What Happened in Our Other Life*. With Megan Bayles, she was awarded a fellowship to develop a Chicago-based online anthology for young women from Columbia College's Ellen Stone Belic Institute for the Study of Women & Gender in the Arts & Media. She is also a member of the Editorial Board of *In These Times* and the editorial advisory board of the Great Books Foundation, and is a blogger for WBEZ Radio's Vocalo.org.

Karen Lee Osborne is the author of the novels *Carlyle Simpson* and *Hawkwings* and the prose poem chapbook *Survival*. She is the editor of *The Country of Herself: Short Fiction by Chicago Women* and the coeditor (with William Spurlin) of *Reclaiming the Heartland: Lesbian and Gay Voices from the Midwest*. Her fiction, nonfiction, and poetry have appeared in many journals, anthologies, and newspapers, including *North American Review*, *American Book Review*, *Women's Review of Books*, *Blithe House Quarterly*, *Columbia Poetry Review*, *Common Lives: Lesbian Lives*, *Conditions*, the *Denver Quarterly*, *Karamu*, *Qreviewonline*, *Sojourner: The Women's Forum*, *Sing, Heavenly Muse!*, the *St. Petersburg Times*, the *Chicago Tribune*, and the *Chicago Reader*. One of her stories was the basis for the independent film *A Common Flower*, directed by Doreen Bartoni. She teaches in the English Department at Columbia College of Chicago.

Coya Paz is a poet, director, and lip gloss connoisseur who was raised in Peru, Bolivia, Colombia, Ecuador, and Brazil before moving permanently to the United States in 1987. Coya is a proud cofounder of Proyecto Latina and the director in residence for the Poetry Performance Incubator at the Guild Complex. A founder of Teatro Luna, she served as co-artistic director from 2000 until 2009. Coya has been a featured reader at dozens of literary events, including Palabra Pura, Revolving Door, and Paper Machete. She is a regular commentator on race, media, and pop culture on Vocalo.org (89.5FM), and holds a PhD in performance studies from Northwestern University. Above all, she believes in the power of performance and poetry to build community toward social change. For a full manifesto, visit her on the web at www.coyapaz.com.

cin salach has collaborated with musicians, video artists, dancers, and photographers for over twenty years in such groups as the Loofah Method, Betty's Mouth, and ten tongues. Her first book was *Looking for a Soft Place to Land*. She has been widely published in journals and anthologies, most recently in *Starting Today: 100 Poems for Obama's First 100 Days*. An Illinois Arts Council recipient and four-time Ragdale fellow, cin is also cofounder of Words@Play, a collaboration with the Chicago Park District and the Children's Humanities Festival. She's living happily ever after in Andersonville with her partner, Chris, and son, Leo.

D. Travers Scott authored two novels, the acclaimed *Execution, Texas: 1987* and the Lambda Literary Award winner *One of These Things Is Not Like the Other*, as well as the collection *Love Hard: Stories 1989–2009*. "New. Great. Revolutionary." is from a novel-in-progress set in 1990s Chicago. A graduate of the School of the Art Institute of Chicago, he wrote his first novel there and gained national attention as a performance artist. He worked as managing editor of *P-form*, a performance art quarterly, co-founded Queer Nation Chicago, and participated in theatrical street activism. After earning a PhD from the University of Southern California Annenberg School for Communication and Journalism, he became assistant professor of communication studies at Clemson University. He and his husband live in Greenville, South Carolina.

Gregg Shapiro, entertainment journalist, writes interviews and reviews for a variety of regional GLBT publications and websites. He has published a collection of poems, *Protection*, and his chapbook *Gregg Shapiro: 77* is forthcoming. His poetry and fiction have appeared in numerous outlets including such literary journals as *Court Green*, *Mary: A Literary Quarterly*, *Jellyroll Magazine*, *Apparatus Magazine*, *Ganymede*, the *Q Review*, *BAC Street Journal*, *Beltway Poetry Quarterly*, *Mipoesias*, *modern words*, *Bloom*, *White Crane Journal*, *Blithe House Quarterly*, and the anthologies *Mondo Barbie*, *Unsettling American*, *Full Moon on K Street*, *Sex & Chocolate: Tasty Morsels for Mind and Body*, *Reclaiming the Heartland*, *Best Gay Poetry 2008*, and *Blood to Remember*. He lives in Chicago with his life-partner, Rick, and their dogs, Dusty and k.d.

David Trinidad's books include *Plasticville*, *Phoebe 2002: An Essay in Verse* (with Jeffery Conway and Lynn Crosbie), *The Late Show*, *By Myself* (with D.A. Powell), and *Dear Prudence: New and Selected Poems*. He is also the editor of *A Fast Life: The Collected Poems of Tim Dlugos*. Trinidad teaches poetry at Columbia College in Chicago, where he coedits the journal *Court Green*.

Rose Tully is a writer and artist and Chicago native. She facilitates memoir workshops with under-published voices as part of an ongoing national project, (In)Visible Memoir, through Memoir Journal in Sausalito, California. She was selected for the RADAR Lab 2010 retreat. Rose is a student in San Francisco State's MFA Creative Writing Program, where she received the Miriam Ylvisaker Fellowship Award and Leo Litwak Award in Fiction, and where she will teach for one semester. She is currently working on a book full of suffering.

Emma Vosicky is a transwoman who holds degrees in law and teaching. In addition to maintaining an active law practice, Emma pours her energies into writing poems, stories, and essays, some of which have been published. She never passes up a chance to speak before school and other groups regarding the reality of being transgender, and she facilitates seminars on using writing as an opening into the world of emotions. Emma and her spouse, Becky, are parents of a blended family of five children. She has completed writing a book of short stories and reflections exploring the experience of gender variance and hopes to find a publisher soon.

Nadine C. Warner is an award-winning writer and performer in Chicago. She has worked as actor, director, and dramaturge for various theaters including Steppenwolf, Court, and Bailiwick, and 2nd Story. She is also the president of The Bricolage Group, a corporate communications company that produces internal meetings and media for Fortune 500 and nonprofit organizations. She holds a BA from the University of Chicago and a JD from the University of Illinois. She lives with her partner and their two children in Rogers Park.

Edmund White is the author of two dozen books of fiction and nonfiction, including *A Boy's Own Story*, *The Beautiful Room is Empty*, *Farewell Symphony*, *Chaos*, *Hotel de Dream*, *City Boy*, and biographies of Jean Genet, Marcel Proust, and Arthur Rimbaud. Among many other honors and distinctions, White is a member of the American Academy of Arts and Letters, an Officier de l'Ordre des Arts et des Lettres of the French government, and a recipient of the National Book Critics Circle award. Raised in the Midwest, he currently lives in New York and teaches writing at Princeton University.

Gerard Wozek's first book of poetry, *Dervish*, won the Gival Press Poetry Award. He received his MA in writing and rhetoric from DePaul University and teaches creative writing and the humanities at Robert Morris University in Illinois. His most recent book of short fiction and travel tales, *Postcards from Heartthrob Town*, was nominated for a Lambda Literary Award.

avery r. young is a writer, performer, and teaching artist. He is a Cave Canem Fellow, and his work has been published in *AIMPrint*, *Callaloo*, *Spaces Between Us*, and many other anthologies and periodicals. He is also featured on *Urban Audiology: The Art of Audio Truism* and other compilations.

Mark Zubro is the author of twenty-one mystery novels and four short stories. His book *A Simple Suburban Murder* won the Lambda Literary Award for Best Gay Men's mystery. He also wrote a thriller, *Foolproof*, with two other writers, Barbara D'Amato and Jeanne Dams. He taught eighth grade English and reading for thirty-four years. He was president of the teachers' union in his district from 1985 until 2006. He retired from teaching in 2006 and now spends his time reading, writing, napping, and eating chocolate.